THE
HIDDEN
WISDOM
OF
PARENTS

THE
HIDDEN
WISDOM
OF
PARENTS

REAL STORIES THAT WILL HELP
YOU BE A BETTER PARENT

by Samuel Osherson, Ph.D.

Adams Media Corporation
Holbrook, Massachusetts

Published by
Adams Media Corporation
260 Center Street, Holbrook, MA 02343

ISBN: 1-58062-164-3

Printed in the United States of America.

J I H G F E D C B A

Library of Congress Cataloging-in-Publication Data
Osherson, Samuel
The hidden wisdom of parents: real stories that will change the
way you parent and make a positive difference in your child's life / Samuel Osherson
p.   cm.
Includes index.
ISBN 1-58062-164-3
1. Parenting. 2. Parent and child. I. Title.
HQ755.8.075   1999
649'.1—dc21   99-35388
                     CIP

This publication is designed to provide accurate and authoritative information with regard to
the subject matter covered. It is sold with the understanding that the publisher is not engaged
in rendering legal, accounting, or other professional advice. If legal advice or other expert
assistance is required, the services of a competent professional person should be sought.
   —From a *Declaration of Principles* jointly adopted by a Committee of the American Bar
Association and a Committee of Publishers and Associations

Cover Image by The Stock Market/Paul Barton.

Author photo on rear cover by Allison Swift.

This book is available at quantity discounts for bulk purchases.
For information, call 1-800-872-5627.

Visit our home page at http://www.adamsmedia.com

Contents

≈

Part I: The Critical Elements of Parenting

≈

Part II: The Development of Family Themes

Part III: How We Grow as Parents

～

Part IV: Enjoying the Rewards of Parenting

Acknowledgments

O ne of the special delights in being a writer is the world of people you get to meet. When you mention to people you're writing a book about parenting, everyone has a story to tell. I treasure not only the stories I've heard but also the support and encouragement from so many friends, acquaintances, even strangers met on the go.

In particular I'd like to thank the following people:

Anne and Ramon Alonso, Stuart Andrews, Chris Anfuso, Nancy and Scott Argeanton, Alma and Jean-Louis Berthet, Donald Bell, Vanessa Benway and her Head Start class, Ann Betz, Susan Berry, Lynn Bergman, Marlene Blumenthal, Kevin Brooks, Barbara Buchan, Michael and Lori Chaikin, Suzanne Cook-Greuter, Martha Craig, Larry Daloz, Abigail DeWitt, Joanne Driscoll Dwyer, Richard Dents, Michael Dover, Wendy Elliott, Laura Englander, Tel Englander, Gordon Fletcher-Howell, Len Fleisher and Erika Radish, Mike French and Beth Williams, Kris Finnegan, Randi Freudlich, Kathleen Garrison, Helaine Scarlett Golann, Mark Goldberg, Ceil Goff, Sharon Gordetsky, Rabbi Julie Greenberg, Willy Hackman, Mary Hackman, Brooke Hackman, Alouette and Mike Iselin, Steven Jacobs, Caroline Jestin, Arnold Johnson, Janice Johnson, Gregg Johnson, Lynda and

Kenneth Laurence, Kristine Locke, Nick and Peggy Kaufman, Alan and Lucy Katz, Mary Koopman, Ann Benenson, Steve Krugman and Suzanne Fournier, Tony LaFargue, Steve Langer, Jim Leone and Susan Gere, Robert Lynch, Jim McGaw, Keith Martin, Molly Mead and Carol Bull, Belinda Mister, Peter Neirinckx, Rob Okun, Dan and Yolande Osherson, Anna Pandolfo, Beverly Panarese, Abby Pearson, Helene Pine, Judy Rogg, Richard and Lisa Rogg, Jean Rekeymeyer and Arthur Brownlow, Bonnie Russ, Joe Schapiro, Sidney Simon, Connie Sioris, Betsy Stout, John Symonds, Ann Taggart, Christine Tauer Martin, Jane Tilton, Richard Tedesco, Lou Temme, Dawn Villarreal-LaFargue, Yvette Yaeger, Lorrie and Ellie Weinstein, and Susan Wolpow. And to those whom I've inadvertently left off the list—many thanks as well!

I also want to express my gratitude to:

Jean Atkinson and all the Parents Anonymous members who contributed help, encouragement, and best of all—stories.

My friends and colleagues at the Fielding Institute—particularly Susan Cortez, April Fallon, Marilyn Freimuth, Nancy Goldberger, Kjell Rudestam, Pat Pasick, Nolan Penn, and Jack Saporta, and all of whom read or discussed parts of the manuscript as it evolved.

Bonnie Harris and all the parents at the Parents Education Center in Peterborough, NH.

Rae Simpson and participants from the Parent Resource Center at MIT.

All my friends at the Kirkridge Conference Center, particularly Bob Raines and Cindy Crowner, and all those who have participated in my weekend retreats over the past twelve years.

My friends and fellow mischief-makers at the Northfield Conference, fellow seekers and mavericks.

All my students over the years at the Harvard Extension School.

I am fortunate indeed that my agent, Jim Levine, combines the best qualities of business acumen and friendship. Ed Walters at Adams Media was helpful, calm, and encouraging throughout—many thanks.

My parents, Adele and Louis Osherson, are the kind of parents who lead a son to be grateful for the many gifts they have given him— and to write about what parents do well!

Most of all, to my wife Julie and my son Toby and daughter Emily: every day with you each is a story, of the best kind!

Listening to Parents

For the past ten years, I have been collecting stories about parents and children. I first saw the power of personal stories at work-shops and courses I taught for parents, and for grown children trying to work things out with their parents. At these workshops, men and women would describe difficulties, bitterness, problems, and ways they despair or feel bad about themselves as parents or as grown sons or daughters to aging parents.

It's very important to listen to these painful stories of betrayal, dis-appointment, and failure. However, I also ask people to tell me about the other side: "Tell me about a moment with your children you hold dear to your heart, maybe something you've never told anyone else," or "Tell me about an experience with your mother and father that you treasure, from any point in your life."

Often participants will be startled by these instructions, reluctant or unsure about what to say. We may remember more of what we do wrong than what we do right! We have our grievances or self-accusations down pat, but it takes a moment to think of successes and joys. Yet remarkable stories emerge when people put aside their skepticism or uncertainty and give it a try.

For example, Elizabeth is a 40-year-old mother, married, with a 14-year-old son, and she speaks with the kind of infectious laugh that seems to make her red hair even more vibrant. She was a participant in a parenting workshop I led one sunny August day at a conference center in New England. Nine of us, mothers and fathers, met in the carpeted classroom to talk about the difficulties and rewards of parenting teens.

For the first hour, Elizabeth was very quiet, though she offered supportive comments to other parents and displayed a lively sense of humor. Yet she protested that she didn't have much to offer "in the wisdom category." She went on to say that "I don't know anything about raising boys," explaining that she grew up only with sisters. Yet she was so engaged with other peoples' stories that several participants encouraged her to talk more about her own parenting experiences. "Be specific. Tell us about a moment of difficulty that turned out well," we suggested. Finally, feeling more relaxed and at home in the group, Elizabeth agreed. She then told a story about the day her son refused to put his seat belt on in their car. The wonderfully creative way she managed to defuse a loaded situation, with such patience and skill, helped us all learn a new strategy for dealing with our own kids!

Until she created her story, neither Elizabeth nor the other workshop members had a picture of her personal resources as a mother.[1] In fact, Elizabeth had much to offer "in the wisdom category," and we all profited once she gave voice to her own creative problem solving.

Hearing stories like Elizabeth's led me to develop Stories for Parents, a workshop that offers mothers and fathers an opportunity to write about their important, treasured moments as parents. Sometimes we start with a simple invitation: "Write about a moment of difficulty as a parent that turned out well, perhaps unexpectedly. The moment can be from anytime in your life, long ago or as recently as today." Or "write about a time as a parent you are most proud of, an experience that you hold dear to your heart."

We take a few minutes to write down a treasured memory on a piece of paper, then go around the room, with each person reading

---

[1] Elizabeth's story can be found in Chapter 3.

theirs aloud without comment until the room is filled with the entire group's stories.

Sometimes we start with *free writing*—writing as much as possible about a prompt that I suggest, such as "I laughed out loud when my son/daughter . . ." or "I was very proud of myself as a parent when . . ." or, "My son's or daughter's skin . . ." We write whatever comes to mind about the stimulus idea for fifteen to twenty minutes, without stopping or going over what we've written. We then read our free writing aloud and use that material as a first draft.

For some of us, *writing* stories—alone in our journals, over morning coffee, or in a writing group with other parents—has a special power, more so than simply telling a story aloud. Writing is a way of interviewing ourselves and gaining perspective on what has happened. Moments of writing can provide a calm, reflective "play space" for parents to deepen their understanding of their experiences. Writing begins more privately than telling a story aloud; we have more opportunity to move between different levels of feeling and thought.

The stories can be surprising—revealing whole new sides to people. One 43-year-old father, Eddie, had talked movingly and at length about his shame over his own father's drinking. When it came time for a treasured story, though, he wrote about the day when he was 8 years old that his father, a truck driver, took him along on his deliveries around the state. Eddie described the joy it gave him to be with his father and to see his father's ability to drive such a massive vehicle, as well as to learn firsthand how respected—even liked—his father was by the people he worked for. Getting this story out at the workshop was a way for Eddie to get his father in better focus, to remember that there was a lot to respect and love about the man, despite the disappointment. Eddie was reconnecting with a more hopeful version of his father and, therefore, of himself.

(For those who might like to tell and/or write their own stories, you'll find a guide to getting started in the Appendix. This guidebook offers you exercises that you can use on your own or with a group of friends to identify and develop your own compelling parenting and grandparenting stories. If you'd like to explore the power of putting personal stories on paper, the Appendix is for you!)

STORIES, WRITING, AND PERSONAL TRANSFORMATION

What is the power of storytelling? There's a transformative power at work. It gives us an opportunity to step back, to reflect, and to see our role as parents with greater perspective.[2]

Personal narratives can help get into focus what parenting really means to us, what the crucial values and visions are that can guide us to a more satisfying parenting experience. For all its power, parenting is a part of life we may not have time or opportunity to really reflect on. We're constantly taking care of the everyday details and decisions. We negotiate homework, bedtime, and curfews, constantly *responding* to the endless routines and accommodations that comprise family life. Who has time to step back and look at what we treasure and want from parenting?

Yet we all need a chance to think about the broader context of being a mom or dad: what parenting is about for us; the central values that guide us; why we're doing it; what we hope for from it, for ourselves and our kids. Telling a story helps put things in perspective and helps us learn more about ourselves. Good stories sharpen our experiences; like dreams they help us sort out what's really important amidst the confusing signals of everyday life. Parenting has its difficulties and bitterness, but it also has treasures that can enrich our lives.

Stories can help us overcome the normal "aloneness" of parenting. For many of us, parenting is an on-your-own activity. So much of parenting happens in the privacy of our homes. What parent doesn't wonder how other parents manage the chronic emergencies and daily dilemmas of raising the young? When we're together in public—with a screaming kid in a supermarket or downtown with a teenager—we may feel as though we're onstage. How often do we think of reaching out and asking for help from other parents?

Despite (or maybe because of) the fact that parenting is one of the crucial components of our self-esteem, I've found that people will talk

---

[2] In the past decade, psychologists and educators have become much more aware of the way in which our personal stories define us. The narrative approach to human development and change tells us, in Neimeyer's words, that "people constitute and are constituted by the stories they live and the stories they tell." (Robert Neimeyer, *Constructivism in Psychotherapy,* Washington DC: APA Press, 1995, p. 175). For more reading about the personal significance of story-telling and writing, see James W. Pennebaker et al., eds., *Emotion, Disclosure, and Health,* Washington, DC: APA, 1995.

more easily about difficulties at work or in their marriage than they will about their confusion, pain, joy, and enthusiasms as a parent. In our culture, parents are supposed to "just know" how to do it. Yet the reality is that we all have much to learn from each other about parenting. Stories reach through the personal, preoccupied bubble of aloneness that many of us live within as parents. They connect us to other parents and to generations of parents. We can identify with these stories. There's an "I've been there too" quality.

Stories are time-honored ways of giving advice, of teaching each other "how-to." There are many strategies for parenting in these stories. We're going to hear about satisfying ways of taking time together, ways of defusing angry moments when we or our kids feel boxed into a corner, recipes for letting our guard down and showing real feeling to our kids, as well as tips on finding a confident sense of parental authority. You can take home the lessons in these stories and try out the same strategies. I've learned a lot of new ideas for my own parenting, and perhaps you will too!

And we also learn that *all* parents both succeed and fail. We may come to be more forgiving of ourselves and our children. Hearing these stories can help lower rigid perfectionist performance standards.

Most of all, we hear about the importance of having a sense of humor with your kids. Parenting is, after all, truly the "impossible profession." It's also a vital one. We're torn in so many ways. We want to be buddies with our kids; we want to be authorities for them. We want to have our own lives; we sacrifice for them. We want to be loyal to our own parents; we want to be different from them. No wonder things get comical rather quickly, and it helps to be able to laugh at yourself. So many treasured moments come about in a funny, unexpected manner. Sometimes we plan too much, and try too hard, when the most valued part of an episode is what we do or say without thinking, unexpectedly, sometimes because we don't know what else to do!

There is a normal unpredictability to parenting. We desire certainty and predictability, but families are not subject to rigid laws. Parenting is a gamble, we make choices without guarantees every day. You may think as you read these stories that you can predict from point A what will happen at point B, but I wager you'll be surprised and touched by the real turn of events many of these parents and children experience.

A major lesson in many stories is that how we parent is intimately tied to how we were parented. It can be very helpful in our own parenting to remember our parents. For example, a woman, engaged in a bitter control struggle with her son, tells a story about her father and comes to realize that she is replaying with her boy the ways she struggled with her father's overcontrolling authority.

Our memories of our childhood are untapped treasure chests. For many of us there are buried treasures and guiding images in our stories about our parents. These treasures are guides to what our own children want and need from us.

For example, when Eddie told the story of going to work with his father the truck driver, he was transforming his own sense of himself as well as his father. Now his father was no longer simply an alcoholic who was not there for his family. The story did not take away the pain for Eddie of growing up in an abusive family, but it deepened Eddie's picture of his father, and ultimately of himself. His father was now also a man with competence who at times cared for his son, who took him to work, and who was cared about and respected by those who depended on him. In telling his story, Eddie is expanding his awareness of who his father was and freeing up the parts of himself that are similarly loving and competent.

Throughout the book, you will find stories from two different perspectives: stories from grown children remembering stories about their parents and stories from parents and grandparents remembering treasured moments with their children.

EMOTIONAL CONNECTION IN PARENTING

Many of the stories are about moments when parents or children make real contact—feel really seen, heard, and valued—moments when a parent or a child (or both) breaks through his or her "role" and connects, if only for a moment, in a human way. We connect on a feeling level rather than just going through the motions, being "good" or "bad" or simply getting through the day.

"Emotional connection" consists of moments when parents validate and respond to their children, with a word of support or acknowledgment, by setting limits in a way that leaves a child feeling safe and secure (even while protesting), or through a soothing activity as nonverbal as buying an ice cream sundae to calm a frazzled child. And connection flows both ways, as these stories make clear: parents too need to feel seen, heard, validated by their children.

Emotional connection is not the same as "being there." You can be physically there and quite disconnected or miles away and very emotionally connected. Parents who are divorced or living in blended families can find astonishingly creative ways to nourish the emotional connection with their children, and parents who live in intact families often find the most joy in moments that transcend the disconnections that are a normal fact of life in our "advanced," changing society.

Many of these stories start with some sort of difficulty or adversity—broken promises, shattered expectations, the shadow of the past over the present—and then lead to wonderful moments, sometimes surprisingly, even unconsciously, in which parent and child see each other more honestly and deeply, as real people. It can be a moment that is achieved with few words between parent and child—a lot of talk is not crucial to an important, transforming experience.

CONTRADICTORY YEARNINGS: SEPARATION AND CONNECTION

At the deepest level, each of the chapters has to do with attachment and separation: with our children and with ourselves. Parenting is more than just setting limits, teaching skills, keeping our kids off drugs, and getting them "launched." Parenting involves also recognizing our profound emotional attachment to our children and their connection to us.

From beginning to end, parenting is a dance of separation and connection between the generations—from the hungry way the infant nurses, to the way the baby responds to her father's voice, to the confusing ways that parents and teens hold on to and let go of each other, through the poignant ways that parents and grown children return to each other—sometimes awkwardly, always hopefully—for "emotional refueling." Some of the most important "silver linings" in difficult moments in families is that they allow us to reconnect in a deeper way, *or* to separate in a necessary fashion.

Parenting also involves connecting with ourselves—with the powerful stirrings of love, anger, hope, joy, disappointment, and yearning that children inevitably stir up inside their parents. The moments that are the most moving and difficult in parenting are those that touch on our own contradictory yearnings—we love our child, we're angry at them; we want to be close to them, we want to be free of them. If we can connect with ourselves, we can better connect with our children. If we can understand some of the splits within ourselves, we can help our children feel more whole themselves. If we can tolerate our "disconnects" from ourselves, we can better tolerate our children's needs to separate from us. And often, if we can live within our discomfort for a while, we can grow ourselves.

As parents we too continue to struggle with separation and connection with our own parents, living or not. The irony is that the generations—our children, ourselves, and our parents—go through this together.

HOW TO USE THIS BOOK

This book draws together some of the most compelling stories I've heard over the years. (The stories have been edited for clarity, and in some cases, specific biographical details have been changed at the request of participants.) Some of these stories came up in casual conversation, on the beach, over coffee, or with a fellow passenger on a long airplane trip; some are from interviews I've done with parents who had particularly interesting stories to tell. The vast majority are from Stories for Parents focus groups or workshops.

The chapters that follow are grouped by themes that kept recurring in the stories parents told and wrote. I've organized the book in a way I hope is respectful of what parents know and have told me. It begins with some basic themes that parents emphasize as important to them and their families, hard-won knowledge bought over time: the discovery that silence and listening can be as important as talking with your kids, how vital appropriate touch can be in family life, and how to best negotiate the issues of power and control that are fundamental aspects of living with others.

The second part of the book focuses on the challenging realities that kept coming up in stories from parents: what to do with the secrets and taboos that are a part of every family; how to hold on to *and* let go of our adolescents; the demands and wonder of the cross-gender relationships in families; how things change between parents and grown children; and the advantages and difficulties of being in a family with a significant, visible difference from the main-stream, such as a major chronic illness, divorce, widowhood, or a history of violence.

In fact, throughout this book, I've tried to pay attention to the realities of difference in families, since the oppressiveness of a too-homogenized perspective can be particularly painful when parents and children feel invisible in what they read and hear from the "experts." There are stories from parents who are divorced, gay and lesbian parents, parents of color, and those who have been through experiences that would test the most saintly or resourceful parent. You'll likely hear language and read about experiences in these pages not often found in books on parenting, some different from your own experience. You may find family choices and values and parenting styles you do not share. There's no one right way to parent. Among those of us who are parents, we *all* have much to learn from each other, and I have yet to meet a parent from whom I could not learn something important.

The third section of this book focuses on how we grow and change as parents, what we may learn from what life has to teach us, if we can only hear it, and how that happens. The last part of the book examines the immense rewards and payoffs of being a parent.

THE HIDDEN WISDOM OF PARENTS

There is a lot of "hidden wisdom" among mothers and fathers, wisdom learned and built up from our experience. We often don't pay attention to what we ourselves know. As parents, it's easy for us to feel we are doing things *wrong*—whatever difficulties we or our children have can seem like proof positive of our incompetence as parents. And our children may often agree!

To complicate matters, we live in a time and culture filled with parenting advice and experts. As parents we often need expert help and opinion; I have been both a provider and consumer of parenting advice. However, the "culture of advice-giving" can also serve, ironically, to undermine parents' confidence in their own ability to find answers to the normal confusion and dilemmas of parenting. Yet parents—everyday ones like you and me, like Elizabeth—also do a lot right. We may find our way through challenging family moments, sometimes by luck, sometimes by creativity, and sometimes by taking risks that startle us. Over time, we accumulate a lot of wisdom that we may hide from ourselves and others, or simply overlook.

This book offers a portrait of the wisdom of parents and suggests a way that you can look more deeply at your own experience. It is a collection of vital stories about everyday life from parents to parents—nourishing, hopeful, real. Most of these stories are about hopeful moments amidst difficult times in our families—times when we feel really stuck with our children and find a way through it, moments of real connection with our children or our parenting partner, or moments when we learn something important about ourselves or our families.

From these stories, you may learn new tricks for managing old dilemmas. And, too, they may help you recollect parenting stories from your own life. By hearing the stories of other parents and finding our own, we invest more deeply in parenting, clarifying what parenting means to us beyond simply responding to the myriad daily details and pressures of family life.

Are the stories from "superparents"? Should we read about moments of success and then feel guilty if our stories don't match up? Absolutely not. One thing I've learned is that all mothers and fathers have times of success and times of failure.

The stories can instruct and nourish us on our own parenting journeys. You may be surprised by them. Although there is much drama in these stories, sometimes high drama, most of them are about "ordinary," small moments, not Big Events—about the day a father took his daughter tobogganing, just the two of them, the daughter's rapturous delight in being alone with her daddy, wrapped up in his big fur coat, speeding down the snowy hill on that cold, cold winter's day many years ago, or about an hour that a mother spent peeling potatoes with her 8-year-old son, just the two of them alone, talking, laughing, the boy watching the calm, gentle, and precise way his mother prepared the dinner. Stories can go way back: One 78-year-old woman once held the group captivated describing the special day when her father gave her a bath, at age 6! Even after twenty, forty, sixty years, these childhood moments are still alive for us.

We often overlook some of the most important moments in our families, thinking nothing is going on. Parents often succeed in ways that they don't take in. You may find that you don't have to try a lot harder, that you need only to look at how you've already succeeded.

To expand our memory means to transform who we are. Often we forget the good that has been buried by the bad, because of our need to become numb to those we love who also hurt us. In giving voice to treasured stories we can reclaim our ability to speak of love and to accept that as a part of our lives. Through story we may transform ourselves, our children, and our parents. Who we are is not carved in stone. We can transform the guiding images of ourselves and our parents, creating new visions of who we and they can be.

Remember: *Parenting is never over*. Treasured stories can happen at any point in the life cycle!

Most of all, though, I hope you'll simply enjoy these stories and take away, as I have, a sense of the wonder of parenting. Think about how much is at stake and how often we succeed without noticing it; how important parents and children are to each other; how parenting never ends, that there is an ongoing rhythm and cycle between the generations; how we always betray each other, and yet also redeem each other; how little need be said; and how much happens that may go unnoticed until we take the time to remember.

And as you read, you may come to remember as well.

p a r t   o n e

The Critical Elements
of Parenting

chapter one

The Healing Power of a Parent's Touch

I t was a cold night in Boston; the forecast called for snow the next day. We gathered around a low table in a school classroom— seven of us, mothers and fathers. From several rooms down the chilly hallway came the chatty sounds and light laughter of an adult education class. Most of the other rooms were dark. We'd gotten past the introductions and reasons why we'd each come here this wintry night to write and talk about parenthood. We needed something to get us going, some way to use the pads and pencils clustered in front of us. I suggested a free-writing exercise to warm us up: "For the next ten minutes, write about 'what my mother's or father's touch felt like.' Write whatever comes to mind, without stopping or worrying whether it makes sense." There were some looks of uncertainty, embarrass- ment, but we began.

Later, Tom, a 53-year-old father of two grown sons and a grown daughter, read the story he had crafted from my prompt.

Tom remembered back to when he was 8 years old, on a fishing trip alone with his father. His father loved the outdoors and demanded a lot from his son. Fishing together was one way that he could be together with his father in a relaxed way.

On this day 45 years ago, Tom and his father were camping in the woods far from home. It was a cold spring day in the Peninsula area of Upper Michigan, and the boy and his father had a good morning of fishing by the edge of their favorite lake.

"We caught some bass, a couple of trout, and we cooked them over the campfire. Then it started snowing. There was a wonderful chill in the air, and the snowflakes came down through the pine trees. My father pulled me between his legs, put his coat over me, and that's how we had lunch. It is the best memory of my entire life."

Do we underestimate the wonderful importance of touch for both parents and children? Many of the most treasured stories of our childhood have to do with times when we felt free to lean against our parents, to rub up, nuzzle, perhaps wrestle with them on the floor, rolling and laughing, or run our cheek against Dad's cheek before he shaves in the morning, or hug Mother and hold on to her.

When Tom describes his father pulling him between his legs that snowy spring morning, we can feel the man's rough warmth, the way he pulls the boy toward him, the son scampering up toward his father's body, eager to lean into him. Did he put his arms around his son's chest and pull him up toward him? The father's legs and chest and coat form a warm cave for the boy, protecting and reassuring him. *You can lean here against the cold; it's safe here. You're precious to me.* Did his father's coat have the wonderful smell of the campfire? Of the outdoors? Imagine the delicious taste of the cold, falling snow from within the warm, protective cave of the father.

Tom's story rekindled a memory for Kathy, a mother of several sons, sitting across the table, remembering back almost thirty-five years.

"I was 9 years old. It had snowed the night before. It was a cold, cold January day. My father and I went out with our toboggan, up to the top of a sledding hill near the house. I got in first, then he, and he wrapped his coat around me for the long, windy ride down the hill. Bundled up like that, racing along, both of us whooping with excitement, I felt this warmth as he held me and the toboggan. I've never forgotten that day."

We live in a time when we are attentive to the dangers of touch. We know the problems when boundaries are violated, when parents or children are overstimulated sexually or are threatened physically. However, have we also lost an awareness of the need to be appropriately held and touched and soothed by those we love? This goes for parents as well as children, grown children as well as young children.

As we'll see in many of the stories in this chapter, there is a normal sensual undercurrent to being a parent. This is healthy and natural and can be helpful for our children. When we allow ourselves to enjoy our bodies—and theirs—we reflect back to our growing children our love for and enjoyment of them. When appropriate boundaries are maintained, our ability to take pleasure in our bodies as parents can only nourish the self-esteem of our children, not to mention *our* self-esteem as parents.

Listening to stories of parents and thinking about my own experiences as a father of a son and daughter—moments when holding my daughter's hand has reassured *me,* when my arm draped around my son's shoulder has grounded *me*—has convinced me that we need to be mindful of the primary importance of skin-to-skin contact that is appropriate and safe. The "touch connection" need not be all "touchy-feely" and definitely should not leave either person uncomfortable. Sometimes very small moments, a brief pat on the head, touch of hands, can make a lot of difference.

Ashley Montagu, the social anthropologist, has concluded that human beings have a primary need for touch.[3] He writes movingly about the importance of skin and tactile contact between people, a fact that has been confirmed over and over by experimental psychologists. In Harry Harlow's famous experiments with baby monkeys, those separated from their mothers would continue to hug a furry "surrogate" model mother monkey rather than eat, if forced to choose.

---

[3] A. Montague, *Touching: the Human Significance of Skin*, NY: Harper, 1986.

THREE BUGS IN A RUG: MAKING CONTACT WITH OUR CHILDREN

When we think about "making contact" with our children, safe and appropriate touch may be as important as any amount of words. Sometimes more so—as the following stories indicate. Listening to them, we can savor the wish of each child of every age to feel his or her parent's body, a father's chest, arms, hair, to be able to wrestle with him, relax in his size and strength and rough softness, to feel protected and safe, to be able to again lean safely on a mother's chest, hold her hand, to have a *piece* of Mother or Father to hold on to.

The following examples are from a group in which parents were invited to write down a brief treasured memory with their fathers, a moment from any point in their lives that they hold dear to their hearts. We wrote for about five minutes on 3-by 5-inch index cards; then we shuffled them up, and each of us read out someone else's, anonymously.

"Throughout childhood, I would sit with my father in church, to his left. I would reach into his left-hand coat pocket for a cellophane-wrapped candy. I would open the candy quietly, which was hard to do, and suck on the candy and fall asleep, leaning my head on his arm."

"I remember my father carrying me on his left arm, and as I was burying my face inside his coat against his neck, smelling the leathery scent of his skin. I felt so good, and safe, and my father felt so real."

"When I was 6 years old and one of four boys (all a year apart), I faked falling asleep on the couch in front of the TV after dinner. This "forced" my father to carry me to bed. On the way to bed, I opened my eyes to see if he was looking at me. He was. He smiled and I closed my eyes again and felt very proud of myself."

"Bits and pieces. Moments. When I was in grade school my dad would be the parent to wake me up. He'd come in and jostle me, rub my back for a few minutes, then announce: "Come on Betsy, school time!" The whole morning routine was really fun. I'd go downstairs with him, and he would shave. He'd be in one of his ribbed athletic undershirts, and I would sit on the potty and just watch him shave. Just like "wow!" the whole thing was so serious. I'd test the shave by rubbing my cheek against his and say, "yup, that's a good one, daddy!" It was just a really nice time."

"I'm thinking back to times in my life when I had physical contact with my father. When I was about 6 years old, he would tell us bedtime stories. He'd invite us to come to his bed, and he was there by himself—my mother was puttering or getting ready for bed. We'd crawl in with him, my brother and I, and he'd start to tell us a story. It was fascinating because it wasn't something from a book, it was from inside him, and it was filled with incredible details and chances of fate, and we'd go along and be mesmerized by the tale he was spinning. Then all of a sudden he'd stop at some critical point. We'd ask, "well, what happened?!" And he'd reply, "that's it—see you tomorrow night!" And the next night he'd remember or ask us where we stopped, and then he'd weave this incredible story from whatever we said. I just remember the moment—the being there in bed with him, the snuggling, the acceptance, and just the wonder of it all— being so close to this guy who all day long was much taller than us, bigger, stronger, louder, moving in and out of our lives in more pedestrian ways. But here we were just like three bugs in a rug, being together. It felt nice, really nice."

Just like three bugs in a rug. How warm and cozy and reassuring the feeling! The instructions for these treasured memories didn't specifically ask for times of being close and held and touched. And of course not all treasured memories have such elements—but many, many do. Rubbing cheeks, falling asleep on Dad's arm, snuggling in bed being told magical stories is part of feeling really cared for and loved.

Many of our memories feature times of safe, appropriate physical contact with father; such times with mother appear less often in treasured memories, in my experience. This is not because Mother's touch is less important—it's vital. My hunch is that we remember treasured moments of touch with father because they happen less often and so become special in the same way that we remember a delicious meal after days of dieting. "Hunger is the best sauce," remarked Victor Hugo. And the hunger of children for physical access to their fathers is very real. As Dads, our sons want to be able to lean on us, get hugged by us as they grow, not just as little boys. So too with our daughters. Many daughters feel considerable sadness that their fathers stopped hugging them when they entered puberty. For fathers and teen daughters to find a way to hug or put an arm on each other's shoulders or around a waist—to retain their ability to touch even as a daughter is becoming a sexual being—can be a great gift for both generations. So too can times when mothers and teenage sons put aside their normal shyness to lean against each other, a friendly arm across shoulders, an acknowledgment of the love between them.

A moment of touch can be worth a thousand words, as Tom's story indicates.

Tom: "He really cared."

After an Ivy League education, Tom went back to help run the family farm and raise his own family. His MBA has allowed him to expand the family's agricultural operations in a difficult time for family farms. His story tells us about a moment as a teenager when being held by his father finally convinced him of being loved.

I grew up on a farm and got into the swim team when I was in high school. My father rarely went. He had all these chores to take care of; it was hard for him to drive and take several days off. Usually my mother or some other kid's parent would take me. Then eventually I learned to drive myself. There was one time though, when I had a big meet in Omaha. It was the night before, and we were in a hotel room, just my father and me. We were watching a basketball game on TV. I was gargling and had just drunk all this cold water, and I stood up too fast, and next thing I knew I was on the floor. I had stood up too soon and fainted. When I opened my eyes, my father was standing over me, with a worried look. I could still taste the saltwater in my mouth; it had spilled all over me. It was the look of deep concern and worry on his face that stands out for me still. At that moment I realized that my father really cared about me. I always felt they worried about me, but this time felt he *really* cared. I vaguely remember the sound of my head hitting the bed, and then my father holding me in his arms. He had a gray beard and was a big man. He generally presents himself as a strong person, and he might have felt this a moment of weakness. He *held* me.

My father's not afraid of touch, though, and that's how I treat my 8-year-old son. We'll rub each other's backs, just as my father did for me. My mother is a warm, touchy sort of person, but with my father, it was always special when I did feel his touch. It's almost a form of greeting in my family. They're retired now, and when we visit them after a few days, over breakfast, his hand will rub my back, a way of saying hello.

There's a language to touch; it's a way of speaking to each other without words, and it doesn't take much—there's no need to be immersed in hugs in order to communicate a lot.[4] *A warm handshake, a back rub, connecting through touch—it may mean as much for parents as for children: Through the touch of skin on skin we find real comfort beyond words.*

THE SENSUOUSNESS OF PARENTING

Is it taboo to speak of the sheer physical pleasure of parenting, particularly in the early years but continuing throughout our lives? Often parents are shy to speak of the sensuousness of parenting, but it is a basic, luscious part of our experience. Becoming a parent means a plunge into the world of bodies and erogenous zones: breasts, mouths, genitals, diapers, and butts. It can be a very sensuous experience, as Ingrid's story attests.

---

[4] See Chapter 9 for the story of Carl, a garage operator in North Carolina for whom a moment of simply leaning up against his elderly father helped soothe the grown son's ruffled feelings at his father's seeming inattention during a long-awaited family reunion.

Ingrid: "I loved what I did with my breasts while nursing."

Ingrid emigrated to this country from Denmark over twenty-five years ago. She now has several children. She told this story after listening to another mother in the parenting group—a young woman from the Midwest—read a tale about the anxiety that breastfeeding her baby created in her. Ingrid understood that fear, but gave a very different perspective on the baby, the nipple, and the breast.

I've never forgotten the experience of nursing my daughter. She's now 17. I hope I'll live long enough to see her have babies and to be able to hold her children. My mother is from a large Danish family. She died when I was in my 20s, and I've missed her so. Many relatives who watch me with our children say that I respond just like her. That feels like a real gift from my mother, and from my daughter, that I can be there for my daughter.

A lot of it does go back to nursing. I remember the feeling of both of us being naked. I loved what I did with my breasts while nursing, spraying the breast milk out all over. I've never met an American woman who's done this, but if you hold your breast, you'll notice that the milk comes out in a wide spray, not a little stream. And there is such joy in the nursing baby, as the milk sprays out into every part of its mouth.

Parenting is a very sensual experience in that we get to experience our bodies in pleasurable ways through our children. At times parenting is a blissful, soupy merger between parent and child. This can be true for fathers as well as mothers: Recall the "three bugs in a rug" all curled up in the father's bed at nighttime. In being able to feel good about our bodies we can help our children feel good in theirs.

Sandra: "I worry I'm too flirtatious."

Sandra's story began in response to the invitation to take 15 minutes and write whatever came to mind about "My son's hands . . ." Her story then grew into an expression of her own yearning to simply know and feel his growing body more. The result is a lovely window into the sensuous experience that is parenting, by a mother who is aware of appropriate boundaries. It is an experience that many parents may relate to.

My son's hands are still small, even though he is 14 years old. Yet they already look like my husband's in the way their fingers are shaped, long and thick. Marco used to bite his nails, and I worried because I didn't know what that meant for him. I had bitten mine for forty years before I could stop. He has started to stop at an earlier age.

I love him reaching for my hand and walking hand in hand with me. It occurs rarely now, and I feel privileged and joyful that it happens at all. Sitting in the bathtub as a baby, Marco loved to splash, arms out-stretched, hands flat. He'd pat at the water as fast as he could, squealing with joy. He'd also fondle his bath toys and carefully put them in his mouth, one side after the other, to look, feel, and explore them tactically and orally. He would try also to reach out with his hands to stroke my cheek while merrily sucking on the breast. His zest for living was awake all over him.

Now my boy sits in my lap, and I can hardly hold him at age 14. He holds hands with me but really only sits in my husband's lap—and that only for a few minutes.

I still can see him as a baby. Back then when I would see him naked, I was always shocked with how male he looked even as a tiny baby. His broad square shoulders that ran straight down to his waist, and his delicious long shining toes! How I loved that little body, so smooth and yet angular and bony beneath the skin. It's been so long since I've seen him naked. Sometimes I want to watch or look when he's changing clothes, just to admire him, how beautiful he's become. We joke in our family about our bodies—he's taller than me now, and I will at times go up to him and flutter my eyes—and I worry I'm too flirtatious, or inappropriate.

Difficult questions surface as our children get older. Often we can take our cues from our children. There's a difference between being open and being seductive, or "flirtatious." Being seductive means to overstim-ulate our children sexually. Being appreciative of the wonder of their bodies, enjoying their development, is not the same as seductiveness.

What do we lose as we get older in simply not being able to touch our children? We may touch our children less as they age—teens are not all that comfortable being seen in public with parents draped all over them, for example. It's a process that starts very early in life. When Sandra finished reading her story, Janine, the mother of a young son, exclaimed, "When you have a young one, you want them to grow up, but when they become independent, you want them back here! I sometimes want to snuggle with my son, and he twists away. And he's only 2 years old!" The group agreed: Treasure the moments of hugging and connection we do get; don't take them for granted!

THE FATHER'S HUNGER

The primary sensuous world of parenting used to be the domain of mothers. Now many fathers may find themselves there as well. We hear these days about the importance for the child of being held and hugged by his or her father. Which is of course very true. But have we overlooked the hunger of fathers for physical contact? Men are often shy to talk about their wishes to be held and comforted; we learn early on to keep such hunger close to our vests. When you ask a group of fathers for their most treasured stories *as a father,* though, an interesting window into the father's hunger for contact opens up. In one such group we wrote stories of treasured parenting moments, again on index cards, then shuffled them up and read them anonymously. Knowing you won't have to read your own aloud provides a sense of safety and security for us, giving validity to Yeat's dictum, "Give me a mask and I'll tell you the truth." Here's what we wrote.

"I shared with my firstborn son when he was around 7 my own experience of his birth. I shared with him the feeling I had of holding him. He was a gift. I remember him crying as the nurse was cleaning, weighing him. The nurse wrapped him up (my wife was nervous) and gave him to me; he immediately stopped crying. I felt a love for him and a connection that I will always cherish."

"I remember holding my son as a baby—changing him, feeding him—physical closeness and nurturing—feeding him in the middle of the night."

"I remember holding my newborn son, 15-20 minutes after his birth, in the chair next to my wife's hospital bed, and falling asleep together with him on my chest, all of us exhausted by the long labor. His warmth and trust and vulnerability at that moment moves me to tears still."

"I cherish my nightly ritual of putting my son to sleep. It's a quiet, open, and fun time for us both. He kissing all his toy animals goodnight and me holding him as he drinks his bottle and falls asleep in my arms. Holding him asleep in the darkness, just him and me, then laying him down in his crib."

Again, touch and skin-to-skin contact were not mentioned in the invitation to story-writing, but are entwined in the fathers' pleasurable experiences. For many of us, fatherhood is an invitation back to our bodies, from which we distanced ourselves growing up male. No wonder sometimes fathers get anxious around infants and growing children; after decades of denying that we need our bodies, our children open their arms to us, reminding us of what we're not supposed to need! We may relearn how to relax into our bodies as our children are growing into theirs.

WE NEVER LOSE THE NEED TO TOUCH
The "touch connection" is vital for grown children and parents, not just the young. There can be great pain for grown men or women who experience hugging their fathers or mothers like "hugging a telephone pole," in the words of one person. Yet often grown children and parents are searching for a moment of embrace, a place to lean, a hand on the shoulder, a kiss on the forehead, at a difficult moment. Parents may go back to their grown children for the sense of grounding that touch brings with it, as the following stories remind us.

Corinne: "After so much time . . . I could touch her and connect skin-to-skin."

Corinne is an elementary school teacher, married to a lawyer. Corinne acknowledges that she and her husband are not as close as she had hoped they would be. "Law is a jealous mistress," Corinne remarked ruefully at one point. In her story, Corinne wrote about an unusual moment of connection during a visit home by her 23-year-old daughter.

Isn't it weird that when children grow up, parents lose access to their bodies, to just being able to touch and hug? It's true for daughters, even as my friends talk about their sons. We change their diapers, feed, wipe them; at first their bodies are almost a part of your own, and then as they grow their bodies become taboo. Judy had just returned from a summer trip to Europe. She had worked at an archeological dig in the south of France for four months and returned exhausted. It had been a great time, but now she missed the boyfriend she had met there, a French archeologist. Judy stayed at my house for a week before she returned to graduate school in California.

One day Judy had very bad menstrual cramps, something she is prone to, particularly when she is under some stress. She lay down on my bed. This was the bed she used to lie in when she was just a baby and a kid. We had a ritual of reading stories to her and her brother there on Saturday mornings. How cozy those times were, all of us snuggled together, the kids between John and me, reading aloud! Even now when we sit there, her father and I, under the covers in our jammies, Judy will come in when visiting and sit on the end of the bed, maybe the newspapers will be spread out; it'll feel like a particularly relaxed and tender time.

So when Judy was suffering so with her period, I told her to go into our bedroom and lie down on the bed. I felt honored that she let me offer that to her, to tell you the truth. She's become such an independent young woman. Then I went and got our iron. A friend of mine had told me that the warmth from the iron on her own daughter's back had really helped when she was suffering with her period cramps. So I put some damp towels on Judy's back and then I plugged the iron in and "ironed" up and down her lower back. It helped her a lot, and it helped me too. It felt wonderful to be able to gently run my hands up and down her back. This is my child, I can remember her in diapers. And I was so proud of her now, a grown woman. After so much time away, it felt great to have this moment of clear and pure connection, when I could touch her and connect skin-to-skin.

As parents, we sometimes need to feel grounded in the feel and texture of our children. Something as simples as a back rub can reassure us of our connection to them, and to ourselves.

Jonah: "He had such a calming effect on me."

Jonah is a 30-year-old father of two young children, ages 3 and 1 year. His wife is a veterinarian, and they live near the coast on a farmstead, where they enjoy life with a variety of animals. At a parent writing group, Jonah read to us a story about how the ability to hold on to his firstborn helped him through a terrible loss.

"A death in the family is misery. My brother died in a boating accident three months ago. I needed my 3-year-old boy, Jack, very much then, after the accident and at the funeral. At the funeral, it's almost like I wanted him to pat me on the back, to comfort me, to reassure me. Several times I had to leave the line greeting people in order to go over and hug my son. He was kind of oblivious, didn't really know what going on, scampering around singing songs. I wanted him to be 8 years old so he'd have some sense of the event. But, still, watching him, holding him, my arm around his shoulder—it got me through.

You don't realize how much parents love their children until you become a parent. My brother had been going through a messy divorce, very depressed, and in fact we think he jumped from his boat and drowned himself. Very sad. My parents have been devastated—sold their boat, the one they used to use all the time.

Jack was great to be with at the search site off the coast. There were several search teams set up, and Jack was a great comfort to have there. He didn't really get what was going on, of course, and hardly knew his uncle. But he had such a calming effect on me—being able to put my arm around him. There were mostly other strangers on the search team boats; my other brother was on a different search boat, and so I felt very alone.

I dreaded finding my brother's body, having to see him drowned. A different boat actually brought his body in, but all through the search I felt so alone. I remember shaking a little. My son asked me, "Daddy, are you cold?"

Hugging him calmed me, to feel how precious life is, to lose it so suddenly. My brother and I were not so close, but it was a terrible blow to us all, and I know that really all I wanted to do was to cling to Jack. Thank goodness he was there and that he let me.

Our bodies ground us, and a child's touch can restore us to the world at times when we are lost in our sadness. For a parent dealing with loss, a hug, a touch, can restore some sense of life, of what's important to live for. Being held can remind us of what is here, and now, and worth holding on to, in the face of a terrible loss.

Paul: "There's such a power to touch."

Paul's story began in response to the invitation to write for 15 minutes without stopping about "My son's hands . . ." A quiet man, who now lives alone while finishing his graduate studies in microbiology, Paul fashioned a testament to the power of touch.

I'm a single father, and the divorce was a pretty horrible experience. My wife basically had custody for the first few months after the separation because the judge just gave Ben to her until the settlement. Now we share custody, but it is very hard not being with him as we used to be.

When my 3-year-old son wakes me up in the morning, I'll give him a little quick rub on his back. Maybe it'll feel as good to him as my father's hands felt to me. There's such a power to touch—a simple touch and you connect. When my son crosses the street, he still reaches for my hand. There's a great feeling to that reach: *yes we're connected; yes, we're father and son at that moment!* There's nothing more pure than that touch; your attention is there. It cuts right through the awful sense of not being there enough, of his spending half the week in his mother's house without me there.

A simple act like holding hands can forge a connection, particularly when we remember the wonderful feeling of holding on to our own parents' hands. For Paul, touch echoes across the generations, uniting him with his son and with his own father, in memory.

Jim: "As I walked in, she took my hand . . ."

Jim is a plumber, a good one. At age 63 he will still come out in the middle of the night if you need him to look at a cranky boiler or drippy pipe. Sometimes wonderful parenting stories are shared in the midst of an ordinary day. That's what happened with Jim—after fixing a plumbing problem at my house, we started to talk about our children, and Jim told me this story about a treasured moment with his granddaughter.

I'm a gruff kind of guy; I know it. My hands are rough, my skin sometimes feels to me like sandpaper—after all these years of having my hands in the muck, twisting pipes and working with 14-inch wrenches. My 3-year-old granddaughter at first would not make contact with me. They were all living in our house, downstairs, and she'd come up to visit and run away from me. She'd go into a different room and play with her parents. Recently, though, my son and his wife bought their own house, in the suburbs, and we went to visit. She came running up to me when we were at the front door, and as I walked in, she took my hand, exclaiming, "Grandpa!" What a feeling, that little soft hand in mine; it seemed so tiny, but it made a real difference to me. She showed me around, maybe she felt more relaxed on her own turf, but I loved how she greeted me, holding my hand as we walked around her new house.

You can't tell a book by its cover, nor a person by his gruffness. Here we have a lovely man, savoring for days a moment when his granddaughter put her little, soft hand in his sandpapery one. And treasure it he should: These moments when the younger generation shows their love is very restorative to the elder one. Touch, in fact, has a restorative capacity—lowering blood pressure, calming us at a physiological level. For elderly people, holding and being held by their grandchildren may be good for their health!

IN AND OUT OF TOUCH

We may grant sensuality to the early years of parenting but edge away from it afterward. With an infant or toddler it seems so unavoidable—the feel of a child's nursing, the skin-to-skin wonder of it all. We acknowledge the bodily needs of infants and young children. We may have a harder time talking about the need to be touched of both parents and older children. Yet being held—and holding—is a real gift and a human need that we have throughout our lives.

The sensuality of being parents and children continues through the life cycle, although it changes, of course, as we both age. Both generations may yearn for this contact. Some of the most powerful childhood memories we carry around are of moments when we felt safe and protected, reassured and comforted, by leaning into our parents' bodies, feeling cozy and sheltered.

The memories of what we yearned for can be important guides for what our children need from us: the safety, exhilaration, comfort, and reassurance that comes from being able to feel a parent's body, lean into a father's or mother's chest, arms, hair, to be able to wrestle with a parent, relax his or her size and strength, a mother's touch, a father's rough softness.

There's a loss of touch that parents too may feel. We may be trying to simply touch our sons' or daughters' bodies and feel unable to do so. One of the biggest losses amidst the pleasure of watching our children grow is the loss of access to our kids' bodies and the reassurances that such access brings, the sense that the world is okay, that we are grounded, we are *in touch.* Jonah holding on to his young son during the painful, scary search for his brother, lost at sea, reminds us of the reassurance a parent can feel in the touch connection with a same-sex child—mothers and daughters, fathers and sons. Feeling a tactile connection with a smaller, life-giving version of ourselves can help us through dark times. At the end of one focus group, Jim, a father of several young children, observed that "I loved the stories about the healing capabilities of something so simple as touch. That's something that many of us I suspect take for granted."

Yet, too, might our need for connection also make a child uncomfortable? Corinne's story of "ironing" her daughter's back while unhappy in her marriage—so needing to touch the girl—raises the question of whether her daughter felt uncomfortable with this gesture. Do parents sometimes turn to their children to satisfy need to touch and be held that are more appropriately for their partners or spouses to meet? If the adult relationship in our lives is not meeting our needs or is not present, we may turn to our children in ways that can leave them uncomfortable or even coerced, feeling that they have to take care of us at the cost of their own comfort. Thoughtful parents need be mindful of such matters, attentive to maintaining appropriate boundaries between themselves and their children. Unwanted touch can be invasive. When a child of any age says no or seems very uncomfortable with our touch, it is important to respect that boundary. Talking to partners, spouses, or friends about touch and what's appropriate can be helpful, as can asking the children themselves. Children give us cues. A 16-year-old son or daughter may not want a parent's arm around his or her shoulder at the mall, while permitting, even welcoming, a hug at home.

What's important is to be mindful of your body and theirs and to remember that we all need the playful, safe reassurance of tactile contact to really feel at home in the world.

Hidden Wisdom You Can Use

- Children have tactile needs to be held and touched all their lives. So do parents.
- Many of us—parents and children—struggle to feel truly comfortable in our bodies.
- Making a "touch connection" does not mean that you need to be touchy-feely. There are many ways to touch. A quick hug,

snuggle, rubbing of hair, or hand of support can be enough to melt the chill of a cold time or a lonely day.

- Take cues from your child—they tell us through words or body gestures what is appropriate distance.
- How did you enjoy physical contact with your parents when you were younger? What didn't you like? Both kinds of memories are good guides to what your kids need from you.
- Is there a way now that you would like more or different physical contact with your parents? How about with your partner, or with friends?
- Are there "touch needs" that you have neglected with your parenting partner or spouse?
- When a child says no, listen carefully: Respect their physical boundaries.
- Talk to your partner, a friend, a counselor, or a minister or rabbi if you have questions about what is appropriate touch or physical contact with your child.

c h a p t e r   t w o

Connecting with Your Child

We try so hard as parents. We want to be there for our kids. We want to help them, protect them from life's hard knocks. Often we try to do that by *talking* to them. *How are things in school? How are things going with your friends? What's it like in your dorm? Is there anybody special these days?*

We live in a time when the worst thing is to be *a silent parent*. I pick my kids up from school and they hop in the car, refugees from middle school and high school. As we drive down the main street of town, I barrage them with questions. Damned if I'm going to be the preoccupied, self-absorbed father who drives along in silence thinking about the baseball scores rather than his kids! So I talk and they're quiet. No matter how I try, I can't get much info out of them. Within minutes, I want to pull over to the courthouse in the town square to have a judge declare my kids uncooperative witnesses and order them to start talking!

Then the thought trickles into my head that *maybe if I shut up they'd say more.* And usually that's true—the better I listen, the more space I give them to talk when they want, the more I hear.

Have we forgotten the magic of silence? There are special opportunities for parents and children when words don't intrude, when questions don't pop out like stop signs and traffic lights. There's a difference between being silent and being unresponsive, between quietly listening and being tuned out, *not-listening.*

What do many of us treasure in our stories about our own parents? We treasure times with few words, when we felt really seen, safe, doing something together with our mothers or fathers. Driving together with Father, watching the ribbon of highway unfurl ahead, or doing errands around town with Mother, or washing the dishes after dinner, Mother or Father soaping up the pots and plates, rinsing them, handing them to us for drying, or being down in the basement with Dad setting up the HO train set, quietly working together on laying the track and putting down the artificial green bushes. These are times that seem like little is happening, but they are rich in nourishment between parent and child.

In one parent group, Marilyn, a grown daughter, now herself a mother, remembered with special fondness the quiet when driving with her father at age 10.

"Saturdays were special times for my father and me. We'd go to the town dump with our trash, together in the truck, just the two of us. Sometimes we'd talk; sometimes we'd just drive along in silence. But I loved those trips to the dump."

Ronald found his memory jogged by Marilyn's story. "I'd spend hours at the dump with my father on the weekends. We'd take the bags of garbage there and then poke around the trash, looking at what other people had thrown out. My father would pick things up, put them down, and every now and then he'd hold up some treasure he found and exclaim to me, 'look at this!'"

Now, at age 50, a father himself, Ronald wondered if his father may have been giving him a lesson about life:

"You have to search through a lot of crap to find something worthwhile. I remember a saying of his: 'With all this shit around here, there must be a pony somewhere.'"

Just father and son poking around in the trash together—in that poking around, though, the boy feels welcome in his father's presence, safe there. It's a time when they can be together without also feeling on the spot, without feeling that you *have* to say something.

CONNECTING WITH YOUR PARENTS

The friendly shared space of silence is important for mothers as well as fathers, daughters as well as sons. For both mothers and fathers, recognizing the nourishing silences with our parents can help us learn to be better parents.

James: "We hardly talked—didn't need to."

Silence can be a shared activity, leaving both participants feeling calmed and soothed after a difficult moment. James, now age 50, wrote this story about the wonder of being with his dad on the golf course, a place where the young boy felt safe, compared to a scary home situation.

I can still remember going to the golf course near our house for the first time with my dad when I was about 8 or 9 on a weekend morning. We stopped at a diner on the way together. It was an old country place, a converted railroad car with wooden booths. I had never had home fries before that day. I can still remember the smell and the texture of those potatoes. My father liked them with ketchup, which I thought was amazing.

For many years after that, once I hit maybe 12 years old, we would go out really early in the morning, and I'd caddie for him. There wasn't much talking between us, the joy and relief was more being away from the house and my mother, which felt really the opposite.

At home my mother would be yelling and accusing us all, including my sisters, of all sorts of crazy things. She suffered from a manic-depressive illness. So sometimes at night, after supper when my mother would be suspicious and yelling at us, my dad would take me out on the golf course, and we'd just walk around, look at the stars, listen to the birds, hardly say anything—just being together was calming and soothing. Once I felt better, my father would take me back home. We hardly talked—didn't need to.

Words between them were hardly necessary. The calm presence of the father, the sweet sounds and gentle starry night, helped soothe the flustered inner world of the frightened boy.

William, in his 60s, spent a weekend at a workshop on Men and Their Fathers: Unfinished Business, where he lamented the difficult relationship he had with his own father, who had died several years earlier. When asked to write a treasured memory of a moment with his father, he offered this brief story—almost a prose poem—about a special time when his father took him to work and communicated without words that he simply wanted his son around.

Dad would take me with him to his chemistry lab on a Saturday morning, and he and I would weigh things—like a strand of hair, a grain of sugar, or a dot on a piece of paper—on the balances in the lab. Sometimes we'd blow glass into intricate shapes. It felt good to share his work world in this way and for him to want me there. Not much was said. We were just there together.

A connection was made without words. The child experienced fascination and enjoyment by simply being with his father in this magical laboratory.

Betty read her story aloud with merriment. She is the mother of several teenagers.

I once witnessed something my mother did that I never forgot. My 5-year-old brother was starting swimming classes at the YMCA, and the three of us were driving him there. I was 9 years old at the time. My brother was up front sitting next to my mother; I was in the backseat. All of a sudden my brother looks up and asks, "Mom, what's sex?"

Well, my mother believes in honest answers and real talk about these matters. So she goes into a big explanation, telling my brother about how when two people love each other, they sometimes want to express that in a physical way, and so they want to touch each other. She went on in this long song and dance to my little brother about sexual feelings between adults and how you should wait until you're married. Finally, after at least five minutes of this, she turned to him and said, "Why do you ask?"

He replied, "Well, here on this card it says 'Sex—M or F?'"

For myself as a parent I've used that experience a lot: When kids ask me questions that come out of nowhere, I first ask them why they are asking. Sometimes the reason that kids ask is very different from what I think it is, and if I know why they're asking, I can figure out better how to answer.

How often do you assume you know what and why your child is asking? There's value in not answering children's questions too quickly.

The following story offers an example of how a mother learned to hear her son better, and feel more relaxed herself, by paying attention to the pleasures of silence in her life.

Ann: "I wasn't being a good mother unless I was pursuing him."

Ann is a 50-year-old mother of several teenagers. She works at a start-up high-tech company in Westchester, New York, the same company where her husband is a senior executive. She came to several lunchtime brown-bag discussions about being a parent at the company. The talk over the weeks had led to many stories about the participants' own parents.

For Ann, remembering the pleasure of silence with her father led to a transformation of her own parenting style. She always listened intently at the brown-bag discussions and at one of the meetings she told a story about her father. She began with a painful memory.

"My father was an angry man, given to strong verbal outbursts. He could be pretty hurtful to me, yelling, criticizing. For most of my childhood in Minnesota, my father fought a losing battle to keep the family farm, and I guess a lot of his frustration came out in his ridiculing us kids, sometimes taunting us. Once he was taking a load of hay out to the fields for the cows, and I wanted to go with him. I must have been 6 or 7. He was in the truck and kept yelling out the window, "Do you want to go Annie or not? Well, are you coming?"—while I was trying to get my boots on. He'd gun the engine and act like he was leaving, saying I was too slow, while I would cry and hurry to lace up my boots.

"Silence was our best time together. Often that was true in the truck, when he was driving, just the two of us, especially. I loved the big old town dump near our farm. We'd find wonderful things there. One summer, when I was 11 years old, we went to the dump and found all these old shingles that had been thrown away; they were all different colors. We took the shingles home and spent the summer fixing up our old farm buildings. My father would go along and put the shingles on while I would follow with the paintbrush, close behind him. We did all the buildings in the course of the summer, including the barn and the other buildings and the house. It felt like we spent the whole summer doing that together. Those were the times that really nourished me."

Ann's words stand out even now: "*It felt like we spent the whole summer.*" There's a timeless, all-embracing quality to the moments of engaged, safe quiet time between parents and children. For Ann the calm silence was a time safe from her father's verbal abuse, but also a time when she was able to feel close to the father she loved so dearly, to see his gentler side.

Of course, a parent's silence can also be hostile or punitive or withdrawn. A parent's cold stare or mute look can wound a child. The key lies in the kind of warm, comfortable silence in which we feel heard and seen and recognized, in which the child feels welcomed and appreciated, as Ann did as she happily trailed behind her father carrying the paintbrush.

The nourishment for Ann came from the feeling of safety with her father. Times were not always safe with him: He was a farmer trying to keep his livelihood in a time when the odds were stacked against him. His bitterness and anger grew every time a piece of his beloved farmland was sold to a developer to pay off debts, and Ann became the focus of his foul moods. Over the years what Ann mainly came to remember of her father was less her profound love of him and more his unpredictability, angry outbursts, taunting of her—those painful moments that are difficult for a child to understand. One activity when her father was predictable and safe was when he was driving; his hands stayed on the steering wheel and his anger under control. During those times she felt able to relax and enjoy him.

One day after lunch at the software company, Ann told me that she had been thinking about some times with her father that she had only recently remembered, memories that had been stimulated by all the stories she had heard during the lunch meetings. Smiling shyly, Ann spoke of a time when she was 11 years old.

My father and I would drive together in his truck while he delivered milk to neighbors from our farm, both of us silent while we drove along, then stopping at farms to look at animals together. I remember spending what seemed like hours together watching baby pigs. Our only conversation would be "Look at that one" or "Oh, that one." It was something we shared very deeply, almost without words.

For Ann, what was shared so deeply was a gentle appreciation and love of animals, of life. On those visits she could see the side of her father that she loved, the side that was almost lost in his desperate battle to hold on to the farm he loved. We can imagine the wonderful calm for both daughter and father, standing in the warm barnyard, daughter sitting on the wooden fence, father leaning next to her, looking at the young animals, admiring them together, the 11-year-old child listening to the gentle tone in her father's voice as they watched the baby pigs, the relaxed way the two of them joked, easy together in the warm summer sun, the pungent, life-giving smells of the farm all around them.

Retrieving this memory at age 50 represented a transformation in Ann's sense of her father, and of herself. The father she remembered now was not only angry and abusive but also a quiet, gentle man, a father different from the angry bitter one who had previously dominated her memory.

Remarkably, as Ann retrieved this picture of a gentle father, something awoke within her; she spoke of feeling transformed, becoming aware of a gentleness and calmness within herself as a mother. When we talked a few weeks later, she told me that she had begun to realize the importance of an engaged silence while with her teenage son.

Because my son is in five-day boarding school I haven't been seeing him as much as I want to. I pick him up on Fridays to drive him home for the weekend, and I go crazy wanting to know how this is going and how that is going and if he has made friends. And recently I've been able to just let go and sit calmly and silently with him in the car for forty-five minutes. The other day he said that he wanted to listen to a *Phish* tape with me; they're a band he really likes. And I could do that and not feel that I wasn't being a good mother. It wasn't that I didn't want to be silent with him; it was that I was feeling like I wasn't being a good mother unless I was pursuing him—finding out what he was feeling and what was going on.

Having found that memory of my father on the farm and how nourished I felt by those times with him makes it easier to be quiet with my son. He is only 14 years old, so it's very hard to be separated from him five days a week. After I recovered that wonderful memory of delivering the eggs with my father, I found I could sit quietly with my son, and there'd be nothing exchanged, and I didn't have to tell him everything going on at home. I didn't have to ask him about everything going on for him. I didn't feel like I had to know exactly what he was feeling or what was happening in order to be close to him.

Listening to him, not talking so much, was a new kind of power, more power really than what I had been doing before. Before it felt like if I was going to be a good mother and I was only going to have this little bit of him, then we had to use this time *well,* and *well* meant getting stuff shared. I wanted desperately to know all that was going on in his life, and yet that was less important than being there for him. Just being with my son brings back the nourishment of being with my father, the two of us so happy and silent. I feel nourished by it too as well as feeling that I can give him something just by being with him.

Ann's story reminds us that some of the best conversations we can have with our kids start with our being quiet, and listening. Often we try to do so much for (or to) our kids, solve their problems and give advice before we've really heard them. How often do we let them emerge out of the quietness between us?

CONNECTING WITH YOUR CHILDREN

Once we ourselves become adults, and parents, the lessons we've learned about listening, hearing, and connecting shape our behavior with our own children. Sometimes, in our hurry to be helpful or to stay involved, we lose track of the best way to connect—the same shared space of silence that we remember from our own childhood.

The following story offers an example of how silence, even unintentional silence, can help us tap into our children's feelings.

Laurie: "We held our breath."

Laurie is a social worker, married to Edward, the senior minister at a large Episcopal congregation in New England. Their sons are grown now. But the story Laurie wrote took place when their then 5-year-old Michael seemed to be behaving outrageously.

One day, when traveling to Maine by car, my husband, son, and I stopped in at a diner for breakfast outside Portland. Michael was 5. We sat down at the counter, and Mike's gaze became fixed on a man seated at the end. Before we knew what was happening, Mike was pointing and frowning at this man, who happened to be the only African-American in the place. Then he said, "You're a bad man!"

Mike paused as my husband and I and everyone else in the diner held their breath, incredulous. He went on: "You're going to die!"

Again we held our breaths. We thought we were raising a color-blind child—after two years as house parents in a local Ivy League college dorm. What was happening? Then Mikey continued: "You shouldn't smoke!"

Everyone breathed again. The man put out his cigarette, took off his hat, and, before he left the diner, came over to shake Mike's hand and reassure him that he would stop. Had I interrupted, none of us would have learned anything. I tend to be a talker and an interrupter, and I was proud of myself for staying silent.

There's a humorous side to conflicts with children, and seeing that has saved me more than once. In fact, it is probably the greatest contributor to my patience, that is, my willingness to suspend judgment when Michael said or did something I didn't expect. By waiting, I was able to learn what Michael's words or actions really meant.

Laurie's husband, Edward, sat next to his wife while she read her story, listening with a look of befuddled amusement on his face. The experience was riveted in his memory too, although he offered a different perspective.

Sitting in the diner, I was in shock when Mike said that. I wasn't being clever in waiting before saying anything. I was simply stunned into silence.

Sometimes shock and silence can be adaptive! For whatever reason, it's sometimes best not to respond too quickly.

Laurie and Edward went on to tell the group that the deeper meaning of their son's words only recently came to light, over twenty years later. At a recent family gathering, they were remembering Ed's father, whom they had been going to visit that same day they had stopped at the diner.

My father was dying of brain cancer, and it was a hard time for us all. The trip to Maine that day was to see him for maybe the last time. Matt really loved his grandpa, and he still remembers sitting on his lap playing with him. We were talking about my father's death and the stop in the diner, and Matt remembered the connection. He told us that he had seen shows back then on TV about how smoking causes cancer. His grandfather had cancer, so he was aware that somehow he was losing people to that disease. And he yelled at the poor man in the diner because of that connection between smoking, cancer, and the pain of losing his grandfather!

Patricia and Marilyn: "I've learned from Pat how to be with Emma."

Patricia and Marilyn have two adopted children, Emma and Rachel. They are a lesbian couple, living in Minneapolis. Together they give a moving portrait of the possibilities for shared silence between parent and child, and the varying comfort levels different parents may have with these possibilities.

Patricia: Our daughter Emma is 11 years old. We'll be driving somewhere and not be talking to each other. There'd be 5, 6, 10 minutes of quiet and reflection, and then one of us might say, "I was just thinking about . . ." It'll be nothing profound; the other person comments on it. It's so different from Rachel, our other child, who is 7. With her in the car, it's chatting, chatting, chatting. With Emma it feels like a totally shared moment, we're comfortable enough with each other to be quiet. When I'm around Rachel in the car; sometimes I feel like just asking her to go someplace and stop talking and find herself.

Recently, Emma and I were driving to soccer, with the radio on. She leaned over to ask permission to change the channel (which I was very happy about because I've asked her not to simply move the channel but to say, "Mom, the radio is bothering me. Do you mind if I turn it off?" Then it was quiet, and Emma said, "Mom, I'm a different person this year."

"Oh?"

"I don't think I'll hate myself if I lose a soccer game this year."

I said, "That's very nice!" I went on: "You know, I *have* noticed a change in you this year."

That was it. Then we had another 5 to 6 minutes of quiet.

Now, Marilyn is always after me to talk more to Emma. She and Rachel love to chatter, chatter, chatter together. When I came home and told her about the conversation with Emma, Marilyn said, "Why didn't you say more!"

Marilyn: Actually, I've learned from Pat how to be with Emma, that I have to listen much more carefully to her and not be so talkative myself. So now we will go for cappuccinos, and I'll just listen to her more carefully. That's much harder to do with Rachel, because Rachel talks so much, and so do I! I wonder sometimes if I'm really seeing or hearing Rachel amidst all of our talk.

One parent may be a better listener than the other. Parents can learn from each other. And the rhythm of silence and talk will vary between parent-child pairs in a family. Sometimes a more talkative style matches a child's temperament better than a quiet one.

Micki: "You learn a whole lot more when you listen."

Micki is divorced and the mother of a 20-year-old daughter, Laura. Micki's a very energetic woman, as evidenced in our focus group by her eagerness to participate in the discussion, often making interesting comments or observations about what other parents contributed. Her verbal facility was welcome in the group; it also lent credence to her story, in which we see that a parent's very ability to talk may drown out a daughter.

I tend to talk a lot, and my daughter has always seemed more quiet. I know that I also tend to assume a lot about her—that she is depressed or worried and for a long time I would launch into a barrage of questions and statements to her about how she might handle her life better.

A few years ago I decided—because Laura was going to college and she had never been confirmed or had a real coming of age cere-mony—that I wanted to do something to mark her womanhood. We talked about doing it at a family values camp that we have been going to every summer for generations. She wasn't real warm or excited about it, but she never said *no* either. She was involved in the planning in terms of talking about it with me, but she was never involved in the creating of it. I told her, "I want this to be something I give to you."

She said okay, but she still didn't seem real excited about it.

When it came down to the time to do it, it was so emotional for me! It was very difficult.

We planned for Laura and me and her grandmother to say a few words at the rite of passage at the evening worship service at the camp. I looked over at her face, and I practically fell to the floor. She looked so miserable. The three of us stood in front of the group, and I read a selection from *The Prophet*. Then played a song from *Sweet Honey in the Rock,* and her grandmother and I talked about how proud we are of Laura, how we trusted her now to make her own decisions.

Afterward I was convinced I had made a mistake. Maybe I shouldn't have asked her to do it. Maybe I should have given her more of a choice.

On the way home, Laura turned to me and exclaimed, "That was the best week of camp yet!"

I asked her about the ceremony. She explained to me: "I wasn't mad or upset, Mom. I was just scared I'd cry in front of the whole community—I wanted to keep it down."

I've learned a lot from that miscommunication and from all my worrying. One thing is to listen better to Laura. I feel I learn a lot now from watching her, really seeing her. We have these wonderful conversations.

Recently Laura has begun to say "Just let me finish" or "Just let him finish" not angrily, but in a clear way. I can't believe how much I interrupt. I've learned it in my family I guess, and I tell her how much I appreciate her doing that because it means that she is comfortable dealing directly with me. It's something she never would have done when younger. She advises me, "You know Mom, you learn a whole lot more when you listen!"

Often we need to learn this new ability to listen as our kids get older—to realize the depth of their insight, of their watchfulness, and not to assume that their quietness means that nothing is going on inside.

Kathleen: "I've learned to breathe and just listen to my kid."

Kathleen gives voice to the difficult process parents go through in learning to be quiet and listen when a teenage child is troubled. She's a 45-year-old mother who works in a large insurance company. She played with a cigarette in her hand during the focus group, apologizing for its presence, saying she's trying to stop and having it around calmed her even if she didn't smoke it.

We're all so invested in our children. We want them and ourselves to have peace of mind. My oldest, Sarah—her personality is just not one to give peace of mind, for herself or for me. My youngest is more easygoing. Things roll off her. With Sarah I've wondered, *what did I do?* You have such power over them when they're young children. She tells me all the time she's her own person and can work things out. You try to mold a child, and if things don't turn out like you hope, it can be disappointing. Yet they are who they are, separate. I'm always talking and trying to give her advice, about boys, jobs, apartments.

A therapist once asked me, "What makes you think you're so pow-erful as a mother, that you can solve everything for her?" Yet when they're young, you're all they've got, so *why wouldn't we feel respon-sible for everything for them?*

As Sarah's gotten older, I've learned she's separate. This is going to sound silly, but once I went to a psychic, when Sara was in her teens. The psychic told me, "You have a child, a teenager, and you need to let her make her own choices and mistakes. She'll be fine."

Sarah was 16 or 17 at the time. Anyone could say that to a parent, but I believed.

Once Sarah started high school I felt I had to separate. I'd pick her up at the MTA, and she'd have such misery—such teen angst. I real-ized I just had to listen, let her have her own problems. I couldn't solve them. Instead I learned to say things like "Sounds like you had a hell of a day" or "Oh, too bad," instead of trying to take over and solve. If you were to ask me what I've learned after almost twenty years of par-enting, I'd say that I've learned to breathe and just listen to my kid when things get tough. It's not easy, but I try.

Often we feel so responsible that we want to make things right. What makes a child feel better, though, can simply be to feel heard and vali-dated, or offered words of encouragement and support.

SHARED SILENCES

It's a truism that there is a difference between listening and hearing. Many parents know about "active listening," a concept that can have mystical and magical overtones. One can wonder just what kind of spe-cial skill "active listening" is. Can I do it?

In fact there is little mystery. Sometimes just letting your children talk is enough. If we stop talking, informing, educating, then they can educate us. Of course you have to truly *listen*. You need to *want* to hear what they have to say. Sometimes no words are necessary; all they need to know—at any age—is that you as a parent simply want to be with them, to witness what they are doing, to share time with no goals, to appreciate what they are doing or have them appreciate what you are doing.

Often with our children, good things happen when some other activity focuses our attention together—when driving somewhere, playing golf, tossing a football back and forth on the front lawn, just spending time together. When doing something with us that they enjoy, kids will start to talk to us. "Shared silences" are quiet times together without a lot of goals for what *must happen,* a time in which you are present and available for whatever comes up between you and your child.

The best lesson of all from these stories is that there's no need for "shared silence" to become yet another agenda for parents. It needn't become part of the Parental Performance Pressure. You don't have to work too hard at this or do it just the right way. Simply being aware of the possibilities of silence and seeing what emerges may bring playful possibilities with it!

Hidden Wisdom You Can Use

- Many good things happen between parents and children in quiet times. Don't assume that you have to talk to be connected. Try being with your child without talking a lot.
- Listen to what your child says in the quiet times: Often they are telling us about what is most on their minds.
- Often children say important things when they (and we) can focus on another activity as well. Too much (direct attention direct eye contact, sitting looking right at each other) can sometimes put kids on the spot. Doing something else together as well—tossing a football, making dinner, watching a river run by—can often lead to wonderful conversations.
- Open-ended questions or statements are often very useful in response, for example, "I wonder what was going on for you in that situation" or "What do you think made that such a good time?"

- Sometimes children may need reassurance that silence is all right. "Is anything wrong?" they may ask. You can tell them that everything is fine. You're just enjoying being together with them.
- Try assuming that you don't know why your child is asking a particular question or making a statement. Instead of answering, ask them "How come you ask that?" or "What leads you to say that?"
- Rhythms of quiet and talk vary between children, and between parents. Some kids and parents are very chatty, others more quiet. Temperaments vary, as do moods. There is no one right way to be.
- What was the rhythm of quiet and talk in your own family growing up? What did you enjoy about it? What did you wish was different?
- Often a gentle word of support or encouragement, a clear sign that you've heard what they've said, can be more effective than long speeches or explanations by you.

chapter   three

Resolving Power Battles and Control Struggles

W
e all know that it's best to avoid getting into control struggles with our kids—battles over going to bed on time, cleaning up rooms, getting homework done, completing college applications when they're due. Yet power struggles are not so easy to avoid. What parent doesn't at times feel locked in a battle in which no one wins and no one surrenders? Rules, routines, responsibilities, and limits are parts of life, yet some of the most special moments for both kids and parents happen when we, consciously or not, find a way to dissolve, even if only for a while, the impossible stalemates of parenting. We become more playful, make a new connection with our kids, taking a new exciting avenue rather than treading down that same dead-end street.

Sometimes we find we've done the right thing without even planning to. Sometimes our kids will tell us how to do it. In the stories that follow, we find parents taking risks, blundering around, trying to find new strategies for connection, ways of defusing confusing and upsetting moments that can get us as tied up in knots as they do our children. Perhaps you'll learn some new ideas to use yourself.

Bill: "No one else knew what happened behind the bushes."

Bill is 35 years old, heavyset, and soft-spoken. He's married and a father of two boys. And he's known as the best soccer coach in his town: He doesn't push the kids too hard to win but teaches them the fundamentals while also having fun.

My story goes back to when I was a child. When I was 4 years old my mother died from ovarian cancer, and 2 years later my father remarried. I was 6, and my stepmother brought with her two young daughters of her own. The first summer after the remarriage, we were all just getting used to each other, and to help make that happen, I guess, we all took a long cross-country camping vacation together.

Throughout this trip, I teased my stepsisters unmercifully. We were all packed away in the hot car, every day going from one campsite to the next, trying to be a family. Looking back now, I realize how uncomfortable it all felt: a new woman up front with my dad, new sisters in the back, my mother gone. I'm amazed at what my father and stepmother (who I grew to love) were eventually able to pull off. However, that day I was fighting with my two sisters in the backseat—and since I was rapidly becoming the obnoxious older brother—I inadvertently threw my elbow and gave one sister a bloody nose. My stepmother insisted that my father stop the car and give me a spanking.

Well, my father stopped the car and pulled over to the side of the highway. He got out of the car and came over to my side and took off his belt and told me to get out. Then he took me out behind some bushes alongside the road. He told me that I must behave better, that he didn't want to belt me, but that I must act as if he did.

Then he beat on the bushes wildly a number of times, while I let out loud yells. We went back to the car and got in. I didn't mess with my sisters anymore. No one else knew what happened behind the bushes, but I've never forgotten.

Sometimes we can speak to the deeper needs under the problem behavior. Bill's father (consciously or not) defused a tense situation by creating an alliance with his son, who likely needed exactly that in order to feel connected with his dad in his newly blended family, trying to fit together in that symbolically small space—the family car.

Connie: "I had lost touch with what I was doing."

Connie is 40 years old and an elementary school teacher.

When my daughter Judy was 2 years old, we lived in an upstairs apartment, attached to friend's house. One night while my husband was away at work, I started to give Judy a bath. This was not a simple task; the bath took place in the shower stall, in a small plastic bin designed for little Judy. It became clear really soon that my daughter didn't want to have a bath. She protested and tried to get out.

I very quickly decided that she had to have a bath that night. Things degenerated from there. Judy would stand up, all soapy and crying, no! I would push her back into the soapy water, saying yes!

There was water everywhere. All of a sudden the phone, which happened to be in the bathroom, rang. Dripping wet, I reached over hurriedly and picked it up, half snarling hello! It was my dear friend Dotty from downstairs. That's when I realized that our bathroom was right above their living room. Did they have guests over who had heard our screaming? I suddenly wondered if their two teenage children were home listening to it all! I felt very embarrassed and didn't know what to say. Without a word from me, Dotty said in the calmest, caring voice, "I hear you, and you're doing fine."

Well, in that moment, I got it. I had regressed—this wasn't just a moment about bathing my daughter. I had lost touch with what I was doing—it was my trying to make her do what I wanted her to do regardless of whether she really needed a bath that night. Did she really have to have a bath? I turned and looked at Judy. I saw this defiant 2-year-old standing in the shower stall, dripping wet, angry, and waiting for the next round of this battle. Well, I laughed. She relaxed when she saw me smile at her. I said, "You don't have to have a bath tonight."

And I pulled her over to me and wrapped her in a big towel and gave her a big hug.

It was something about Dotty's quiet voice that calmed me down. Without scolding, she communicated to me that I should think about what I was doing, and it was alright.

When we get locked in a bubble of our own preoccupations and need to win with our kids, a fortuitous "break in the action" can pop the bubble, helping us see reality more clearly. A phone call to get encouragement from a friend, counting to ten, taking a deep breath, and leaving the room and coming back are all ways to get a different perspective during a too-intense moment, when we as well as our kids are near the edge.

Lilith: "I really met my father as who he was, not just as my dad."

Lilith is 43, and you can tell from the muscular thinness of her body that she was a professional dancer for many years. She now teaches dance from a studio in her home outside New York City. She's married and the mother of two young girls.

I have two older sisters, and the general form of punishment when my sisters and I wouldn't get along would be spankings. We would fight constantly and my father would always get very, very frustrated with us. You know how the youngest in the family is—always wanting to make sure there's enough attention on them.

I grew up in Florida. The Sunday morning ritual in our family was my mother and my sisters and I would go to church—my father was Jewish, my mother Catholic—and then we'd pick up Dad at home and all go to the beach. We'd play on the beach for hours and hours and hours, then we'd go get hamburgers and cherry pie and come home. On this particular hot fall day we were driving home; my sisters and I were just screaming and yelling and bickering with each other in the backseat of our convertible. My father kept turning around and warning us to be quiet—but it was no use. We didn't have enough room, and I hated the way my older sister Jane leaned against me. Or she'd complain that I was humming or singing too loud. We were all so tired and full of sand from the beach. My father kept warning us to be quiet and putting his hand in the backseat; at one point he kind of waved it back at us, trying to grab someone. Then he warned us: "Now listen, if I have to tell you one more time to keep quiet, I'm going to spank you when get home!"

Well, I was the little one and definitely a part of we, instigating things. Finally my father yelled at me, "Okay, that's it. You're getting a spanking when we get home." When we walked in the front door my father said to me in this serious voice, "Okay, you need to go to your bedroom. It's time for you to get your spanking." I went in there ahead of him, and I put on my pajamas.

Then I had a thought: I decided I was going to put books in my pajamas—hardcover books from my reading shelf. I figured that if my father spanked me he was going to be in for a big surprise! So I wedged several hardcovers into my jammies and waited, ready for my spanking. I didn't know if he was going to think it was funny or whether he was going to get angry with me. He walked in looking all stern, and I remember his arms swinging back and heading toward my bottom and me holding my pajamas tight against my waist so that the books wouldn't fall off. Well, he walloped the books, which made this big noise. It was one of those moments where I started giggling and then he started to. We both ended up on the floor just laughing and giggling with each other. It was such a sense of recognition for me. It felt like that was one of those moments where I really met my father as who he was, not just as my dad. It stayed our secret, too, so that sometimes when I got spanked, I knew I could put books in my pajamas and get away with it.

Dispensing justice and limits as a parent does not need always to carry with it a sense of Godlike retribution. Sometimes a playful response can do more for a child's self-esteem than a Draconian follow-through. While consistency and appropriate limits are very important, it's precisely a parent's willingness at times to suspend or bend the rules that gives children the crucial sense of being seen and valued for who they really are.

Elizabeth: "I'd be calmer if I had it to do over."

Consider Elizabeth's story of a time when a parking meter became an unexpected prop in an old family drama. In her mid-40s, Elizabeth and her husband had several teenage children, two daughters and a son. Her lovely red hair shone in the bright August sunlight that filtered through the spacious room at the conference center, where a group of parents were gathered. Several of us sipped from mugs of coffee. I was surprised at Elizabeth's nervousness; she's a bright, articulate, self-confident woman, yet she seemed shy when talking about parenting her 14-year-old son.

My moments of difficulty have mostly been with Bobby. I don't know anything about boys and their growing up. I only had sisters; Bobby's our only son. We have a good relationship, but he does a lot of testing and experimenting with what he can get away with. Friends tell me not to do power struggles. They just don't work, but still . . .

I had picked Bobby up in town and we were headed home. He wanted me to stop at our favorite jewelry store, because he wanted to buy an earring. He had gotten his ear pierced the week before. So we did stop there, and I even bought him a cheap silver earring. We were having a nice moment, and as we were heading back home, I noticed that he wasn't wearing a seat belt. So I commented to him about that, and he smiled vaguely back at me and said, "that's right Mom."

I said, "I need you to wear a seat belt."

And he said, "I'm over 12! I don't have to wear a seat belt." He quoted the law to me: "Under 12, buckle up."

I replied, "Well, my rule is that if you're in my car you need to wear a seat belt."

The seat belt lay limp by Bobby's seat. Storm clouds gathered in the car.

I pulled over to the side of the road and parked in front of a parking meter on the main street of town and said, "I'll wait."

Bobby said "I'll do my homework."

He got out his backpack and flipped open his math workbook.

I said "I'll meditate," which I did. I just sat there behind the wheel of the car and closed my eyes. After a few minutes, I remarked to him, "By the way, I just want you to know that parking tickets in this town cost three dollars."

"I'm not paying for a parking ticket!" he replied huffily.

I said, "Well then, I suggest you put money in the meter. We're waiting for you, after all."

After a few minutes of thinking about that, he got out and put forty-five cents worth of change in the meter and got back in the car. That bought him over an hour of time for us to sit there!

So . . . Bobby sat there and did his homework, and I sat and meditated. Then I read some of a book I had in my purse. Every now and then a friend would drop by and ask what we were doing.

After a half hour or so, Bobby closed up his book, put away his pencil, and put on his seat belt. We drove home without comment.

The whole thing was light. We didn't have an argument. There wasn't any teeth-gritting or fist clenching.

I was grateful for the slack I felt. At other times, I feel stressed—that I have to get here or there, or that Bobby has to put on his seat belt right now, that he's being pushy or willfully disobedient, pushing my buttons, and then I get mad at him, and yell or guilt-trip him. I often feel like I am in a power struggle and have to win or give in.

One source of wonder in these moments may be that we calm down the bullies within ourselves and can really give ourselves and our kids the space to work out a new solution to an old battle.

We can imagine Bobby's struggle: to be like an adult and not have to put on a seat belt ("The law says I'm grown up!"). What teenage boy wouldn't be hungry not to have to submit to a mother's words, especially after having had a moment of closeness with his mother, buying earrings together? Maybe now Bobby needs to demonstrate his independence and perhaps even to provoke his mom.

Elizabeth in turn struggles with her need to keep her teenage son under control, literally as he grows by leaps and bounds in his ungainly powerful body, piercing his ears one day, going out on dates the next. The car is a perfect flash point for both of them. If the boy won't follow the rules now, what'll happen when he's 16 and, gulp, driving!

The most painful control struggles with our kids usually reflect unfinished struggles from our own childhood, and this is true for Elizabeth. Her battles about rules and limits with Bobby are rooted in her own childhood with a colorful, erratic father who broke many rules.

He was a passionate, troubled man who drank too much, fought too much, drove too fast, and who deeply loved his daughter. Elizabeth grew up both attracted to and scared of those men who test limits and get away with it. And now, as fate would have it, she has a son who also is fascinated with pushing the edge of the envelope.

What's so delicious about Elizabeth's story, and about such playful moments for us all, is that she sidestepped the familiar battle about rules with her kid, and maybe the old one within herself as well. Elizabeth gave her son a face-saving way to put on the seat belt.

She finished her story with a personal insight about her parenting.

My youngest child is 12, my oldest 26. When I look back, if I could erase the tape and start over, I'd work more on serenity and having more slack. I've been pretty grumpy as a mother. All the stuff I got grumpy about wasn't worth damaging my relationship as a mother to my kids. Kids are irresponsible because they're young, whether they leave their clothes all over the floor when they're 10 is really not such a big deal. Eventually they stop doing that, whether you nag them or yell at them or not. I would live with more. I'd be calmer if I had it to do over.

Colleen: "The idea of a parent negotiating with a kid—whoa!"

Colleen, a single mother, sat poised in her chair at the parents writing group that cold winter night, eager to read her story. Her grandparents came over from Ireland, and a picture of the small town near Dublin to where she can trace her ancestry is on the wall—next to an old photo of the great Irish actor Henry Irving, whom her grandparents had seen perform in the early 1900s. Colleen, a freelance copy editor, hosted this event. Her living room is lined with books; manuscripts are piled on her desk.

This past summer, between TV, Nintendo, and computers, my 8-year-old son, Frankie, was always in front of the screen. After he's been on the screens for over half an hour, he's a total crab. It's like his mind has been fried. I worry he's not reading enough. He's at that place where reading is still a task, not an enjoyment.

I work as a copy editor. I love reading, and even more than that, I like things to be in control. I hate disorder in my house. I get frantic inside when that happens. And whenever I'd go into his room, Frankie was playing video games or watching some stupid TV show. So we'd start to argue. I'd yell, "No, no, no! No more TV! Turn the screens off!" I'd come into the room angry before I even saw what he was doing.

So the other day, I heard the familiar Nintendo music coming from his room and got really upset. When I rushed in, Frankie looked up and stopped me. He said, "Mom, wait. Listen to me, now just listen."

I paused in my tracks and he went on.

Why do I have to stop just this minute? The Nintendo didn't work right when I first got started, and then I took a break. I haven't been playing so long.

So we looked at the clock and figured out that it was only fifteen minutes that he had been playing this game. I asked him how much longer he wanted to play, and then we sat down and talked about the problem.

I said to him, "This is what I want. I want you to read more, and I'm having a hard time telling you that you can't always have the TV on and you can't always be playing Nintendo and computers."

Frankie said to me, "Why don't I do some of that and then some of the other?"

That seemed reasonable. We made a plan: time on his choice of TV or Nintendo and then equal time doing reading. Over the summer, he's been reading books and a game magazine with short stories and mazes and hunting for things and stuff like that.

Frankie is only 8, so I don't mean he just said and did all this in one easy moment. It took us a couple of days to talk about and work out an agreement. But, you know, I've had to do as much learning as he has.

Growing up in my family it was my father who laid down the rules. He was a real Irish patriarch type. He had a touch of the brogue in his voice, and he could yell. Then, when I was 15, I remember my father yelling at me to do something, take out the trash I think it was, after I had just spent hours on my homework, and I started to cry hysterically. He backed off, and that was the end of that. He got his way by yelling until I got my way by crying. It was all yelling and crying in my household. So the idea of a parent negotiating with a kid—whoa! What a new idea!

I've learned to ask Frankie what he thinks would be a fair way to do this, and often he'll come up with an idea—like I'll do some reading and then some computer. Then I have to come up with a more refined version of his original suggestion, some of this, some of that.

Parental authority need not always be hierarchical, nor do differences always have to be negotiated with "affect storms": parent yells, child surrenders, or child buffaloes parent by crying and yelling, until parent gives in. Colleen and Frank are negotiating a new style of authority, more interactive and responsive to the needs of both parties. Negotiating replaces bullying.

Steve: "I had to let my will drop away."

Steve is a hearty man, who seems resigned to the thinning of his hair as he approaches his 50th birthday. He's the president of a suburban bank outside Cleveland. He graciously hosted a writing evening, inviting over parents from his son's school and their church. The walls of the family room in his large house are lined with plaques thanking Steve for his community involvement. He's chairman of a fund-raising drive at his alma mater. He's also up three mornings a week playing basketball at six a.m. with the guys at the Y. Steve laughed often reading this story, as if surprised at his own resourcefulness.

"This is the story of the ten-hour seventh-grade homework marathon. A few years ago, one night after dinner, my son Teddy showed me his seventh-grade history assignment sheet. He had a report due in a couple of weeks. He decided he wanted to write a report on Greece, and, in the weeks beforehand, I helped him find a few articles from our town library. Then nothing happened. Days went by. I forgot about it. About a week later, on a Friday afternoon, I asked Ted what was going on with the report, and he replied, "Oh yeah, it's due Monday.""

He told me he would get to work on it "sometime." That felt familiar. Teddy can get so scattered and vague, you know how 13-year-old boys are. To be honest, getting him to focus on his homework felt like an old battle—to not leave everything till the last minute, and most of all, not to do a sloppy, hasty job.

Is this story about me or my son? I'm not sure. I know I push myself. I like to get things done. I remember one of the worst moments of my junior high school was the time that my father tried to help me learn better handwriting. He came to the dining room table while I was working on an English assignment and began to show me how to write more neatly! I was humiliated, and furious. I got so sullen and angry, until he just gave up.

With Ted I wasn't sure how much to push him. He had just started junior high, and the stakes seemed higher than in elementary school. So, when he came to me on the Friday after school, I suggested to him that he start working on the report right then, or at least by Saturday. Teddy looked aghast. He told me he'd worked hard enough all week already and that he wanted to see his friends that night. Well, we had several arguments over the next 2 days about his starting his report! I was trying not to force him, even though I wanted to chain him to a chair in front of his desk!

That Sunday he got back from a sleepover at a friend's house late in the morning. While he was eating a bowl of cereal, he remarked, "Dad, I do have to get the report done. I don't want to get another detention."

Another?

"Well, there was a French assignment that I didn't get done in time, and I did it in detention last week."

Then he asked, "Dad, want to give me a hand with this report?"

So, Ted went over to his study area in the living room and looked over one of the articles on Greece and started to copy it word for word. I watched this and told him he needed to do a first draft and to write it in his own words. He replied that all the kids just copy out of books to do their reports.

Well, I was getting pretty steamed. First I got angry at the teacher for not teaching him how to write reports. But then I began to feel guilty myself for not paying enough attention to what Teddy needed in his middle school environment.

"Would you like some help?" I asked.

He said sure and asked me if I'd type up the report for him! I said no, no, I wouldn't do that, but I'd help him organize information for the report.

I felt myself getting angry and impatient. But somehow I felt like I had to let my will drop away. I decided to go pretty much at his pace. I kept remembering that day when my father tried to correct my hand-writing and how *I had bullied him.* I didn't like backing down with my own son. But I did. I took my time.

We sat there together on the bed in his bedroom. I decided that I was going to give up the whole day, if necessary.

I got Ted milk and cookies a couple of times, rubbed his back. He wanted to take a break and listen to his favorite band, Pink Floyd. At first I said, "No, no, got to finish the report first." Then I thought, *Why not relax, take a break?* He put on the CD for me, wanted me to listen to the songs, which I did.

Ted yelled at me a couple of times after we wrote an outline and a first draft. He complained that I made it much harder for him. It was okay. I weathered it. I didn't get hooked. These battles can be deflected when we let our will slip away.

Instead, I developed a sense of drama about the project. I'd go and make periodic reports to his mother and younger brother downstairs about how it was going. I made it exciting, telling how we're doing, where we were. We were going to get this done! It became a big deal in a good way. He typed out a first draft around six p.m., after four hours of our talking and reading and outlining. We had dinner all together. Then I proofread it while his bedtime came and went. We ignored it. Ted started to type the final draft around eight p.m. So slow. He'd type a sentence, then gaze off into the distance, lost in a thought about Pink Floyd.

By ten p.m. he had finished spell-checking his essay. It took us ten hours, but he did it! Ted was very proud of it, and so were we. I learned a lot from that episode—that yelling doesn't accomplish much, about the need to control myself, the tiger inside spoiling for a fight. That's okay for business—banking has gotten pretty competitive—but not with my son.

We have to woo our children sometimes. We need to be clever and to engage them. Younger children don't have the mental resources that we do. We can sometimes drop the need to force them to submit to our way and playfully, gently lead them toward a new approach. We don't always have ten hours to devote to our kid's homework, but that may not always be the kind of wooing that's called for, as the next story suggests.

Spencer: "I've learned not to push too hard and fast."

Tall and lanky, Spencer is a 60-year-old college professor who can see parenting from several perspectives. The children from his first marriage are negotiating college while his young son from a second marriage is still just in elementary school.

This story is one still in progress, actually. It's a sort of "diversion" story about power struggles—the way we resolve a tug of war over Spiderman with a 2-year-old by offering an Incredible Hulk. It happened about six weeks ago with my 18-year-old, Peter, and we're still playing with the Hulk.

He's a freshman at college in the Midwest, and they have a winter term for individual work projects. You're supposed to go out for four weeks into "the real world" and do something that will further your education.

Peter decided that he wanted to spend the month "fronting the essential facts of existence" in our Vermont home with three other kids—another guy and two girls. We thought that they were too young to do that, and besides as he knew fully well, we had weathered turning down a similar request from his only sister two years before. "No," we told her, "it's not okay for you to spend your work term shacked up in our vacation house with your boyfriend!"

"You'd say yes if it was Peter," she had accused us.

And we had said, "No we wouldn't."

So now I was stuck—I could hardly say yes to him after having said no to her!

Peter and I have a pretty fierce relationship, going right back to my divorce years ago from his mother. I wasn't looking forward to his coming home to talk about his plans.

Over the phone I knew he had all his arguments lined up and would put up a struggle. We needed an alternative proposal, or we'd be in the same old battle, where he wants to push at the edge of the envelope and we're saying no.

A few days before Peter arrived home, my wife and I were talking with a friend who is on the board of a program that sponsors educational trips for college students to the third world. It turned out that there was a trip available at just the right time, going to Nicaragua. Peter, it happens, speaks a little Spanish—he had spent two weeks at language school in Mexico—and so we checked on that trip. It turned out it was full. But our friend then suggested that we talk with the director. He could use an extra hand, she said. Maybe he could cook something up. As it turned out, he could. Peter could go as a "leadership intern."

So the other night we sat down to talk in our home. I just listened to him and didn't come right out and say no. I wanted him to know he could make a coherent argument to me and that I would listen. In fact, he didn't have a very strong argument. He had no study plan for that month, no good explanations (educationally) for why he was going to spend work term in a vacation home in Vermont with his buddy and their two girlfriends. He began to see his arguments were weak, I think, and so by listening to him, I didn't have to criticize him.

Silence descended. I didn't say no. I've learned not to push too hard and fast. Instead, I said, "I have an alternative proposal."

I told him about the position we had found through a friend, that he could be a "leadership intern" helping to run a group of students doing a village sanitation project. As I described it, I saw the twitch of a tiny grin crack the corner of his mouth. I couldn't tell whether it was that he saw the diversion and intended to deflect it, or whether he liked the idea. But a few words later, he breathed, "Awesome," and I knew we had made it through.

I think he felt some relief. I'm convinced too that my describing the position as a *leadership* intern made him feel valued and important and made it appealing to him.

The trip doesn't leave until January so that's why I say the story isn't over.

Instead of locking horns with his teenage son like two bull moose, Spencer found a face-saving alternative for his boy that he presented in a respectful way that reinforced Peter's self-esteem and sense of partnership in the dialogue.

KING KONG MEETS GODZILLA

"These battles can be deflected when we let our will slip away," Steve wrote. These wonderful stories underscore our vulnerability as parents. While we may prefer to deal with our children from positions of strength, authority, and hierarchy, where we're on top, that's not always the most productive way. The stories point to the importance of validating our kids, letting them know that we see them as people and can respond to them, instead of simply being single-minded and having to win.

In these treasured stories, parents calm down the King Kong within themselves so as to woo the Godzilla within their children. We get hooked in control struggles because they reflect unfinished battles within ourselves, a part of ourselves we can't get comfortable with and can't let go of. Watching her son in front of the TV, Colleen was able to restrain the frantic part of herself, the part who knew how to respond to frustration only by yelling like her father or weeping and storming out like the 15-year-old girl who learned to dominate her father with angry tears. Miraculously, Steve was able to woo not only his son but also the angry dominating part of himself who learned at the handwriting lesson as a teenager to respond to the embarrassment of slow or sloppy work by becoming angry and shaming those around him. Getting out of what I sometimes call The Swamp of Frantic Emotions or past The King Kong Meets Godzilla Approach to Parenting is a life-long struggle for us all, one that is never entirely solved.

Yet when we can find a calm space within ourselves, we can see that often the "power struggle" is about *connection*, a moment when the child (and usually the parent too) struggles to feel validated and seen and loved by the other. Elizabeth's teenage son needed to assert his independence via the seat belt law just at the time he spent a lovely, cozy afternoon with his mom, buying earrings together. Sitting in the car by the parking meter, Elizabeth was able to let her son find a face-saving and respectful way back to her after asserting his independence from her. In her playful transformation of a spanking, Lilith found the moment of "special" connection and attention that she coveted from her father, and that may have been at the root of the misbehavior with her older sisters in the first place. And Bill at age 6, packed into a car with his new "family," missing his lost mother—how could a young boy not want to poke and prod and make more room in that car, maybe even dissemble the whole vehicle to make enough space to put his lost birth mother back into it? The true lines of gravity in the car connected the son to his father, the two survivors of the original family, the only ones who really remembered the mother who was no longer there. Bill's father, maybe inadvertently, found a way to make an alliance with his son, to say to him that yes we are also the old family here even as we are becoming a new one. We have a secret alliance behind the bushes; it's you and me kid. With this secret between them, he found a way to get the message to his son (*quiet down!*) without forcing his son into a humiliating surrender. With this playful strategy the father gave the boy what he needed: something special from his father, the surviving parent.

Of all the many kinds of parents stories, tales of power and control that work out well have a special poignancy, perhaps because they truly are magical, not in a nostalgic way but because they describe moments where we as parents are as surprised as our kids when *something in ourselves and them changes*—or, as one mother began her story, "Finally one day it occurred to me." Something just clicks, breaking old gestalts and perceptions. We may not completely transform ourselves and our children, and we surely need to relearn these lessons over and over, but the moments in these stories are special to remember.

Hidden Wisdom You Can Use

- You don't always have to win as a parent.
- Never underestimate the importance of saving face for kids of all ages. Try to find ways for children to go along with what you want without leaving them feeling humiliated or too exposed.
- Being attentive to the connective yearning of your child underneath the provocative behavior can defuse tension. Sometimes a child's unwillingness to be quiet or settle down has to do with his or her wish to sit in your lap, or have your attention for a while, a friendly hand on his shoulder, a word of encouragement. Sometimes, too, it's because she feels unsafe or frightened in some way.
- We often get into control battles with our kids when we are rushing or distracted. Stepping back, taking a deep breath, and devoting some time to listening to your child for a few moments may actually save you time in the long run.
- Think about your image of authority as a parent. Is it hierarchical or more egalitarian, or a mixture of both? Is it an all-knowing Robert Young in *Father Knows Best*? Is it Bill Cosby, who manages to have just the right mix of humor and authority? Maybe it's King Solomon, who gives edicts that are always obeyed. Can you think of relationships with authority figures—at home, in school, at work—that left you feeling good about yourself? What did you hope for authority figures as a child? These memories are often helpful guides to what our children want and need from us.
- Time-outs can be as helpful for parents as for kids——counting to ten, taking a deep breath before speaking (or yelling), making a phone call to a friend. Remember, you have the more difficult task—you're the parent, not them! We need to be calm ourselves during tense moments with our kids.
- Breaking rigid internal sets or gestalts is very important when you feel in a power struggle. When you are stuck, try to come at things from a new angle.
- Humor and playfulness that is not seen as mocking or shaming can be very helpful during control struggles.

The Development of Family Themes

Family Secrets

W e inevitably confront with our own children what couldn't be talked about growing up in our families of origin. All families contain secrets, distortions, masks, and evasions—parts of life that are too painful or threatening to talk about directly. Often we are not aware of what the secrets and taboos were in our childhood families. Sometimes we only become aware of our own denial when we trip over it with our own children.

Denial and silence can be as painful for parents as for children. We may struggle with generational legacies: Do we provide our children with a different future or continue the silence? Sexuality, violence, authority, alcoholism are all issues that provide the opportunity to redefine the past and the future in new ways, for ourselves and our children.

We may choose to keep silent to ourselves, our children, or our spouses, or we may try to bring to the surface what couldn't be dealt with in earlier times. Doing so can be helpful for our children and healing for ourselves.

Andrea: "I've had a horror of creating hang-ups in my children."

Andrea is 48 years old, with two daughters now in their early 20s. Andrea and her husband run a working dairy farm in Vermont and have lived in New England all their lives. She is a smart, lively woman who often shook her long red hair as she read her story.

Sexuality was never discussed in our family when I was growing up. I'm not sure how well I did with my kids either, but there's one conversation with my teenagers that I want to tell you about.

My mother was never told anything about sex by her parents. She didn't know how to make babies until she first had sex with my father. If her parents had been more up front, she probably wouldn't have had sex so carelessly after marriage. One story I heard after her death was that she had gotten pregnant without expecting to. Getting pregnant so young must have been horrible, an absolute no-no. Another story has it that she was forced to have an illegal abortion. And I've heard from an aunt that my mom was forced to get married. Obviously that's not a good way to start a relationship. My oldest sister said, after my mom's death, that she always had this sense that she was illegitimate but could never figure it out because our parents' wedding date covers the territory. But there was this date in October when, inexplicably, Daddy would send Mother flowers, every year. I noticed that. The wedding day was supposedly in June. So who knows what was being covered up? As you can see, little was talked about directly in our family. It was all rumor and gossip.

I grew up with this great awkwardness about sexuality. My mother made it a special point to explain to me where babies came from. She came into my bedroom when I was 11 to explain to me the facts of life, as she called it. It was very awkward for her, and for me. She wanted to explain to me that sex was a wonderful thing that took place in your lover's arms, a marvelous thing—but she didn't mean a word of it. What I got was that this was a very scary, bizarre thing that happened. Another thing I got was that it was not okay to be in any way sexual before marriage, to dress provocatively, to behave in any way provocatively but that there was this switch you could flip when you got married to suddenly become sexual. It's weird.

It was not in what was said specifically. It was in the air we breathed. *"If a girl loses her reputation, she never gets it back." "Guys can do whatever they want. It is okay for guys. People expect that from them, but you're a nice girl. You don't do that."* She'd just make these observations, driving along.

When I started to get breasts at age 10 or 11—I never really did get very much in that department—she got all worried, starting talking about guys just wanting to hang out with girls with breasts, just wanting to fondle you. It was a bizarre conversation. All my friends got their periods before I did, got their bras before I did—not that I ever really needed one, but I wanted one just to be part of it all. I kept wondering why my mother thought the boys would pick me for my breasts when everyone else in the high school was more interesting. Finally, I just told her that I can't believe you're saying this to me—the flattest-chested person in New England! She just laughed. Then she competed with me for that honor. She said she was flatter chested than I was, but, in fact, she wasn't. I was definitely the flattest-chested member of my family, and I still am! She was just so worried, and I could never understand why. If she could just have been up front with me, if either of them could have, it would have made sense.

It's a precious thing for children to learn about how they were conceived and made. My parents could never talk about that. At our vacation home, my father said once, "Well, you were started here in this house. Your mother and I got together and you know about all that, right?" That's as close as he could get to talking about *that*!

So, I've had a horror of creating hang-ups in my children. We live on a farm, lots of animals copulating all over the place, and the kids have seen that. It's always been clear how animals have babies, but I've never sat down and explained anything. I've been so afraid of being awkward or communicating the wrong things, so I've never communicated anything at all.

Except I do remember this one time with my girls, Allison and Joan. We were going someplace in the car together, both girls and two of their friends, all older teenagers. We were talking about something, and, out of the blue, Allison, our eldest, started it by saying, "You know how after you have sex you get all wet and drippy and you just want to clean up right away?"

Wow!

And I said, "And how would you know that?"

"What, Ma! Think I haven't had sex?"

"Well, I don't know."

"Well, I have!"

"Oh. With who?"

"I won't tell you that."

"Was it good?"

Then everyone cracked up. They were so embarrassed that I asked that question. They all tittered and said, "I can't believe we're having this conversation!"

Then I turned to her younger sister Joan and said, "Well, what about you?"

"I've had sex too."

"A lot of times?"

"No, just a couple."

I told them that I worried a lot, especially about AIDS. And I told them that I wanted to be sure that they were protected.

"Oh Mom, come on. What do you think?! There's little else we talk about besides being careful sexually!"

And that was sort of it. They've never asked me for advice, and I've always figured they didn't need it. But they wanted me to know, and they were cool about it. When I asked if it was good, they just laughed. In fact, they may not know. It may be years before they know or can really answer that in a real way. But I hope at least they'll be able to talk about it in the same way we did in the car, when they're ready.

Sometimes small changes in family patterns can bring big consequences. We may think we have to completely rewrite the family script, but, in fact, most often we take small steps as parents; we are different from our parents by degrees. Andrea was able to respond when her daughters gave her an opening. What may seem a small step was actually a big one for Andrea, one that took considerable courage on all their parts. By being able to laugh together, rather than making sexuality into a heavy, scary event, Andrea offered her children an image of their mother different from the awkward, hesitant, scared mother that Andrea knew as a child. And her children are helping to free Andrea, to reassure her that they are not as intimidated or ignorant about sexuality as she herself may have felt at their age.

Parents who didn't feel very enabled by their own parents may find great satisfaction in helping enable their own children to sidestep or overcome exactly what blocked them years ago, as shown in the story that follows.

Megan: "The way I was brought up and the way I am now are miles apart."

Megan is 33 years old, married, with two young children. She's a decisive, organized person who works as a project engineer for a software company along the Hudson River in New York. There's a thoughtful, warm tone in her voice, as well as a touch of Irish lilt. Megan's a particularly open-minded person, whose parenting style may differ from some parents but which reflects her desire to offer her children a less shameful, closed relationship to their own bodies than she herself experienced as a child.

I really enjoy my little girl's self-exploration. She always has her hands in her diapers! I probably enjoy it because the way I was brought up and the way I deal with it now are miles apart. None of this was ever discussed, and it was all bad. Don't touch yourself! Don't ask about your body, about sex—it was all bad stuff.

When I was 8, one of my friends in school told me about sex, the mechanics of it all. I went to my sister—who is six years older than I am, so she's the authority on everything—and asked her, "Is this the way it goes?" She said, "No, no! I don't know where you heard that. It's not true." That was very typical. And I *had* been given the right information.

Once I found tampons in her purse, in one of those little white compacts for carrying them around. I must have been around 8 or 9. I asked, "What are these in your purse?"

She replied, "Well, you know when football players get a nose-bleed? That's what they use to stop them."

Can you believe that? And I asked, "Well, why do you have them in your purse?"

She and her older friends just laughed, and I felt so stupid, like there was something obvious here and I wasn't getting it! That's the way it happened in my family.

I'm just really enjoying allowing my children to have that openness with their bodies. Kelly, my 2½-year-old, *loves* to touch herself. She just loves it! Know what? That feels so free to me. She *hates* wearing clothes. We make jokes because I don't know why I bother buying clothes for her. She insists on taking them off all the time. All last winter she used to unzip her sleeper in her crib, just throw it out of there. And I know it was because she wanted to get her hands in her diapers. Now we're working on potty training and stuff, so in the summer we've allowed her to not even have a diaper on lots of times. Today she was running around without a diaper on. She stands in front of the TV and lifts her leg and gets her hand down there as far as she can. I guess I'm very proud of my husband for being able to allow her to be herself. It's really humorous. It brings smiles to both our faces. She's really enjoying herself, and I think that's just fine.

My husband's not always so sure, and he cues off me sometimes. We've had talks about it. There's a piece of him that's uncomfortable, but he talks about it in a humorous way, for example, "I can't believe I'm sitting here witnessing this."

I'm far from a perfect parent. I can be a real control freak, put lots of pressure on my kids. But this is something I can look at and say, "I have come so far!" This is one thing I am proud of.

What gives us the most pleasure may be freeing our children of what trapped us when young. Megan is appropriately proud of being able to help her daughter feel comfortable in her body and also to support her husband's sense of humor, in which he relies on his wife for guidance in this matter of bringing up an uninhibited daughter.

Other parents face the generational aspects of life and death issues—such as violence in their family or community. Can parents change the direction of their family's future when the problems are so difficult and the stakes so high? The stories that follow give examples of parents who have tried.

Anthony: "If my kids and I didn't talk, it was going to happen all over again."

Currently divorced and living with his girlfriend, Anthony is in his mid-30s, a friendly African-American man who works as a high school gym teacher in the public school system in Brooklyn. He is large and muscular—picture Mr. T. He is divorced and has two children, Chantelle, age 8, and Atticus, age 6. We talked after school, alone in the bleachers of the cavernous school gym.

The tragedy of my stepson Gary being brutally murdered a year ago was one of the hardest things I've gone through in my life. He was 14, shot to death one day, in a friend's house, not a mile from here. His mother had told him that she didn't want him playing with this certain boy, because he was in some type of a gang. But he was still hanging out with this kid. I had lived with Gary and his Mom since he was 4 years old. Even though his mom and I were separated, I was like his father. His real father was long gone. I'd be telling my ex-wife: "Diane, you need to have that boy come and stay with me." I told her that if kids reach a certain age, 13, 14, 15, and you let them do whatever they want to do, after awhile, they're pretty much raising themselves. They're going to lie to you, do anything they can to stay in the streets with their friends. They won't learn anything about mortality or limits. Well, Gary started to do all of that stuff. Many times he had witnessed me fighting with his mother, drinking, calling her names. But we had started working through those issues.

I've seen a lot of bad shit in my life. My mother killed a man, and all of us kids saw it happen. It was horrible. We were never allowed to talk about it because that's my mother's way. If something bad happens and we don't discuss it, she can pretend it never happened. So we learned to hide, keep secrets, even from ourselves. All that stuff flashed back through my head after Gary was shot.

He was shot to death by a 16-year-old boy. One afternoon his mother let him go out, and he was hanging around with this boy. Chantelle was outside and reminded Gary that he wasn't supposed to be hanging out with him.

But he told Chantelle to be quiet. He had told his mother he was going to the mall, but instead he took off with the 16-year-old boy to the home of a 13-year-old. I think the gun already was hidden there in the boy's room and that they were setting Gary up. Somebody heard over the police scanner that a little black boy had gotten shot. They said the boy had long braids in his hair. Gary's mother ran outside to find out where Gary was. Chantelle already knew. She ran over to the 13-year old's house. By the time she got there, the police had put up the yellow caution tape, and they wouldn't let her in. My daughter kept saying, "my brother is in there, my mother wants him to come home!" I'm sorry she had to see all that. The boy shot Gary in the side of the head; he died right there in the house.

I was at work that night, running a sports program in the school. A policeman showed up, and told me that my wife was at Harlem Hospital.

Well, instantly, I had butterflies in my stomach, sweaty palms, and heart palpitations. I figured something happened to my wife. When I finally found Diane, she was lying on the floor. I could see that one of her eyes was swollen. There was a doctor and a minister in the room.

The doctor said, "Anthony, it's about your son Gary. He was shot and killed tonight."

I remember saying, "Oh, my god." I took my coat off and got down on the floor where Diane was. I asked her if she was okay. She said she wanted me to view her boy's body. I said okay.

Diane just freaked out after that. Five people had to drag her out of there. I moved that little boy's head, and blood leaked out from him on to my hand. That did a number on me. I still have flashes of it to this day. It was awful.

I was 8 years old when I first saw a man die. My father was long gone and this was some guy living with us in Chicago. He and my mom had been having a fight. They did a lot. And he had hit her in the shoulder with the pick end of a hammer. They were drunk. She always kept a gun in the house, and she got it and shot him. She killed him. There was blood everywhere. It happened so quickly.

That wasn't the only time. When I was 22 I watched a friend of mine get knifed in the heart in a fight with some Mexican dude over a girl, in a back alley in San Antonio, Texas. I held him in my arms while he died. I remember saying, "I'm never going to let anything ever affect me again. I thought I had numbed out completely. But instead of feeling, I did drugs, alcohol, you name it. Now I'm a recovering alcoholic and drug addict. I've been clean for five years.

Everything I had ever seen that was violent came back to me when I looked at my dead boy. I almost called up my mother on the phone and yelled, "Why were you so weak? Why didn't you help us!"

No telling where I might have ended up if I hadn't gotten help. I hit someone's car while I was under the influence of alcohol and was forced into a rehabilitation program. Eventually I learned that my problems went all the way back to my childhood.

I realized after Gary's murder that if my kids and I didn't talk about all this, it was going to happen over again to them.

I know how therapy worked for me, and it made me feel alive, worthy, like a responsible parent, to be able to get my kids the help they needed. My ex-wife wouldn't go.

The therapist was very good. She saw Chantelle and Atticus together once a week. I even missed some work days so that I could take them.

I didn't want Chantelle and Atticus to grow up without a chance to really work through the death of their brother. I know how people can push their feelings down and never really be themselves; they can just mask everything. I want my kids to be able to deal with whatever comes at them, rather than to hide their feelings.

Sitting there with the therapist the very first session, I watched Atticus play on the floor with the toys while the therapist talked to Chantelle about the loss of her brother. She asked about the fun things she used to do with Gary. And Atticus was on the floor saying things like "I miss my brother" and "Gary got shot." Just to have them expressing themselves like that made me feel really good inside, to the point where I cried. My baby boy looked at me and said, "Daddy, are you crying?" and I said, yes, as much as my ego wanted to say no. He asked me why. I said I was crying because I was happy. I didn't say much more. I didn't want to get into anything that was going to inter-fere with the conversation that Chantelle was having with the therapist. But I kept thinking that I wished my mom had been strong enough to do this for us. That's why I was crying. I realized how much I was doing for my son and daughter.

My son talked about his brother while he played with the toys. He told about how they'd play hide and seek and Batman and Ninja Turtles. Chantelle talked about how they'd play tricks on their mom.

I had to hold back the tears. A lot of stuff I couldn't share with them because I didn't have the relationship that Atticus and Chantelle had with their brother. Even though I was seeing all of them on a reg-ular basis, I wasn't there when they were sharing like kids do. I wasn't there for any of it—that really hurt. I became aware of what I had missed out on—their smiles, laughter, when they'd get angry at each other, sad times.

Now, when they come over to see me, we keep Gary alive. September 8 was his birthday, and we had a party for Gary—me, Atticus, and Chantelle. We even bought a cake. Everywhere we go, whether it's just riding around in my car, or to karate classes, Gary is right there. Sometimes I'll even say, "Gary, quit hitting me!" when we're driving. It might sound crazy to some people, but it keeps his spirit alive, It also keeps the door open and allows Atticus and Chantelle to talk very freely about Gary.

They can't do that at home with their mom. I can't even imagine the pain that she's going through. She's become very silent. I got her to go to therapy a few times, just her and the kids, but I don't know if she's kept it up.

We can give to our own children what we didn't get ourselves. Anthony is helping his children learn how to grieve, and in doing so he hopes to break the cycle of violence in his family. By getting help and participating with them—in therapy, by his instructive playfulness in keeping the memory of Gary alive—he is helping them feel less embedded in the violence, impulsiveness, and despair he knows so well.

Anthony clearly struggles with the residue of his own exposure to violence—his story hints of flashbacks and PTSD-like symptoms. Yet he is still able to do the right thing by his children.

Darryl: "Oh my god. I can't hide this from her, she knows!"

Darryl, a 37-year-old African-American man, tall and trim with a slight mustache, lives in Toronto, where he runs an auto repair business. He is married to a Canadian woman.

Last summer I took a trip with my 8-year-old daughter, Daphne, to see my mother down South; they had never met each other. My relationship with Daphne was suffering. I had been working long hours at the auto body shop ever since I bought the place two years ago. I didn't see much of her; it was not the way it used to be when she was younger.

Her mother was working hard, and things seemed to be running smoothly at the shop, so I said to Daphne, "Where would you like to go for a vacation? Montreal? Somewhere in New England? Go see the grandmother you've never seen before?"

To my surprise, she said she wanted to meet her grandmother, down in Georgia. That's where I grew up. So I bought two round-trip tickets on Amtrak and arranged for a two-week trip.

I come from a messed up family. But I was hoping to hide it from my daughter. My father was a woman-hater. He beat my mom. She landed in the hospital in Atlanta after he hit her in the head with a shovel. We all had to see that. And, he ran around with women. One night my mother threw red-devil dye on him. It melted off part of his fancy suit and scarred part of his face. It was a real horror show.

Now she's filled with anger and distrust. I haven't seen my real father in twenty-five years. I picture him old and decrepit and wanting someone to come to his aid and no one will. My brother and sisters can't stomach him, and I can't either.

My stepfather died in 1988 from cirrhosis of the liver. The only time I really knew him was when he drank and could be whoever he wanted to be. When he didn't drink, he was as quiet as a mouse. I wasn't very close to him. I found out after he died and we went through his belongings that he kept pictures of us from when we were young. He was okay; he took all of us kids and adopted us. But he molested one of my sisters. And my mother pushed it all under the rug. My sisters don't have a relationship with my mom because no one wants to get into it. Basically, I'm the only one who will still call my mother up and say, "How are you doing?" And I'm the only one who is willing to visit her.

So my daughter and I took the train from Montreal to New York down to the Georgia coast. At first everything was really nice, the grandmother and granddaughter meeting each other. She asked us to stay at her house. Pretty soon, though, my brother came over, high on drugs. I had a problem with him because he gets violent; he'd just done time for armed robbery and had been out of prison less than a year.

He was still waiting to hear our mom say, "Bobby, you're a good boy." But he's *never* going to hear it. My mother is afraid of him. She's filled with paranoia and fear because she sent him to a reform school when he was younger. They never really had a relationship. What a mess. I found myself trying to keep it all from Daphne. I wanted my daughter to believe I had a good family. I didn't want her to see any of this stuff.

One day my aunt came over, and started gossiping about our family. And my mother got to running off her mouth about my brother and one of my sisters—how they're no damn good and how he's lower than whale shit at the bottom of the ocean. My mom's got a mouth on her like a cesspool. Daphne and I were in the back room. I turned the music up, and she asked me how come I was turning it up. I knew she was listening. I said, "Let's go for a walk down to the ocean."

"Daddy, how come we can't stay here in the house?"

I said, "Daphne, I know you hear the way your grandma's talking. Sometimes she gets carried away and doesn't know how to deal with her anger and stuff, so just kind of ignore her."

Daphne told me: "I'm scared of her because she yells a lot. Even when she talks on the phone, she's yelling and screaming."

I think my mom's nuts. So I tried to drag my daughter out of the house or make up stories for her. I told her that her grandmother worked at a sewing job for this family in town, and that she cleaned the house of that family. I just made things up.

Then one day my brother Bobby came over. He had been bugging my mother all day, knocking on the door. Someone had gotten him a fix, and he needed more money. That night Daphne and I slept in the living room. All night long we had to keep getting up for the door and saying, "Bobby, go away, please!" But he just kept coming back all night long. Finally, he showed up that next morning, wanting to borrow money for drugs from my mother. Daphne and I went to sit outside on the porch. Then Bobby asked *me* for the money. I told him: "Hey, I came down here to visit with you, and I just have enough money for me and my daughter to get back on the train."

He started yelling and screaming. I told Daphne to get inside, and then we started to get into it. I looked up on the porch and saw my daughter looking through the venetian blinds. I thought, "Oh my god. I can't hide this from her. She knows!"

Just the week before I was in Toronto, away from all this, and now I was about to have a fistfight with my brother. It had to stop.

Finally I broke down and talked to Daphne. "Daphne, it's not all it's cracked up to be down here. It's very crazy." And do you know what my daughter said to me? She said, "I thought something was wrong, Daddy." She already knew!

That afternoon I had a long talk with her.

"Daphne, a lot of things have gone on in your family and you know how I used to fight and drink and fuss with your mom and everything like that? Well, the same things have happened in your family here, too. Your uncle kept coming back here last night because he's on drugs."

Daphne is so smart. She said, "He does crack, too, huh, Daddy?" And I said, "Yeah." And I just went on and on. My mom's had a lot of problems; the whole family has been divided up many times over; my mother would get into trouble, and we'd all be separated. I told her that mom's had to pretty much raise us by herself, that she's had a lot of hard times and has a lot of anger built up, and that she doesn't even know it.

She was making circles on my hand with her index finger while I was talking, not really looking me in the eye, but just sort of looking down at my hand. I told her about her uncle using drugs. When she told me that she already knew there was problems it was phenomenal because Daphne was only 7 at the time. I guess that's about the age I was when I knew there were problems in my family. I'd bring friends over to the house, and my mom would yell, "You get those goddamn no-good jerks out of the house." That's just how my mother would talk to us. It wasn't till I was 16 that I started telling her, "Mom, you're crazy. Something is not right with you." And then she threw me out. That's when I started to drink and use drugs. Basically I've been on my own since I was 16 years old.

I didn't know if I should tell Daphne all that. I worried that it was too much for her. I gave her a big hug—and told her our family was different from what was going on down here and that it was important for her to know about it. She gave me a big hug back. On the way home on the train, we were even able to laugh some and joke about it all. "Boy, Grandma can really yell, can't she!"

I felt that the trip rekindled a close connection between Daphne and me. It worked something out for me. We've been able to joke, laugh, and hug. When I talk to Daphne, I don't see us as a grown adult and little child anymore. It's more like big folks and little folks. And I try to talk to her like she's an adult. The most important thing is that I don't keep secrets from her, and I don't get upset with her when she tries to keep secrets from me, which rarely happens.

I've realized that I put too much energy into worrying that I won't be good enough and that my family will wind up all messed up. What really matters is that I am there for Daphne, no matter what.

Has Darryl put too much on Daphne, given her age? Sometimes we want our children to go through what happened to us, in the hopes that this time it'll be different. We may desperately wish to "undo" the past through our children. Darryl's confession to Daphne may carry with it his unspoken hope to be forgiven for his own family violence, present and past. We can make our children into little versions of ourselves, with the roles reversed: They become the forgiving parents we wished we had our-selves. On the other hand, Darryl is trying to break a family silence, to make his own struggles known to his daughter. In doing so, Darryl provides a powerful model for his daughter of the very human struggle of parents to give voice to parts of themselves that they learned—at some cost—not to talk about.

It can be hard for parents to know how to talk with their children about affect-filled parts of the past that are still unresolved. Sometimes filling in information for kids can be healing in itself, as the following story reveals.

Harriet: "I feel happy I can give it to her straight. No one did that for me."

Harriet is a 33-year-old accountant. Her husband works for Bell Atlantic. They have two young children. She comes from a large family in Maine.

I have several nieces and nephews in their teens and I get some gifts from them about silence and taboos. I come from a . . . dysfunctional family. Let me just say that and leave it at that. My brother's and sister's children come to me now with questions because I am a straight shooter. As a kid there were so many things I was told I had to leave the room for. There was the time that my brother died in an automobile accident—I was 9, and he was 22. No one would talk about it. His car evidently went out of control and hit a telephone pole. There were several passengers in the car. I didn't know they had been drinking and driving until my stepmother told me recently. I was told he was killed in a car accident, and I still don't even know where he was sitting in the car. Evidently a cop found them and pulled my brother out and tried to resuscitate him, but he died there on the street. At the funeral, my sister-in-law sat in the pew motionless, not showing any emotion; everyone was whispering, hands covering their mouths. I wanted to understand why she wasn't crying. The same thing happened when my mother died. My father wouldn't let us go to the hospital to see her. I wanted to talk to her, hold her hand. I didn't see her until at the funeral, in the casket. It was a horrible sight. I still shake from head to toe thinking about being in church with that casket, looking at my mother's body.

It's a gift for my nieces and nephews to come to me; it frees me of the past. When they do, I want to shake my sister. She left them when they were very young. My sister had three beautiful kids, now 19, 16, and 14. She was a drug addict in our nice suburban town. While she was stoned one day, the oldest child got hold of some matches and started a fire; the house almost burned down. My brother-in-law grabbed the kids, and told her to get out. She said okay and just went about her life without showing any interest in the kids.

My 16-year-old niece Gloria was visiting this summer with her father, and she saw me playing affectionately with my son. She came up to me and asked if she could talk to me.

She told me that her father wouldn't hug her at all. She wanted to understand why. I knew the reasons why—I knew about the abuse and pain he suffered as a kid, why he would stay away from hugs, not know about them, be afraid of them. She also wanted to know about my sister.

"How could she leave me?" she asked.

We talked. I answered as honestly as I could. I knew she was ready to hear it.

It's a gift to me, knowing my niece and nephew won't grow up without any explanations. They're old enough to know. I'm happy I can give it to them straight. No one did that for me.

Silence can be very loud in a family, as can "hints" about difficulties. Children often fill in pieces of the puzzles with false conclusions or with misinterpretations. What they take away from our half-truths may be different from what we intend. Age-appropriate explanations that reassure children and tell them what they need to know in order to feel that things are safe and secure for them in the world often do a lot better than pregnant silences or confusing allusions to things that can't really be asked about.

Grace: "There's a real draw to being crazy."

Grace, 43, and her husband are lawyers. They have two teenage sons. She's from a large Irish family.

I wonder whether to tell my children that there is mental illness in the family. I spent some time in a mental hospital, and although I'm fine now, I still keep it a secret. I want to share with my sons that you can overcome tremendous odds, but I don't.

My psychotic episode was a reaction to my mother's death. I was so symbiotically attached to her. I left for college, on scholarship, soon after she died, but when I got there, it felt like nothing mattered if I didn't share it with her. I was very smart and was able to use my intelligence to go to many wonderful places. I still do. But intelligence doesn't replace your mother.

She died in an automobile accident—broadsided in a busy intersection by a truck, alone in the car—when I was 18. It was so hard. I just wanted to hold her hand and be with her. After she died, I was supposed to stay home and take care of my father and my younger brother. Instead I told them that they could take care of themselves, that I wasn't going to stay trapped in Philadelphia. We were a very tight family; there were many aunts and uncles around. What I did was certainly a taboo—you're never supposed to turn your back on family. Part of me, though, was bent on not living anymore. I abused sleeping pills and wound up finally in the university clinic, an excellent treatment center that helped me tremendously.

It's very hard keeping both feet in this world. I'm drawn to that other world, the dark world of my mother. Part of me I cherish; part of my strength comes from that world, and it's one that I haven't shared with my children. There's a real draw to being crazy. The crazy world is so interesting; all the rules go; you can be as bad as you want, eat when you want. I feel my children are too young, that they won't understand, that they'll be frightened and not love me, find me too weird.

I hint at it. When we watch a story about a woman having problems on TV, I'll say, "I understand what it's like to feel so hopeless, so overwhelmed, worthless."

As a parent you have to maintain the illusion that you're in control. Maybe I'm afraid if I speak it, it'll be real. It's so easy to go over to the other side. I can still feel the attraction.

How much do we tell our kids about difficult parts of our past? Grace struggles with a question many of us can relate to (and which we'll return to at the end of this chapter). The question often becomes more pressing as our kids reach the age at which we most struggled with whatever our demons are. Since Grace's mother died when she was 18, as her kids approach their mid-late teens, fears of patterns repeating themselves repel and attract her.

LIES, SECRETS, AND "THE TRUTH"

What is "the truth" about our pasts? *How* we tell our children what they need to know is as important as *what* we tell them. Telling "the truth" out of a need for revenge on the past or particular individuals can be damaging to our children, just as withholding a "truth" that is not relevant or necessary for a child at a particular age can be a loving act. These are difficult decisions for parents who want to be mindful of their motivations and the needs of their children. Getting support can be crucial. Talking to trusted family members, friends, a minister or rabbi, or a counselor can be very helpful.

Kids need basic information about their past and their family lineage. It should be delivered with love, in an appropriate fashion, in ways that they can understand. A young child may simply need to know that his or her parents or grandparents are okay now or, if not, that they are getting the help they need. They can be told that difficult events happened, and may continue to happen, and that the adults around will watch out for and protect them. At the deepest level, young kids (like grown ones) most want to know that those they love are, or will be, okay, and that they themselves will not be abandoned or forgotten. We all need to feel *hopeful*.

It's important to listen to your children's concerns and worries about difficult events and to validate the anger, fear, and sadness that they express. And it's important to let your child know that these events are not the child's fault, that they didn't happen because of something the young boy or girl did. "It's not your fault," cannot be repeated enough.

With teenagers, discussions may become more complex and detailed, more philosophical and speculative. Teens can profit from discussions about motivations and causes. Remember too, though, the tendency for teens to become overly moralistic, to want to take sides or make black-and-white judgments. Teens too will want to know if difficult events are "their fault"—and it is important to let them know that whatever happened was not "because of them." By doing so you can "depersonalize" the past. Often, too, children will want to know whether the difficulties of the past will befall them too. If my mother was hospitalized for depression, does that mean that I will be too? If my grandfather was an alcoholic, will I become one too? An open discussion about risk factors and a mindful attitude about family vulnerabilities and how to cope with them can be vital to a child's self-esteem and sense of being able to manage themselves in the world.

For children of all ages, it is important to avoid demonizing the past, or individuals who are beloved by them. Talking about family secrets and taboos does not mean discrediting a child's history or those who are dear to the child. Yes, a father or grandfather was abusive, per-haps, but there were also other parts of the man as well; he may have been a fine mechanic or a loving grandfather or member of his church. These "truths" don't change the painful reality, but they need to be acknowledged as well. It can be vital to a child's self-esteem to find parts or pieces of beloved figures to hold on to, and "the truth" includes a full portrait of the complexity of those whom we love. Demonizing or overidealizing people is not "the truth."

"*I have come so far! This is one thing I am proud of,*" advises Megan. What gives these moments their power for parents may be the way that we feel *we* have really changed, done something different, changed the future so it is not a replication of the past. Remember that learning that pain and difficulty can be overcome is a vital lesson for children. In being joyous and proud of what we've dealt with, we pro-vide our children with an important model.

Parents in contrast often try to look perfect for their children. "We didn't deal with that" or "just say no" or "buck up"—whatever. What kind of lesson does that provide our children? It's doesn't really work in terms of teaching our kids survival skills for adult life. Many children lament to their mother or father that "I can't be perfect like you." By telling children about the difficulties in our lives, we are showing them how to persevere and manage.

The stories of Anthony, Grace, and Harriet remind us that not everything is solved perfectly in families. That's the truth. What is important is the emotional atmosphere surrounding difficult moments. An honest, frank, caring acknowledgment of difficulty goes much further than shame-filled silences, where questions or fears scream inside us but cannot be spoken.

Confronting taboos and silences that span the generations can be among the hardest moments for parents. Such moments bring with them the fear of betraying those we love, of doing something wrong, of exposing our deepest shame. Ironically, too, when parents find the courage to surface a shameful silence, it can lead to a deeper honesty between themselves and their children and give children the hopeful knowledge that difficult parts of the past may influence their lives but need not determine it.

Hidden Wisdom You Can Use

- You don't have to be completely different from your own parents. Often small changes across generations can have a big impact on children.
- Children need to know about the past of their parents and grandparents in age-appropriate fashion. Talking to young children is different from talking to teens.
- Kids need to know that adversity can be dealt with and that and they can break away from negative family patterns.
- "Depersonalize" taboos and secrets: Kids interpret hard times as their fault, and need to know that whatever happened was not directly because of them, or because they were "bad children."

- Show the good points as well as the bad ones. If at all possible, try to communicate love for difficult people as well as honesty about the hard times. Kids need to know that there are some redeeming, lovable features about all their family members.
- You don't have to have all the answers in order to be honest, reassuring, and supportive of your kids.
- These are hard matters to take on alone: Get help and support if you are burdened by family secrets or taboos. Talk to your spouse or partner, if possible, and/or a trusted friend, minister or rabbi, or counselor.

c h a p t e r   f i v e

Families Under Pressure

W hat does it mean to be brave as a parent? There's an old saw, drawn from stories of soldiers in combat, that tells us that to be brave means to be able to do what is called for even though you are very, very scared. Bravery is not the opposite of being unnerved or frightened, it's rather being able to do what has to be done in the face of fear.

What's true in battle may also be true in the family. Our inner demons bellow and moan, frightening us, but we *have to do something.* There are many battlefield moments in parenting. For example, after months of driving lessons and watchfulness, you let your teen for the first time take the car alone to a dance; you're enraged at something your young child said or did and worry about being able to control yourself but you know that you have to respond somehow to them; or your grown child makes a career or family decision that doesn't easily reconcile with your own values or choices, yet you know that this is the time to be supportive of them, not critical.

Bravery as a parent, then, may lie in the effort to look clearly at ourselves and our families in moments when we are besieged by our inner fears and demons. We can't get rid of those demons, but we strive to see what we and our children really need despite the shrieking from dark places inside us, and around us.

The stories in this chapter have been contributed by parents who have encountered dark times with ample demons: a mother struggling with the survival of her newborn, and the impact of medical choices on his development; a father confronting the life lessons of his divorce; a single mother alone with her children in an unfamiliar town; a father left widowed with his young daughter and son; parents who are lesbian dealing with their daughter's self-esteem as she encounters a painful "attitude" among her classmates.

These are different circumstances, yet with common threads. The dark times for these parents put them on the edge of "mainstream parenting." They are families with a difference. The bravery of these parents has much to teach the rest of us. One lesson has to do with shame and passivity and isolation. Shame refers to the sense of defect, the painful feeling that something is wrong with us, or our family. The essence of differences that become toxic is that we experience them as evidence of our own "badness" or "stupidness" or worse. So too in families: When we feel different from other families around us, we may internalize a sense of being defective or wrong or bad. The power of shame is that it makes us want to hide, to get out of the spotlight, to cover up our defect. Imagine that your child doesn't hear what's said, he responds to sounds but doesn't respond to language, while all around you families are chatting away or another mother tells you how tears of joy filled her eyes when her son said his first word—"ma-ma"; imagine that your sexual orientation differs from what is called "normal," and your child struggles to understand the meaning of that in our world where heterosexuality is still taken to be the norm; or imagine that you have no wife in a community where every parent seems to be married.

If we experience a difference as a defect—my child's cognitive functioning makes him "less than" so-called "normal" kids or my sexual orientation makes me "weird" compared to others or being divorced feels like something is wrong with me—we become isolated and alone and may even deny the reality or our needs and our kids. On the other hand, we may find in our family differences a source of pride and strength that allows us to feel more empowered and real as parents, to become true to ourselves and our children.

All families struggle with difference. All parents experience some shame. We all fall short of internalized ideals in some ways: Perhaps our kids struggle in school or at work, or they're not as athletic as we hoped, or we worry about their social life or family choices, or everything seems great but they struggle with *us*. Every parent is limited in some ways, even as they succeed in others. The tension between feeling proud and feeling ashamed is one we all share. What parents don't want to both turn away from their families and to connect with them to grow more masterful?

The following stories teach us about building confidence and mastering the lessons of life amidst adversity that tests us, beckoning us to be brave. As you read you may hear the sense of difference from "normal parents" that these parents struggled with on their journey to remain loyal to the integrity of their own defining experience.

Joan: "I didn't want to see him."

Joan is 48 years old, and a psychologist. Tall and elegant, with lovely, long black hair, smart and confident, she cuts a striking figure walking into a room. I know this because I've had the pleasure of seeing her at conferences over the years. She's a friend. Her 5-year-old son's medical condition has confused and intrigued doctors since his frightening, premature birth. Larry recently has been given a diagnosis of "agnosia," which means that Larry is "functionally deaf"—his brain is able to hear sounds and noises but unable to process the words he hears as having any meaning. Joan is quite verbal and sophisticated, and the dawning realization that to her son her voice was simply an unrecognizable jumble of noise caused her considerable pain. Yet Larry is healthy and alive, a reality for which Joan is grateful, given her awareness that her boy almost didn't survive his birth. He is also smart—his nonverbal IQ is 119, a fact that Joan underlines: "Too often 'deaf' and using sign language is associated with being dumb."

Joan is married, and also the mother of an 8-year-old son of a normal birth. She graciously offered to tell me a story about her experiences. We talked for several hours one sunny summer afternoon at a conference, alone together on a bench just off the entry lobby of the conference center. Busy people bustled around us, hardly noticing the intense conversation, punctuated throughout by tears from both of us. Joan seemed unperturbed by the bustle not twenty feet away.

I had gone to the doctor during the twenty-sixth week of my pregnancy, and I *knew* something was wrong. There had been no movement for three to four days. But when the doctor took out her heart-rate monitor, she heard the heartbeat, so I thought everything was okay.

She sent me down to the lab for a routine glucose tolerance test to screen for diabetes during pregnancy. I feel so stupid for having listened to her. I know now that with such elevated glucose in the blood, we should have expected movement from the fetus.

Twenty-seven weeks into the pregnancy with Larry I had a dream I've never forgotten. It was about those exquisite porcelain dolls. I dreamt one was looking right at me, and it was all porcelain except it had human eyes. And all of sudden the eyes opened up and looked right at me. They were the deepest blue eyes. Everything else about the doll seemed dead—porcelain, nonhuman. That dream was a message, I'm convinced. I shot up awake in the middle of the night, scared. But I went back to sleep. It's so hard to believe your baby is really in danger.

Early the next day, though, at the Laundromat, I was reading a baby book and came across a passage cautioning that if your fetus was older than twenty-six weeks and you go a day without movement, you should get to your doctor immediately. I almost fainted right there. It had been *ten days* since I last felt movement. I called my husband and said we needed to go immediately to the doctor. He knew something was up. At 9:15 a.m. I had an appointment for 10:30 at our small local hospital.

The doctors took one look and went into their "Why didn't you tell us sooner?" routine. They stopped, though, after looking in the charts and seeing that we had been in the week before and sent home. They weren't sure what to do. The OB-GYN doctors got several neonatal specialists on the phone. There was no movement at all on the fetal monitor.

The sonogram showed Larry just floating there, with nothing moving. His gradually declining heartbeat, was unresponsive to stimulation.

That stillness on the sonogram was the worst. It upsets me still. At twenty-seven weeks, you see your entire . . . *baby*, you see everything. Just how still it was.

So we hustled into a C-section. I said I wanted a local, but my husband wanted me to have a general anesthetic and the doctors listened to him.

So I didn't see Larry when he was born, but my husband said he was just this purple little thing. The first thing I remember is waking up back in the room and the nurse asking me if I wanted to hold my baby before they sent him to Columbia Presbyterian Hospital in New York City.

I said no—I didn't want to see him. They went nuts. Next thing I know there is a social worker in my room, worried that I'm a rejecting mom. I only wanted to hold on to my fantasy of my new baby rather than seeing what I knew the reality was.

I'm crying now but its not tears of regret or sadness. It's like a scary movie that turns out happily; we got through all the difficult stuff. Funny—no one wanted me to cry back then. In the hospital they wanted me to bond with my baby and not cry.

How did I get through those first few weeks, when Larry was so pale and limp? Well the woman in the next room gave birth to a dead baby, so I was grateful for what I had, that's how. Someone else always has it worse.

But it was hard on the maternity ward those next days, with all the mothers parading down the halls with their babies, all the babies in bassinets right next to their beds. And I didn't have my baby with me.

The first time I cried was when I first saw him in the NICU, the Neonatal Intensive Care Unit. I was not prepared. He weighed 2½ pounds, his skin almost transparent, no muscle, scrawny and skinny and see-through. You could see his veins. Bobby, our firstborn, kept saying that "Mommy gave birth to a giraffe." The worst part is that something was poked into every area of his body: monitors on his scalp, hands, and feet, with IVs his arms. The nonhuman, the mechanical, seemed more important than the child. *I* felt the pain of being poked and prodded. I couldn't touch him in his plastic incubator with its plastic cover. He was on oxygen with a respirator up his nose and in his mouth to keep him breathing.

I still remember his eyes, like in my dream. They *are* deep blue; they were the only thing you could see with him so covered up with his hat and swathed up in a blanket.

I was in shock. I cried standing there, and an intern said to me, "Don't cry; everything's going to be alright." Imagine!

Larry spent twelve days in the NYC hospital NICU. All the time he was there no one really knew what was wrong with him. He couldn't move; he could really only blink his eyes.

Then Larry was transferred to our local hospital NICU. We drove home from New York City, and he rode in a little ambulette to our local hospital. We waited for his arrival.

He spent all day under a heat lamp, hooked to oxygen monitors, only five minutes at a time out of the incubator. We were really lucky with his brain. One problem with premies is hemorrhaging in the brain. Larry only had a level 2 bleed. That was minor and cleaned up. But no one knew how destructive the anoxia—the oxygen deprivation—was before his birth. The doctor said, "He could be a complete vegetable, have severe cerebral palsy, or simply have some learning disorder."

I must have been suffering from the general anesthetic aftereffects because my husband knew better what going on day to day. He said to the doctors, "If he really is a vegetable, let him die. We have a healthy son, a family." He didn't want the shame of being a father of a boy in wheel-chair, having to push him around in public. That wasn't it for me—my shame had to do with the possibility of Larry being retarded. Neither of us wanted to be parents whom others *pitied.* I didn't want the rest of my life tied to this *thing.* I know now that Larry is far from *a thing*, but it is not easy having such a special child. It's manageable, its fun, and it will be okay, but in terms of my life story, it's not what I imagined.

The big problems began when it was time to bring Larry home. The lore in the NICU is that the child goes home on his due date. Well, that date came and went. Larry had been there over six weeks but they weren't willing to send him home. They worried about his blood oxygen, the monitor with the red line. What if it went too low and he stopped breathing?

We began to argue with the doctors. We had done all the procedures, knew when he was blue or not, how to hook him up to oxygen at home.

Deep down I desperately wanted my son home. We wanted to be a family. Maybe it was just a fantasy, but we thought if we could only get him home, it would make it okay. We'd all be okay.

We explored our legal rights to take him home AMA, against medical advice. In the end, we couldn't do it—we still wanted them to say it was okay, like Big Daddy giving us permission. And in fact the medical staff had to write the prescription for oxygen tanks and they wouldn't do it, so they had some power there. Finally, we worked out a compromise that got Larry home three days to a week earlier than they ultimately wanted.

From this event my whole view of medicine has changed, and I've changed too. We wanted Larry home because we had a sense that the doctors really didn't always know what was best for him, that they didn't know what was going to happen. All along I had expected the Big Daddy doctors to know the answers and to take away my anxiety. But I've realized that they don't always know, that you can't always get away from anxiety.

What's become clear is that you know your child better than anyone else. Medicine doesn't say that, but special education teachers do. We've been struggling with what school placement is best for Larry now. In special ed you see all these kids with the same label but they are all so different in profound ways. Special ed teachers tell us directly that "you're the expert on your kid; you decide." It's empowering but scary. You feel you don't really have the knowledge. It's scary to be empowered. But I've learned the importance of being an advocate for your child.

One of the hardest tasks of growing up is to take responsibility for our lives. What parent doesn't struggle with exactly that? It can be vital for parents to make their own decisions, to mature past the wish that somehow other people know best. With so much at stake, it's easy for parents to become passive around doctors, therapists, teachers, and other authorities. Yet who best knows the child? Of course, there are many times when you need to be able to ask for help, to listen to other people's judgments, to see if you are so emotionally involved that you have lost perspective. Yet, too, it's vital to remember to hold on to your voice, to nurture it and listen to it.

Joan's story also reminds us that hard times are not forever. "This too shall pass" can be a most important thought to keep in mind. Joan found herself in a situation that "in terms of my life story, it's not what I imagined," yet she comes to find deep joy and satisfaction in her life with Larry. A year after telling me her story, Joan wrote me a chatty letter, sort of an update. It was full of life and energy, and ends with a different dream: "Today is a good day to write you. It is Larry's birthday. Instead of dreaming about a porcelain doll with alive eyes, I dreamt that our iguana was trying to bite her tail!"

Raymond: "I felt like I was walking around with a big X on my head."

Raymond cut an imposing figure in the parent focus group. He was six feet tall with dark black hair and an athlete's bearing. He laughed easily and participated readily; he was used to working in groups. Yet he read his story with a certain shyness, a tentativeness born of difficult times. He wrote of a journey that began when his carefully constructed world fell apart—his marriage, a successful real estate business—because of major substance abuse, all the while trying to maintain a connection with his son who lived thousands of miles away.

My son Jim is now 17 years old, just starting college. Since he was a toddler, I've been a long-distance parent. And I *mean* long distance: For most of my kid's life, he lived in Paris with his mother, I've always been here in Portland, Oregon.

When Jim was 2 years old, his mom and I got divorced. I had gotten heavily into drugs and lost a real estate empire of about a million dollars, both my parents dropped dead within six months, and then my wife asked me for a divorce. It took me years to get myself straightened out and to stop being so angry at Jimmy.

The shame of being a single father was overwhelming to me. I could write a book for single parents called *The Pickup and The Drop*. Before my wife moved back to Europe, we spent a year shuttling Jim back and forth between our homes. When you wake up on Sunday morning . . . Ugh!—living by myself I really didn't have that feeling of home, like you do when you're married. I'd go out with my kid and there was always a sense of having two left feet, like you're an outcast, a failure. You're with your kid and you're a failure. I felt like I was walking around with a big *X* on my head. The worst memories are of taking Jimmy home and my ex coming to the door naked, just with a housecoat over her. I knew someone else was there, and she'd come to the door and peek out, and I felt like such an outsider!

That's when I was really into coke. After I'd drop off the kid, I'd started my coke run—pick up some coke and lock myself into my room and go on a run until Monday morning, then Tuesday use none, Wednesday just about into focus, and Thursday it'd start again, that awful hollow pain, and I'd use some more coke to fill up. All this time I ran several miles every day, and so thought I was healthy—the persistence of the illusion is astonishing.

After several years, I began to get sober. Then my wife decided to move back to France. That was my worst fear. But I didn't fight it. I knew her life here was not happening as she wanted. I was a pretty crazy, rageful guy back then, and in some ways it was easier having them far away rather than close by. At least I didn't have to deal with The Pickup and The Drop. I'd visit from time to time, and it was clear I didn't have to come and go every week.

My ex-wife could be pretty crazy, but she was also very loving. I think it's the mother who really conveys the image of the father to the child and so to have a good relationship with your ex-wife is *very* important. I knew things were working out because I'd call Paris from Portland and she'd answer in this lovely tone: "Jimmy, Daddy's on the phone!"

My heart soared when she did that. I felt like I was just calling home from work, like they were around the corner, just down the block—as opposed to "Jimmy, your fucking father is on the phone." No matter what's we've gone through, she's always painted a picture of me as a marvelous father. That's very important to me, and I've thanked her many times for that. Jimmy and I talked three times a week on the phone, come hell or high water, and I'd visit every five to six weeks.

For years all I hoped was that he made the airline connection in New York City. At a young age, he was flying by himself. Parents talk about the pain of putting their kids on a schoolbus for the first time— imagine on an airplane by himself! As he's gotten older it's gotten easier. When he was 7, 8, 9, 10, he was traveling as an unaccompanied minor, with a stewardess watching him.

My year is planned around the time I will see him. Once I looked at a calendar and counted the number of days I would see him in the coming year. Then I tried to figure out how many hours I'd see my father in a week when I was growing up—you know, actually *saw* him. Even though I'm divorced, I think I've seen more of my kid than my father did of me.

My father commuted to his furniture business in New York City all the years I was growing up. He worked six days a week and finally by Sunday morning was relaxed a little, and then it was back to work. He was very demanding and rejecting, and my mother was a pretty angry lady. I've worked hard to justify in my mind that I am a good father, or at least as good as my father, because I spent more time with my son, at least if you add up the actual amount of time we really saw each other.

It's been very difficult, though, not like coming home every night to your family. Whenever he came to visit, there was this build up for me beforehand. Then I'd see him, and there would be this tremendous love, and after it was all over this tremendous loss.

Every time I'd leave him off at the airport, I'd go to my car and cry, just cry, for a good ten minutes. Then after a day or so I'd be back in my routine again, and it'd be okay—high, then low, then okay.

When he's in town, I stop pretty much what I'm doing, and we just hang out together. So we had two weeks of total intense time at Christmas and Easter and six weeks in the summer.

It took me years to get myself straightened out. AA helped tremen- dously. I loved my wife so much—it was devastating to be divorced. I got over by it by finding another woman. I'm happily remarried, have young children with my second wife, and this is the first time I've expe- rienced being and living in a family. Growing up I really didn't know how angry and rejecting my parents were, and I wasn't capable of real love when Jimmy was little. Now that I'm remarried and have a new baby, I've wanted to wave my wedding ring around when I'm walking little Mary in the park. With Mary I have a second chance, and I just feel so grateful that I live in the same house with her and her mom, wake up and see them, come home to them.

I feel so lucky to have Jimmy as a son. Just the fact that we have been able to maintain and grow the relationship is so satisfying to me. It's like we've come full circle, my crazy anger way back then has not destroyed him or our relationship.

So I've learned a lot about what I need to keep my head straight: a wife, a family to come home to, a good connection with my son. I'll go to great lengths to stay married! There are times I'll get furious at my wife, we'll fight, but I've learned that I can't be in control all the time, that I have to let her lead as well. This is the first time I've given my paycheck over to my wife, let her take care of the money, be attentive to what she needs to be in a marriage. This time I'm staying married!

So, Raymond was able to bridge a point in his life where the familiar definitions and structures were lost. As his real estate business and family fell apart he dropped into his own emptiness within what looked like a successful life. Through his long effort to pick himself up, he managed to stay in connection with his son.

His story points to the pain around connection and disconnection within the parenting experience for a parent who is divorced. The "pickup and the drop" can be a time of separation and loss for the parent (as well as the child) built right into the childcare arrangement for the entire family. There is a kind of sheer bravery for many parents who are divorced in simply "showing up," holding on to the relationship with their children in the face of at times overwhelming shame and loss that can leave a parent yearning to turn away from those he loves.

Raymond developed a number of useful strategies to manage the adversity in his life: He became aware of the real separation and loss at times of picking up and dropping off Jimmy and structured those times so that he wouldn't be plunged into more loss than he could handle; he identified his own anger, which was connected to the pain about his childhood and found alternative ways—through AA, for example—to manage it; he realized that it helps to have a wife who understands a son's need for a good, honest image of his father, and he played a role in making this happen—by expressing gratitude for what his ex-wife did right. Raymond advises us that making room within your awareness for your own anger and neediness is important, as is taking responsibility for the parts of you that are out of control and need fixing.

Often divorced fathers and mothers find adventurous ways to stay connected across physical distances. For example, one father described to me weekly phone calls to his son that took place while his angry, grieving 13-year-old boy would sit on the toilet to talk with him, sometimes flushing it while they talked. The father was most proud of not hanging up on his son but rather staying on the phone to work at bridging the emotional distance between them.

Most important, though, was the "inner work" Raymond did in the face of his shame, his feeling of being branded as a failure—finding ways to manage his shame, to stay connected nonetheless, and to finally "own" his need for connection and family rather than a drug-induced isolation: "I've learned that I can't be in control all the time . . . this time I'm staying married!"

After reading his story to the group, Raymond's voice became softer. He told us enthusiastically about a new kind of "pickup"—meeting his son at the airport to drive him to his freshman year in college. "Watching him come out from the gate, my eyes made contact with him. He's now about 6 feet 2 inches, very good looking—he has his mother's beauty. There's a real sweetness about him, bright, good student, athletic—just started surfing about two years ago. He's a very funny person. I can laugh with him in ways I don't laugh with anyone else. We just crack each other up."

Rachel: "I had two strikes against me in town."

A 45-year-old single mother, Rachel brought an ironic, playful tone to the story she told me as we sat on the screen porch of her house one summer night remembering an experience that has never completely gone away. Proclaiming that "I haven't done too well with men, and now it's time to give them a break," she lives alone with her 12-year-old son Wally. She laments some of the weight she has gained recently, though she still has some of the athletic trim associated with her love of biking and outdoor sports. Her daughter is now in college, and Rachel has recently obtained her Ph.D. in English Literature. She teaches literature at a high school for gifted students.

When Wally was 6 years old, we were living in a small town in Ohio. There were some very tough things going on. Several years before I had left my husband, whom I had married when I was quite young, and moved across state with my 2-year-old son and teenage daughter. After several years I went back to graduate school to finish my studies for the Ph.D. Then the relationship I was in broke up. My boyfriend just could not handle my being in school; he wanted me out making money, not back in school. But teaching English has always been a dream of mine, and I was determined to go for it. He had been very supportive after my marriage broke up, but once we moved in together, he really couldn't handle it. So I had two strikes against me in town: First I was an unmarried woman living with a man, and then I was a single mother living in town without a man.

Have you ever heard the expression, "little town, big hell"? Well, that's what it was like. Most of the people were in families, and that's how it had always been. And here I was "a fallen woman" who on top of it was in school far from where I lived. I had to commute every day 1½ hours back and forth, teaching a triple load as a graduate student so that I could support my family. So we really stood out there. My neighbors were watching the house. They'd see me coming and going and tell me that they saw my son playing in the front yard with no jacket or that he was crossing the street with no one there. They'd ask whether I knew what was going on in my family and whether I should work so far from home.

My son was always in a battle with the teachers. He was too fidgety, he wouldn't sit still in class, he was always dropping his pencils. Then one day I got a letter from the teacher, who was very upset. She had asked the kids in Wally's fifth-grade class what they wanted to be when they grew up, and my son said he wanted to be a drunk! All the kids had laughed, but when the teacher asked why he said that, Wally replied, "Because my mother lets me drink beer at home."

Well, you can imagine what the teacher's letter did to me. She reported how concerned she was that I was letting him drink and wanted to know what was going on in the house. The first thing I did, of course, was to sit down and ask him why he had to jab it to the teachers like that. He said, "It was just a joke!" In talking with him, he pretty much told me that he knew how scornful of our family they were and that he did indeed enjoy yanking their chain. I went in and saw her and told her that my son was not drinking in the house at age six, that maybe once or twice he had a sip of beer and that was it, which is the truth. But in fact, they were turning me against my own son, the constant picking and watching, feeling so scrutinized. I wondered if he really was an annoying kid.

Later that year I called the principal one day to tell him that Wally was sick and wouldn't be in. I asked the principal if it would be convenient for me to pick up his classwork for the day at three p.m. when I returned from work. Several days later I received a letter from the State Child Protection Agency notifying me that the principal reported that I had left my sick 10-year-old alone in the home all day. The letter warned me to get my act together. I hit the roof! You know, the custody battle with my husband had only been a few years earlier and you really never get over it, I think. "How could I prove that I'm a good mother in a situation where no one knows me?" I wondered. It felt like, *here we go again!* The whole town seemed to be watching us, disapproving. But in fact I *hadn't* left Wally alone.

I went into action. I told the principal that I had never said my son was alone, that it was just his assumption. In fact, my ex-boyfriend was there a part of the day and a trusted neighbor was there the rest of the day. It turned out though that Wally had said to a teacher earlier that "my mother leaves me alone sometimes"—what he was doing was bragging to her about how capable he was, how proud he was of himself. In fact, I did leave him alone sometimes, not when I was at work, but at times when I had a short errand to do. And he is quite capable and trustworthy alone in the house. So I explained to Wally that maybe in a town like this you really can't exaggerate.

I replied to the state agency, and I called my lawyer who contacted them. The horrifying thing is that it all made no difference. The school sent the police to our house one day soon after, when my son and teenage daughter were home alone. The police arrived, and Melanie, who was 16, answered the door and told them "*Look at me*. I'm 16. I'm watching my brother, and there's nothing wrong going on." The police called me at the university, right in middle of one of my classes, and wound up apologizing.

It turned out that one of my neighbors, who knew the principal, called him, even though he knew Melanie was home with Wally. He told the principal that my son was home alone. Instead of checking with me, the principal immediately called the police, who came to our house. The police were very embarrassed.

I went over to our next-door neighbor and confronted him. He justified his lie by saying, "I know that something very wrong is going on in your house." He insinuated that I was a bad woman and that it didn't matter what the truth was. I reminded him that he had never been inside my house and didn't at all know what was happening there. Then I told him to stay away from our home and that if he did see anything that concerned him to talk to me first. He looked sheepish and said he would do that.

But I was in a rage. That's what the town was like for an unmarried woman with kids. Some of the neighbors wouldn't let their kids play with my son. Some of them have boyfriends who are twenty years younger than they are, some of them drink and smoke dope, yet they are so sanctimonious. I don't want to sound too angry. It's just that here were all these people who felt like they knew how life is to be lived: you stay married, don't divorce, and certainly don't live unmarried with a man. We were very different.

Notes and letters from the school continued. I can't tell you how awful it was to get them. My heart dropped to my toes. I felt so vulnerable and hounded. I worried that maybe I didn't know what I was doing. I had metal taste in my mouth.

Finally, one day Wally came home and told me that his teacher had hit him because he was wiggling in his seat and had dropped a pencil while squirming around. I cried. I was so upset. But now too I knew I had them over a barrel. I was livid. I insisted on a meeting with the superintendent, the principal, and the school psychologist.

I went in there with my briefcase, the one I had used in graduate school for my papers. I brought it on purpose. I dressed up in a business suit. I didn't want to go in there simply as an upset parent. I'd seen parents lose power, get all quiet. I wanted to scare the shit out of them. So I kept looking at my briefcase as we talked, and I mentioned the name of my lawyer and invoked several of the relevant statutes that forbid teachers hitting students. But I also told them that that was not my major objection. I said that I was sick and tired of their attitude. They kept asking whether I would agree to visitation by the Child Welfare Bureau. I said absolutely not.

In fact, we had talked to the school psychologist a lot. She was very supportive of us, and said the system was a mess. She supported us, but she didn't do anything. I liked using the therapist she recommended. I was happy to have Wally go see him. The school may have thought they were punishing him by sending him, but Wally liked it, and I liked having another person involved.

So at the meeting, the school psychologist talked about Wally's strengths and weaknesses. We saw that he had issues but that also he was getting a lot of grief he didn't deserve.

The school eventually asked us to please keep Wally in the school system. The principal told me he was one of the brightest kids in the class. I began to visit the school, to go to his class. I began to volunteer, and that made a big difference.

I came to realize that I can't hide away from a terrible situation hoping someone else will fix it. I learned not to avoid a necessary confrontation, but rather to take effective action.

A painful sense of shame can accompany the feeling of being on the edge of a community, perceived as deviant by those around us. We all struggle with such feelings in some ways, falling short of idealized notions of what is a good enough parent or man or woman. Rachel's story struck me not simply because she was fierce in defending her son. After all, we can be fierce in defending a position that really ought to be more carefully examined. Was she in fact messing up in some way or misperceiving a threat in other people's honest concern or desire to help? Possibly.

What comes from Rachel's story is her human struggle to take responsible action. A silver lining in Rachel's loneliness and struggle to make it through her "big hell" was that she learned not to roll into a cut-off, defended posture, avoiding confrontation. She tried to stand up for herself. But she also listened to what the voices of concern were trying to say. She became very "strategically smart" in fiercely defending Wally in the climactic meeting—dressing and behaving in a way that would not make her a victim. Yet she was smart enough to listen to and use those around her, such as the school psychologist. Her story ends with a focus on active involvement—by volunteering in the class, Rachel became more aware of what was happening in her son's school and let them know her more as a real person rather than a fantasized "fallen woman." By her choices, both Rachel and the community in which she lives may lose some of their scary fantasies about each other and finally see each other as real people.

Meg and Karen: "My world cracked open."

Meg and Karen are dear friends of mine who live in Boston. Both of them are busy professionals with active careers, as well as being "the two moms" of their 11-year-old daughter Ellen, adopted when she was an infant. They eagerly accepted an invitation to contribute a story to my project and suggested that they tell their story while we have dinner together, without the kids. I welcomed their participation because they have a wise perspective as well as a deep interest in parenting. In addition they bring a sense of humor and irony to daily life. Meg describes herself as having grown up "a privileged WASP observing the ordinary bigotry in my town" and notes, about her coming out, "I don't want to say it's a relief to be in the outgroup but it's not the worst place in the world to be. I've had just about every privilege you could have. And when I began to come out, I knew I was going to give up some of that privilege but realized I could live without it."

As the three of us talked over a delicious meal of angel-hair pasta with grilled shrimp and roasted vegetables, I was aware that for these two women, being parents took place within the context of their being lesbian. How important to being mothers was that feature of their life?

Unsure of how to ask, I said, "I want to include attention to your being lesbian parents, if that feels relevant, but I don't want to make it more than it is." Both women thought about this for a moment and then, with some energy, Meg began their story.

Meg: In the moment I don't think of myself as a lesbian parent. I'm a parent who happens to be lesbian. However, when I'm out in the world meeting a new doctor or teacher for my kids there is always that question. *What are they thinking? Do they know?* There is this kind of public self that kind of catches your breath. *Who do these people think we are? Are they going to see our complexity?* Will they see that we're Meg and Karen and have been together so many years and are raising an 11-year-old? I always worry that they're not going to see that and put us in some kind of bizarre category of unnaturalness.

Karen: Well, I perceive us as a lesbian family a lot, similar to what you said, Meg, about being in the public realm. I feel we're in the outsider realm because we are gay parents. We look in at a straight world. Sometimes I feel that I look into a world I'm just not a part of because we're gay, like this morning going to school with Ellen, for example. In our community, being a single mother is probably the norm, but I don't feel it. I perceive homophobia like anti-Semitism: You can smell it a mile away.

Meg: I remember feeling as a kid that my family was not very cool. We lived in Westchester County, outside New York City, in a town with much wealth. We were not poor by any means, but my parents lived in a social strata where everyone had more money than us or at least acted like it—bigger houses, better dressed, more vacations. Plus I was a gawky, awkward kid who got by on my brains but maybe not on much else. I often had the feeling of being odd, or out of it, or exposed.

Now, sometimes when I take Ellen to school, I see these blond, white-skinned, heterosexual moms, and it replays for me some of that childhood feeling of "I'm out of it" because I am a lesbian. Who knows? Probably at 8 a.m. those women are not thinking about whether or not I'm a lesbian. But it's a moment when I feel I have LESBIAN emblazoned all over me. So if they don't talk to me, I'm sure it's because I'm a lesbian.

The way being lesbian shapes our parenting is really expressed by the story of Ellen's coming out to our new neighbors. For years Ellen was proud of having lesbian moms; this was before she got shit from people for it. She did understand that there was something different about having gay parents, so she was pleased to go to Gay Pride Day with us, and she wanted to know about Gay Pride and what if it was. She even said, "I have gay pride." In her third grade class, the kids made personalized nameplates for their desks. Ellen made a pink triangle with her name on it; she thought that could be okay because other people wouldn't know what it meant.

We had lots of talks with her. She knew that she could have gay pride and lesbian moms but that not everybody in the world was okay with it. She knew she needed to be a little careful about whom to tell and whom not to tell.

Then she had several hard experiences with friends. In the fourth grade, a girl she had been friends with for years said one day to several other kids in the hallway, "Stay away from Ellen She has AIDS." In the way kids do, they taunted her about being creepy. They'd say things like "Ellen has cooties." Then they went on to this crazy confused thinking that she has AIDS because she eats hot dogs. Ellen's friend had been going through a hard time in her own family—her father had just left—and she must have felt very angry, very vulnerable and exposed and so lashed out at the person who seemed most vulnerable: Ellen.

Then it became clear to the kids that Ellen has two moms. In the fourth grade, another kid stopped Ellen in the hall. He was a classmate of hers, walking with his younger brother, and he grabbed the younger boy, pushed him at Ellen, and said, "Tell Ellen what *we* think of *her* family!"

These events really shook Ellen. They made her realize that fear and hatred and bigotry aren't theoretical concepts but could really affect her. So she tried to figure out how to make the world safe for herself. She approached us, and her teacher.

Actually, at first she didn't say anything. We noticed over time though that all of a sudden her friend Joanne stopped coming over. We asked Ellen about it, and then the story started to come out. Joanne had been mean to her at school; and she had said Ellen had AIDS.

Then Ellen told us about one of the boys taunting her in the hall. We talked to the teacher, who said, "I take behavior like that very seriously. I'll talk to the boy."

He called the kid's father, who simply replied, "I support my kid."

The teacher told him, "Well, every time he does it he is going down to the principal's office."

The principal is great. He's suspended some kids because of their offensive language.

Ellen expected the adults to control this behavior and prevent it from ever happening again. But then she discovered that as kids get a little older, they learn how to say things out of the teacher's earshot. She learned that hateful language against gay people would continue, that kids would be sophisticated enough to not get caught, and that the adult network was not going to protect her.

Karen: We learned about that from asking her why she left my name off the class address list last year. One day she came home with a list of her fifth grade students and parents. It had Meg's name on it and not mine. When I asked, Ellen said that she had not put my name down "because I'm going to get harassed." I said "no you're not!" and she replied, "I told you to stop it before and you didn't."

It was like the world cracked open for me. I said to Meg that we were going to get active in this school. So we went right in and did some workshops on homophobia for the teachers. After that the principal, who had come to the workshops, suspend, some kids for using the words *fag* and *gay*. The teachers loved the event, so that made us get a little more active.

When I first heard Ellen's words, I felt so sad and hurt—oh my god, someone trying to hurt my kid. That obnoxious connection between AIDS and being gay is worse than the homophobia, as if everyone who is gay has AIDS—it's so stupid. I went through a period of feeling hurt for Ellen and for us.

Then I realized that Ellen was absolutely right. We hadn't been helping in ways that we could. So I confirmed for her that she is right, that we can't stop it completely, and that this is something she is going to hear the rest of her life. There is homophobia inside our culture and inside all of us. Regardless of her own sexual orientation when she's grown, she has to confront a hatred of gayness, inside her and outside her.

Ellen wanted to cut off everyone who had hurt her, and we had to work very hard on that. We told her that kids say these words and don't even know what they mean; sometimes they want to be hurtful, but sometimes they're just mimicking their parents. We went over the whole spectrum of what these words mean.

The bottom line we tried to communicate to Ellen is that we can't make it stop forever, but that we CAN stand up for ourselves and educate other people. That's what we tried to do through the workshops we did in the school. I felt that that was important for Ellen to see us doing them. And it's important for her to see other friends who also have gay parents: It helps Ellen see that she is not completely alone.

Meg: This story has an uplifting ending of sorts. Recently, Ellen was very concerned when our next door neighbors Betty and Ralph said they were leaving. They were parents with older children, and Ellen felt very close, particularly to Betty, who is a warm, friendly woman who has done a lot of baby-sitting for us. Their house has always been a very special, safe place for Ellen. She was very concerned with who would move into it. At one point, Betty told Ellen that two lesbians with young kids were looking, and Ellen was very hopeful that another lesbian family would move in. But that fell through. Then a mother and teenage daughter bought the house and moved in. Ellen was so anxious to meet the people. As soon as the moving truck pulled away, she went over alone, rang the doorbell, and introduced herself.

Within two minutes, Ellen told them that "my moms are lesbians." The women responded, "Oh. Well, that's fine."

Ellen came running back to tell us: "Guess what! I introduced myself and told them my moms are lesbians, and they said that it's fine!"

In fact, today Ellen came home from school all animated and lit up. She said, "I told Thomas today that I had two moms, and he said, 'Oh, cool'!" So our daughter is trying to make safety for herself in the world. And who isn't?

By way of their active engagement with Ellen and their community, Meg and Karen are helping their daughter deal with stigma, both the stigma of community suspicion and dislike and the "internalized self-hatred" that we take within us when we feel part of a "family with difference," whether that means being Jewish in a largely Christian culture, being gay within a predominantly straight community, being less well off within a town where money seems to come easily to other people, or feeling less intelligent amidst high achievers.

Meg and Karen give voice to the familiar, painful feeling of shame, that feeling of being in the spotlight, exposed and naked for all to see. It makes us want to hide and isolate ourselves. Instead though, Karen and Meg choose active engagement, with the school and with their daughter. They speak the truth to both, educating the teachers about the reality of gay life, showing them that in many ways we are more alike than different regardless of our sexual orientation. At the core, most people are just struggling to be decent.

Most importantly, Meg and Karen validated Ellen's reality: Yes, she will suffer some from having two moms in our culture, but there is also much to be proud of. They show their daughter ways to manage and understand the hatred and suspiciousness and stupidity of others.

The painful dilemma that their daughter presented them with—how to feel safe as a daughter of lesbians, and how to come to terms with this part of her family—became a fulcrum of growth for the two women, helping them take more active control of their lives and integrate this part of themselves in a fuller way. Ellen's struggle became a window of opportunity for Meg and Karen to grow as well.

James: "I spent months staring at the ceiling late at night."

James, in his 30s, is the owner of a paper products firm in New York City. He became a widower with two young children to care for when, several years ago, his wife died of pancreatic cancer, a very aggressive form of cancer.

After my wife died of cancer at age 32, I spent months staring at the ceiling late at night in our bedroom, taking stock, wondering what to do with my life. I had a good job, nice house, was managing okay. I realized after several months that I was trying to replicate the same life we had before my wife died, and it was not working. I was doing everything as if nothing had happened.

I needed to redirect the pattern with my neighbors. I was faking it, fooling myself, co-opting my children into the charade. The only way we were going to succeed was to realize our uniqueness in the situation. Acting "normal" was not healthy, at the time, for our family. That was an existential insight: We had to recognize that Judy was truly gone. I decided we had to move out of the old neighborhood. It was an intense neighborhood. When you're a single father, you're in the minority. By some strange statistical anomaly in our town, there are few divorced people around, much less widowers. It's mostly made up of two-parent families. Few women worked in this affluent suburb. My wife had an advanced degree and worked in the schools, and the other women there had pity for her. They felt it was only about needing a second income; they didn't get that my wife liked her career.

If we had stayed there, we would have been surrounded by wives in Dodge Caravans. There were no husbands involved with getting their kids to school. I thought of moving to a different town, out of state, to where friends lived. They encouraged me to. We wound up staying in town, but closer to the center. I really didn't want the kids to be any more uprooted by moving away from all they had known.

A quarter-mile made so much difference. It's amazing. I had much more personal freedom; our neighbors showed more respect for me and my family.

I realized I had to turn the whole thing around—make our uniqueness a positive to survive. I had depended so much on Judy as my wife, and I knew I had to become both the mother and father. But, in fact, I didn't always know how to do that. I didn't always know what was best for my 6-year-old daughter or how to handle my 9-year-old. Growing up, my sister was much older than me, so much so that in fact I was raised as an only child. My wife had four sisters and grew up in an environment of combat. I didn't. She had astonishing verbal skills and was very clear about what should happen in the home.

Now here I had to deal on my own with a family. It can feel like Bosnia in our house when the kids are squabbling about this and that. I'm not at all sure how to be peacemaker. Through the miracle of the DNA chain, the children have gotten my wife's verbal talent—for the first time in my life, I am arguing with my children. You can't not argue when you're a single parent; you have to deal with whether to eat cereal, what to wear, whether to give up religion.

At work I never had to argue. I'm in a senior position, and I can just tell people, "Off with their heads!" At home it's hard; children marshal arguments. I'm old, and it's hard to teach an old dog new tricks. There's a skill to fighting.

Sure, I went into therapy and that was helpful, but I needed to involve my kids more than I had when I was simply the Dad and had my wife to depend on. My kids and I had to become a team, a group.

I explained that over breakfast one morning, amidst the boxes of cereal, to my kids Janie and Willy. Here's the deal: We're not a family anymore, we're going to be a team. We're going to operate in a different way. We're going to take better care of each other, look out for what we all need, share the tasks and chores. Everything is not going to be coming from the parent to the kids. I told them that *I* needed *their* help, wanted their opinions, their advice, to know what they needed. I solicited their opinion. They liked it.

So I felt so proud of myself recently when Willy, out of the blue, decided to give a present to his sister. It was something she really wanted, a hairbrush that he saw when the two of us were shopping at the drugstore.

It may not seem like such a great event, but they fight all the time. Janie often gives in to him but manages to do so on her own terms. Willy often attempts to bully her and often hurts her. I've tried very hard to foster the team concept in order to demonstrate the necessity of our interdependence. It is important that we all take care of each other at the level appropriate to the individual. Although Janie is only 6, she has a clear understanding of this. Willy has been reluctant to participate and, in fact, has recently entered a phase of challenging me whenever possible, maybe because 9-year-old boys go through a rebellious phase. Everything recently is a difficult challenge in getting him to be responsible. Therefore, when out of the blue he insisted that we pick up the hairbrush for his sister—he *thought* of her and remembered it and then presented it to her—I was overwhelmed and felt positive. Evidently my talk had affected him. He was willing to go and buy that present, to momentarily step outside himself. He had taken what I said to heart.

Moments of adversity can allow us to find a deeper, truer voice. James is still finding his voice as a parent. He's had to acknowledge the loss, rather than acting as if it never happened and going on as usual. The death of his wife meant a new version of James was called for. For James that meant finding a different way of being in the family. He had to become less passive and more active and present, to grapple with the flux of feelings that he had not had to experience in his own family growing up. His fatherly voice is still emerging, he makes clear. He's becoming able to tolerate conflict, argument, not always having his way. And most powerfully, perhaps, James is finding that he has influence over his son, that amidst the rebellion, his son also takes to heart what his dad says.

James came to the focus group with the hope that creating a story about this time would help him make some sense of what had happened. What emerged as well was that reading the story in the group was in itself a supportive, life-affirming activity, one he did with humor and spirit.

A WORLD CRACKED OPEN

"The world cracked open for me," observed Karen, when she realized how different her daughter felt from other children because she had "two moms." For Karen and her partner, Meg, this realization led to a greater integration of being parents who are lesbian into their lives— giving workshops, becoming involved with the school, talking with their daughter, and taking ownership of who they are in a fuller way.

For both women there was a deeper personal integration as well. Each struggled in a new and fuller way with what it meant to be in the "out group" (lesbian parents) and the "in group" (white professionals with many privileges), with their *own* ability to tolerate differences and respond to them, and with the intertwining of shame and privilege in their own childhood histories. Parts of themselves that had been disowned were brought closer into their sense of self, made less toxic by participating in their daughter's struggle.

It is very important to be aware of a child's sense of difference from other children. Differences in skill, talent, temperament, looks, and intelligence are of course what give us our individuality and can be the source of great joy and opportunity. However, when kids feels they stand out in ways that make them a target, or the sense of difference is accompanied by a feeling of being strange or alone or devalued, then their self-esteem is at risk.

There is much that parents can do to help children with the feeling of being painfully different. Validating their struggle by an open acknowledgment of differences between people can be helpful. So too can a kind and receptive listening to the pain of a child who feels injured or hurt for being "different." Having a dialogue with a child about the meaning of people's reactions to differences is important. Without trying to talk them out of their pain, it may be possible to depersonalize what feel like very hurtful reactions of other kids by looking at the underlying ignorance, intolerance, and vulnerability that provokes scapegoating and shaming. Clarifying what the child is doing as well to provoke the scapegoating is important. It can also be crucial to identify empowering behaviors that reduce the sense of victimization a child feels. Might the child use other peers for help? Teachers? Counselors within the school? The parents' active involvement and efforts to help can model empowerment for children, if such efforts are not perceived as overly reactive and leading to further shaming.

We help our children as well when we become aware of our own attempts to hide from *our* sense of difference in the world. Our individuality and character lies in what is most unique about us, yet there is a part of us *that doesn't want to go there*. We may want to hide from our sexuality or from our ethnic heritage or from our aloneness or from our ambition. Identifying your own masks, disguises, and ways of getting isolated can help you empathize with your child's wish to hide.

And there's a part of most of us that wants to stereotype those we don't agree with who make us feel uncomfortable. To help our children understand the painful experience of feeling different we can look at the angry, frightened part of ourselves that wants to dismiss others who seem uncomfortably different from us.

"It's scary to be empowered," observed Joan, who struggled so long and hard to not give over power to her son's doctors. We may all in some part yearn to live in a sleepy, slightly numb world, where we can be comforted by the fact that someone else knows best. That way we don't have to worry or take risks. Let the doctors deal with this, they know how! Let the teacher handle this; that's what she's paid for! Let the therapist talk to my kid; he's the expert!

The parents in this chapter reached a place where there *was* no one else. They had to confront the reality of making choices, finding resourceful parts of themselves, being brave by not letting their fear paralyze them for too long. They remind us that there is no replacement for being involved with and knowing your child, and listening to your intuition and that of your partner. Sometimes we have to do something, even though we don't know what to do. Not only may your child profit from your bravery, but you may grow and discover new parts of yourself as well.

Paradoxically, we also learn from these stories about our limits. Ultimately, we are not able to fully protect our children. In fact, often our kids are exposed to difficulty that we ourselves may have caused by our choices and behavior. As one parent remarked in a focus group, "Forget protecting my kids from the hard world. Sometimes I can't even protect them from me!"

How important it is, then, for us to teach our children skills for managing difficulty—by validating their feelings; putting into words what causes pain; feeling shame when appropriate, but taking steps to reduce it when shame feels toxic; not getting too shamefully isolated when things get hard, but rather finding sources of support, understanding, help, and perspective.

And perhaps too we all need to see past false dichotomies. Adversity and happiness, bravery and cowardice, shame and pride, empowerment and paralysis are not either/or parts of our lives. We may often feel both. As children and adults, we don't simply "get past" difficult times into a carefree sort of Happy Valley. Rather, we grieve and things get better but the grief stays with us. When you divorce, for example, there is a reminder at times throughout our lives of that pain; or when you're part of a marginalized group (parents who are gay or lesbian, single parents), you will confront over and over little reminders of difference. Such times can also be a moment of acknowledging what makes us particularly who we are. We can remember, respond, and move on.

Hidden Wisdom You Can Use

- Feeling different in some ways is a part of life. However, when children feel "too different" from their peers, their self-esteem can be effected.

- Listen to and validate your children's pain when they feel "different." Without dismissing their reality, help children find sources of pride in their difference, or in other parts of their lives. Pockets of competence and self-esteem can protect against toxic shame and self-doubt.

- Often adversity helps us find our true voices. Adversity may be a real part of the integrity of your life and of your own development.

- Be mindful of how much power you give to "experts." Doctors, counselors, teachers, friends, and ministers and rabbis can be helpful allies, but they don't always know more about your child and family than you do. You know your child better than anyone else.

- There is anxiety as a parent that relying on experts won't take away. There are many moments when choices have to be made with inadequate information.

- Become an advocate for your child and your family. Don't simply accept whatever people in authority tell you to do. They don't always know better than you. Question them, ask for the reasons for the recommendations, look at their logic and information gathering, and pay attention to your intuition and to how much they seem to be attending to your child. Don't be afraid to ask for a second opinion.

- Hard times are not forever—remembering that "this too shall pass" can be a helpful boost to our morale during moments of adversity.
- Shame and sorrow can be mastered; they need not control our life.
- Active involvement rather than shameful withdrawal can sometimes turn around hostile situations. Find out more about the concerns of those who are suspicious of you, and volunteer to become involved in situations that seem foreign or strange. Sometimes more simple human contact and interaction can reduce a sense of difference, and of suspiciousness.

c h a p t e r   s i x

Coping with Teenagers

A s parents, we know the story about the teen years of our children: Adolescents are in a process of finding themselves and experimenting with new roles, new opportunities. They become young philosophers, true grouches, and risktakers who want to push the envelope. Adolescence brings with it difficult choices about sex, drugs, music, and driving—all the new possibilities that coming of age brings with it.

What often catches parents by surprise is the parallel process we go through with our teens. As they struggle with new roles, so do we. How do we manage the chaos of the new that our teenagers bring with them? You want to protect them, but you can't entirely. You want to wrap your arms around them, but you're not sure how much. How much should we loosen our protective embrace?

We know about the dependency of teens but much less about the dependency and vulnerability of their parents. Our children need to go, but it's hard to let go of them. In fact, there is a mutual interdependency in families of teens. Parents and teens are redefining their attachments to each other in a way that both separates and connects them.

For many of us, there is a large elephant in the house that we hardly know how to talk about. How do we manage our own terror as we experiment with how much freedom and control to let our beloved child have? Amidst the tension between holding on and letting go of them, how do you find sure footing?

One of the key challenges, I believe, is to find ways to respond to the real attempt of our children to hold on to us even as they seem only to want to let go. Being anxious and teetering and tottering to find your way in a new world is a normal part of being the parent of an adolescent. It's a different world in some ways from being the parent of an infant, a toddler, or a latency age child, where your authority is much clearer. Becoming mindful of your anxiety and the reality of change can help you and your child better manage the new terrain. Consider the following story.

Julie: "Boy, was I nervous that night!"

Julie is a thoughtful, 38-year-old mother with a lovely smile. She lives in a suburb of a large midwestern city. One unexpected night, while her husband was traveling on business, she found herself in very new and challenging emotional terrain with her 15-year-old son, Norm. We sat and talked over coffee in a parents group, after she wrote about her experience.

Next to a busy downtown subway stop is a plaza that the kids call the Pit. It's a lowered concrete area that's cut off from most of the pedestrian traffic around there, so it's a great hang out for street people, druggies, and all the teens who are fascinated by them. Lots of green hair and pierced ears, eyebrows, lips, noses, whatever. Because there are so many bookstores, arcades, and movies down there, Norm has been allowed to take the bus from our suburb down to the subway stop.

The deal was that he was to be home by 10 p.m., which he has been very good about doing. Norm looks pretty straight: He has an earring in his ear but no purple hair, no body piercing. But he begun to meet some new kids in the Pit. One Friday night a couple of months ago, he called at 10 p.m. and told me that he had missed his bus. So I told him, "Okay, no problem. Get the next one."

Then at 11 p.m. he called and said that he didn't get on the bus. "I'm in some kid's house downtown," he said.

"Okay, tell me where you are and I'll come get you."

"I want to spend the night here."

"Just tell me where you are. I'll come down there, and we'll deal with it then."

Well, I got into my car and drove down to this very dilapidated section of town and found the apartment where Norm was with this guy named Bobby.

Bobby's mother was there too. The apartment was tired looking but not really shabby. His mother was sitting at the kitchen table in her bathrobe. She grabbed my hand when I walked in and exclaimed, "You have to let your son go. Give him more freedom!"

I had never met this person in my life!

Then she started to cry: "At least the kids are here in this apartment and not out on the street!"

I looked in the other room and there were a whole bunch of teens from the Pit—green hair, purple hair, no hair, hardware all over the place, through all parts of their bodies—lips, bellies, ears, tongues. The woman spoke with an odd accent, and I later learned she was from Poland, and really didn't know what to do with her kids in this country. She was single mom really overwhelmed.

Then Norm came up to me and said in a serious tone of voice, "Mom, I am *really* behind. I need more experience. I'm too sheltered. I need to know more about what's really going on in life." He told me that he really wanted to stay that night and hang out. "Come here and I'll introduce you to the other kids. They're really nice." Some of them shook my hand, said hello. Then he took me aside and said, "I really want you to let me do this. They're okay guys."

I didn't know what to do. The mother was in the other room, drinking coffee and crying, talking to her friend on the phone about how hard life was. She was a sort of hysterical, off-the-wall person.

But I trusted my son enough. I looked around carefully—this was not a drug scene. Several of the kids were playing a video game; some were talking. I even found myself sniffing the air, trying to smell marijuana! Nothing like that was going on. Norm was honest and open. I thought, *oh boy, here we go into teenage-hood,* and perhaps Norm was right. It was time for him to know about some of these things. This scene was something he wanted to check out, and he was capable of it.

So I agreed and drove home. My hands were sweating on the steering wheel that whole way home. *What had I done?* Ninety percent of the time I'd just talk with my husband, but I couldn't reach him. It was a spur of the moment decision, and I felt close enough to my son to see who he is, what he's doing, how his mind works. He'd come home in the past on the hour that he was supposed to. He'd called me that night; he negotiated.

I wanted to keep the channels of communication open. I'd already told him that we both know that kids experiment with drugs and sex. I did. It seemed most important to be talking together, not to have rigid rules based simply on my fears.

But, boy, was I nervous that night! When I got home I called my sister across the country: "You won't believe what I just did!"

She listened and said, "Good job!" She's raised some teens, and it was really important to me to have someone to share my anxiety with. The next morning Norm came home:

"How was it?"

"It was okay, I guess." He didn't say a lot about it.

Two weeks went by and he came in one day when his father and I were having coffee. He told us that he stopped hanging out at the Pit:

"It was okay, but the kids there were too stressed out."

He had heard a lot about their lives, and he told us about some of the kids who were runaways, another who'd been abused by his uncle, and one kid who had alcoholic parents. He found out some things and made his own decision about what he wanted to do.

I'm just glad that I found the courage to give him the responsibility to explore and make good choices. We've kept open the lines of communication, and I'm convinced one reason is that I've controlled my tendency to go off the wall and come done really hard, when so much of what he's doing I did too.

Julie's decision is only one way of handling the situation. There are many different ways for parents to respond to their teenagers' desires to experiment and for more independence. Some parents might not have let their son or daughter stay. There is no one right way to respond. In this chapter we will hear other stories, other fine ways of handling a teenager's desire to push at the envelope of his or her life. First, though, we need to consider the pressures parents feel at such moments—pressures that can leave us reacting in ways that achieve results the opposite of what we intend.

THE VULNERABILITY OF PARENTS

"Just tell me where you are," Julie asked Norm. In those words were both a deeper request and the parent's vulnerability. He could *not* tell her, he could hang up and she wouldn't even know where he was, or he could "forget" to call her. We lose some of our ability to protect and control our kids, of course, when they become teens.

Julie had the presence of mind to go to her son. She didn't demand that he come home right then. She decided that she needed to be with him. That decision allowed her to see what her son was actually doing and make choices based on reality, not on her frightening fantasies. "I looked around carefully—this was not a drug scene," Julie says. Often we have stereotypes about what teens are like, based sometimes on how they *look*. "Green hair, purple hair, no hair, hardware all over the place, through all parts of their bodies— lips, bellies, ears, tongues." We may then assume that something scary is going on. After all, part of the "project" of the adolescent is to look different from adults, even to shock them, thereby asserting a sense of identity and developing selfhood. How do we get past the ways something or someone looks? As parents, we need to consider what we need to know to have some confidence that our children are safe. It is very important for us as parents to ask ourselves these questions: Where am I getting my information, where is the uneasy feeling coming from? What are my assumptions? Be as specific and precise as possible. That way you can frame clear questions to your teens or be clear as to what you need to know to make decisions about what and what is not allowable for your child.

When Julie walked into the downtown apartment, she was making a voyage we all have to make when we have adolescents, one from *our* comfortable or familiar assumptions into *their* ways of experiencing the world.

In one way, Norm is leaving. He's saying that he is not just her little boy anymore. Part of the normal parent-teen struggle is the sound of the preadolescent bubble of adoration between parent and child being shattered, as it must be, by the teen's firm message that he or she is different from us. From that separation process, a deeper connection between us can come. If we don't let them go too abruptly or hold on too tightly, our teens will hold on to us even as they let go, miraculously.

And what about the word *terror* that I used in describing the experience of being the parent of a teenager? Julie remembers her experimenting with drugs and sex as a college student, and part of her may imagine only the worst for Norm. Similarly, one father, Arthur, in the same focus group, with a teenage son himself, remembered his own frightening experience driving one night while having smoked marijuana. Now a respected businessman in his 50s, he remembers ruefully how "pure, dumb luck" was all that saved him from a terrible automobile accident:

"I had smoked marijuana for one of the first times and then drove with another guy from one party to another in the college town where I was in school. It was winter, piles of snow on the dark streets. I drove down a one-way street, the wrong way. Another car just swerved to miss me. I remember the guy honking his horn, blinking his lights. I was terrified, and pulled over. The other guy with me was so scared that he got out and walked to the party by himself. I opened my window to try and sober up in the cold night. What if the other driver hadn't reacted so fast? What I had been in an accident, stoned? That scared me so much I was much more careful about what I did. But what a way to learn!"

Arthur talks to his kids but doesn't know if they listen.

"What happened to me was ancient history. They imagine they're invulnerable. It won't happen to them." He sighs: "I just hope I've instilled in them enough common sense not to do the stupid things I did. But part of me knows that they will. I pray they have the good luck I did not to have something terrible happen when they're being stupid. So much of it is good luck."

We know how much dumb luck it takes to get through life in one piece; *they* don't. Perhaps the terror that comes from parenting adolescent children excuses us when *we* act crazy as parents. We need some reality grounding, sometimes from trusted friends or other parents, as Julie sought in her phone call to her sister. Sometimes we need to hear from another adult that we're doing the best we can. It grounds us, keeps us from drifting away into our worst imaginings about our kids, or ourselves. That's why the stories that follow can be so reassuring and instructive.

As the parent of a teen, redefining your authority does not mean giving up authority. The language of connection shifts as our kids grow from toddlerhood to adolescence, and what is asked of us changes as well. We need to avoid being *too* reactive to what our teens stimulate in us. That means acknowledging their views and values and separate perspective perhaps more than you did when they were younger. Acknowledge when you've been off base. Engage them in dialogue about choice, decisions, and values. Make sure they know where you're coming from and why.

The task for parents of adolescents is to really *see* their kids, to be close enough and observant enough to really *hear* them. Then we can sort out when our fears are taking over in a way that blocks us from seeing what our kids need. That means knowing our kids—their limitations, strengths, hopes, and needs. Julie was able to make a courageous decision because she knew Norm. That's not to say we can't be mistaken or let down in our assessment of our children, but if you have the information, you are less likely to act from your own fears rather than their reality.

In the following stories, we're going to hear from fathers and mothers who stumbled into new ways of talking to their teens, of accepting differences that define us as individuals, of setting limits that work, sometimes without even realizing it. These parents left the door open as their kids separated so that the teens came back, even as they said they were leaving.

Stan: "The conversation was going very wrong, and I didn't know how to stop it."

Stan and his wife Jane are the parents of two children. Their daughter is just finishing college, and their 15-year-old son, Terry, is this year beginning to think about what extracurricular activities in high school will strengthen his college application. He's trying to decide whether it's too "dorky" to join the high school band. He loves the drums, as does his father, who at age 45 still plays in a local jazz band. Stan is an intense man, though not without a sense of humor. He speaks slowly as he tells his story, as though he is still ruminating about the lesson he learned.

I apologized to my 15-year-old son yesterday. That may sound like a small thing, but it felt like a big change, and it had a big result.

Yesterday was Friday. Terry hadn't come home on the school bus and called from a friend's house to say that he planned to stay there overnight. He also wanted to go skiing with his friend's family the next day, which meant we likely wouldn't see him till Sunday.

I was upset because my wife and I had planned for a Friday family night, something that has become rare because our son spends a lot of time these days over at friends' homes on the weekend. We wanted to light the Shabbot (Sabbath) candles and have a meal together.

When I explained this to him he protested, telling me he really wanted to be at his friend's house to watch a TV movie starting at 6 p.m. I got mad and said we had bought food for dinner and made plans. Terry got heated. He said that he was home every night of the school week and Friday nights were special to him. He really wanted to hang with his friend and have pizza for dinner with his family. He half-jokingly offered to call during the candle lighting, which didn't assuage me. I persisted. Finally he blurted out angrily: *"I don't care about Shabbot. We light those damned candles every week!"*

I was seething inside but felt blocked. I didn't want to just order him home, since it seemed pointless to have him sitting resentfully like a captive at our Friday night family dinner. Then my mind somehow settled on his chores—he's responsible for taking the garbage out when he gets home from school on Fridays. He said he would do it on Sunday. That wasn't good enough for me, or the nagging anger I felt. "Don't make promises you won't keep," I snapped back.

"When don't I do what I say I will?" he asked, sounding confused.

I mentioned a small house project he had taken on to earn some money and which had yet to happen.

He exclaimed, "Dad! I said I'll try and do that, and I haven't gotten to it yet. I'm planning to."

Terry's pained and defensive tone registered most of all to me. I realized I had hurt his feelings and that in fact I was off base about the work issue. He'd actually been working quite hard both at school and at home. My last desire was to make him feel bad about himself.

What I most felt was sad. He was growing up and moving out into the world. The conversation was going very wrong, and I didn't know how to stop it.

So, I said, "Terry, I'm sorry if I sounded like I was claiming you don't work hard. That's not what I meant to say. You are a good worker and trying hard. I just wanted to make sure the chores get done."

It felt really weird to be apologizing, like fathers don't *do* that, as if I *had* to be right—if I say he doesn't work, then he doesn't work! Yet it also felt really good to apologize and make things right.

Terry didn't say much in reply. I knew he heard me. It's the next thing that he said that almost made me weep. "Dad, it's not because I don't want to be home; it's not because I don't love you. I just want to have some relaxing time with my friends. I want to have pizza for dinner here and watch TV with Dan."

He was right and I knew it. What more did I want to do at age 15 than hang out at a friend's house on a weekend night, without having my parents hovering over me?

Terry agreed that he'd do his homework over the weekend at his friend's house as well his chores when he got back on Sunday. I said, "I know how much you love us, Terry, and I hope you know how much we love you. Go and have a great time, enjoy yourself." He said, "Thanks, Dad!" and that was that.

Deep down, I knew I had to deal with his growing up! I needed to hear his love and his directness. The wisdom of what he said touched me. That he could speak so directly to me. I can't remember talking like that to my father.

By the way, Terry came home on Saturday evening rather than Sunday, telling me, "I wanted to hang out a little here, it's not so bad to have you on my case." And he took care of his chores!

A father's apology—heartfelt and real—repaired the injury to his son and left the door open for the boy to come home without feeling that he had been shamed and defeated.

Andrea: "That looks terrible!"

Andrea and her husband Bob live in Virginia, where they manage a restaurant.

My son Adam is 16 years old and has always had a struggle in school. In ninth grade, his teachers told me that he just skulked around the halls, wearing a Mohawk, and doing other provocative things to his body. For example, he'd go over to a friend's house and come back with his head shaven. Then there was body piercing—ears, eyebrows. I figured he needed to do some testing. He'd come home with purple hair, and I'd say,

"Okay, you've got purple hair."

I didn't get on his case, and tried to be ho-hum about it. Then he started to fail in school, and I figured that he'd been so success oriented that maybe he needed to slack off. We were real laissez-faire. The school guidance counselor called and shocked us by saying that Adam was not doing well, that here was a kid with real potential who was not doing the work.

My husband and I really struggled. When you push Adam it only gets worse; he's real stubborn. Over the years, we had been through the whole assignment book routine and all.

The teachers acted like we knew nothing about this and were just space shot parents who didn't know what was really going on. But we got on Adam.

One day he was doing his homework, and the phone rang. It was his girlfriend. I told her, "He's doing his homework. He'll call you back later." Adam jumped up and grabbed the phone, pulled it off the wall, slammed the door, put his foot through it, and stormed out. That was a very scary incident. It's the kind of behavior we expect from 5-year-olds, but here was a big strapping 16-year-old. We waited till he cooled down and then told him that he needed to repair everything that he had broken, which he did.

My husband and I were really stumped. He had no siblings growing up and I had three sisters and feel like I don't really always get where boys are coming from. His ninth grade teachers were saying that he was clinically depressed, and I was telling them that "you're only seeing a part of him. There are other parts of him."

At one point Terry asked to see a counselor. We made an appointment. He then said he wasn't sure if he wanted to keep it. We said "Go and see Dr. B., and if he decides there's nothing to talk about, then fine; but maybe it'll be helpful." He came back from the appointment with his eyes on the floor and said, "I think I need to go back, there's some things for me to talk about."

My husband and I alternated weekly appointments with Adam with the doctor. It was very helpful to have someone outside the family to be supportive of us all. He found an extracurricular activity at school in floor hockey. That gave him some pleasure and a self-esteem boost. His grades started to get better, and he was doing his homework. His teachers, though, were acting as if nothing changed. We had to tell them to *recognize him, acknowledge him*.

Then one winter's morning Adam was in the bathroom for a while, and I was in the kitchen alone. He came downstairs and . . . he'd shaved off his eyebrows.

My stomach sank. I felt a queasiness in my gut. I knew what I wanted to say. I looked right at him and said, "Adam that looks terrible! I don't know what you were trying to do but you look like a skinhead."

He stopped and looked at me.

"Mom, you're right. I know it does. I'm going to let them grow back. I was just experimenting, wanted to see what it looked like."

He heard my directness, and he didn't resist and fight. Adam wore a hat down low over his eyebrows until they grew back. It even became kind of a joke. His best friend brought over two caterpillars he found in his backyard and said that Adam should glue them to his head.

What was really nice was that here was a moment when I knew what needed to be said. He needed these limits, and he heard them. He was really crying out for some comment from us. From that experience, my husband and I became convinced that Adam needed us to create structure for him. We established a rhythm of getting him to do his homework, being on him, and telling him that ultimately we wanted him to be able to monitor himself, but that until he could, we would do it for him. It's not a miracle cure, but he is responding. We're hoping that high school is a whole new start for him.

Sometimes a direct and honest response from us is what our children are most waiting for. His mother's direct reaction to Adam's experimentation gave the boy an honest, nonshaming response that helped him sort out what he wanted for himself. Andrea's words were strong but her tone and her directness must have communicated love. Andrea's story offers a nice counterpart to the way Julie handled her son Norm's experimentation. Limits lovingly offered can be very reassuring and help define us.

Chloe: "We went through a horrible struggle that was ultimately a gift to our family."

Chloe has lived in the same town outside Philadelphia all her life, and her family goes back generations in the town, to its settlement in the 1600s. Her husband, Benson, is the founder of a successful mutual fund investment firm and spends long hours growing his business—at the office and traveling. As in many small towns, gossip spreads fast where Chloe lives, and the drug and school difficulties of her son Michael seemed to "violate a taboo" in the town: Everyone graduates high school and no one drops out. And certainly no one does drugs. She told her story shyly in our focus group, as if the other parents present might judge her. Nonetheless, there was an unmistakable confidence in her tone—of someone who has weathered a hard time and knows she can get through it.

When our son Michael was in his teens, we went through a horrible struggle that was ultimately a gift to our family. He's now in his 30s, and at 6 feet 3 inches still has the bearing of a soldier. He has difficulty purchasing suit jackets and blazers because his shoulders are so broad, and his waist narrow. He can cut a striking figure, but his shoulders have had to bear their share of burdens.

Michael got involved with drugs in high school. He never went too public. He was very clever. He was never picked up by the police, never caught in school, never in any trouble. People in school knew there was a problem—his grades were terrible. I'd call the teachers and they'd say that he was just not doing his work.

We finally hit bottom when we sent him to boarding school. He was doing beautifully, or so we thought. Then he fell one day and broke his wrist and couldn't play that season on the school football team. He started to go downtown, hanging out with the local kids, doing drugs. I'll never forget the day the headmaster at the fancy private school called, a few days before Christmas break: "This is Jim O'Brien at the academy. When you pick up your son tomorrow, take all his stuff. We don't want him back here."

I was totally devastated. I had failed as a parent. I hadn't done the job. So he went back to high school and did terribly, something that had never happened in our family. He finally dropped out of tenth grade, another taboo. In the suburban town we live in, you don't drop out of school. I didn't know anyone this happened to. There was a great deal of shame in our family.

Michael worked doing odd jobs that year. Finally we were desperate so we checked him into Jefferson Hall—a drug rehab unit. We sent Mikey to an alternative school after that. Both things were very hard to do: my family has lived in this town since the 1600s. How could I explain to people?

Jefferson was an experience of healing. We learned how to communicate. There were a lot of behavioral exercises. We learned how to say, "I have an issue with you" and how to listen to the other person's answer. Mike and his father did a lot of work together there—hugging, crying, confronting. Mike really suffered from Benson being gone so much at work, and he worried that he couldn't fill his father's shoes. That's still an issue. Mike's chosen an alternative route as a schoolteacher. He's complicated, not an entirely happy young man. But we are all connected now, love each other, and know it. That experience kept our family whole. I often wonder if it hadn't happened whether we would have become really fragmented as a family.

Sometimes the darkest moments with teens can be the beginning of a rebirth for the whole family. This family's perseverance paid off, as each person learned to talk more honestly with the other.

Rachel: "It felt like I was really going to lose him."

After her divorce, Rachel, an attractive 35-year-old woman, started her own travel agency business in the Hartford area. She and her ex shared custody of their son. The arrangement was amicable until Rachel's ex-husband moved out of state and their teenage son had to make a decision about where to live.

The most difficult thing I've ever had to do in my life as a parent was to let go of my son two years ago and let him go live with his dad down South. Billy was in high school at the time. It was horrible, and I'm proud of the fact that I was able to do it. His dad and I were divorced when Bobby was 11, and for years it was pretty amicable. He lived down the street, and Bobby went back and forth between my apartment and his dad's. It was working out really well. But Malcolm's from Georgia, and he wanted to move back home.

I kept saying to my ex, "Please stay!"—because everything was working out so well in terms of parenting. But I wasn't successful in convincing him. People talk about how adolescent boys will gravitate to their fathers. Well, I'm not convinced of that. Bobby and I are very close. But he was having his adolescent thing and was struggling, in school and socially, not feeling very successful with his peers. He was a little in the out group, not getting invited to the cool parties.

After a Christmas visit to his father in Georgia, Bobby came into our living room when we were alone and said,

"Okay, I've found the place I want to live—down South with Dad."

I thought my heart would break. But I put on a cheery face and said, "Well, okay. Let's talk about all that." That led to months of negotiating. It was just a horrible time. Most painful was that my son *wanted* to go. At 18 he was supposed to leave home, not at 16, just starting his junior year in high school! I was so angry. It felt like he was going to become a Southerner, like his father. My whole family has been raised in the North, and he was going to a part of the country I don't know very well. It felt like I was really going to lose him.

One climactic night, my son and I were going out for pizza. It was at a pizza joint we often go to, a favorite place of ours. I was miserable inside and didn't want to show that to him. I didn't want him to start taking care of me. But it's hard not to feel like you've done something wrong. *How come he wants to leave here? Was I just a bad mother he wants to get away from?*

Being in our familiar pizza place made it worse in some ways. I imagined not eating there with him any more. I started to push at him, "Why are you going, really? Are you running away from your problems here?"

In fact I was angry at his father and didn't realize it. His father was like that, I felt—running away from problems in his life. He was always talking about wanting to get away from Hartford—it was too tough here, unfriendly, if only he could get back to the country, where things are peaceful. Give me a break! The man lives in the country now and has the same problems that he had up here!

Anyway, Bobby got more and more defensive, "No one here likes me. Down there is good energy; it's rural."

I was hearing all the things his Dad said, like a party line!

I just spoke to him as honestly as I could. "Please make sure you are not running away from your troubles here. You could wind up having the same difficulties with friends down there as you do up here."

Bobby didn't want to talk about it. "I just want to do it. I'm old enough to decide. It's my life."

I left that restaurant and knew that I was going to have to do my own grieving. I have a good friend who I talked with for hours—I did a lot of screaming and crying. "This is not the way things are supposed to be!"

All that yelling helped me sort out a few things. I realized that my son is actually quite adventurous. He's liked challenges from the youngest age. At age 9 he wanted to go to summer camp for two months; his counselors said he did great, and he was very proud of it. He was one of the first kids in his group to learn to ski and the first to become really good at skateboarding. I knew that his job as a child was not to live for me but to live his life.

I realized that he needed me to say to him that it was okay, that I trusted him to make the decision. One night at home I told Bobby, "It's okay. I know you can make the right decision. I will back you in whatever you feel you have to do."

I had to say it several times, over several weeks. What was most important for me was to see that it was not a personal attack on me. I so often question myself as a parent. Am I doing a good enough job? I began to see that Bobby also wanted to try his wings, that he had an adventurous streak and wanted to try something new, and that it was not *my fault somehow.*

He decided he did want to move and that he would fly up to see me each month and on holidays. Boy did I grieve! I remember packing him up. As they were driving south, I was on the phone to my friend, crying for an hour. Then I said to her, "Okay. I gotta go to work."

One thing that really helped was that Bobby and I spent that summer together before he left. We fixed up my house. I had bought a new house and was going to get some roommates; he would have his own room there, ready for him when he visited. Friends came over to help from time to time. It was fun setting up this house I own. Bobby worked that summer part-time at a convenience store down the block from us, and we spent part of each day working on the house.

I really cherished that time we had together. He helped paint several rooms, did some carpentry with me. It was getting close to the day he was leaving, when he came into the living room and asked me if I'd help him build some new shelves in his bedroom, and a new bed. He said he wanted some shelves to display his camp and soccer awards and to keep things "for when I'm living here too." He even joshed me about the bed: "C'mon Mom, I've outgrown the old one, and I need a place to sleep when I'm visiting here." I felt so grateful to him,. We built the shelves and the bed together, and it was an acknowledgment that he was indeed coming back, not just fleeing the coop.

It was hard, but it's worked out okay. Bobby hasn't disappeared from my life. We talk a lot on the phone, spend time together on holidays and visits. Most importantly, he is starting college this month, at Emory University. He's moving ahead in his life. He didn't get stuck in battles between his parents. That's what I'm most proud of from all this.

Rachel worked hard—with friends, her therapist, listening to herself and her son—so as to depersonalize Bobby's decision. We depersonalize a hard time when we see that how others are behaving is not an assault or judgment on us, but comes out of their struggles and needs. In seeing that her son's choice to leave was not because of her failure or some wrong she had done, Rachel was able to grieve and to create a ritual good-bye (the summer project together) that strengthened the relationship and affirmed their connection.

Monica: "I had an hour commute each day to work, and I was crying in my car."

Monica is a smart, lively woman. Even at age 40 her strong wiry body still looks a bit like a gymnast's, revealing the athletic interests she has pursued for years. She spoke quickly and laughed a lot as she told her story.

When my eldest daughter Marty was 16, she was accepted for an exchange program to New Zealand. What a hell of a time we had before she left! New Zealand! You can't go much further away and still be on this planet. We were both so sad, and we couldn't talk about it.

Things hadn't been easy for Marty since my messy divorce when she was 12. She and her sister and brother had left their childhood home and friends to live full-time with me when I moved halfway across the country. Marty in particular missed her father, who really wasn't there for her in important ways. I didn't handle the tensions of the divorce well, either, and she was often angry with me, too. But we had always been very close, and her going so far away was extremely difficult for both of us.

I was very proud of her and had supported her right from the start when she talked about applying for the fellowship. She was one of ten out of two thousand applicants chosen. Marty really embraced this opportunity and felt positive about it. In my head I did too, but my heart ached at having her away for so long. Finally, it was only a few weeks before she was leaving, and I didn't want to break down and cry in front of her. I think she didn't want to do that in front of me either.

I had an hour commute each day to work and I was crying in my car, back and forth. I kept a box of tissue on the passenger seat next to me. I don't mean to sound creepy, but it felt to me like someone was dying. I was beside myself, so scared of losing my daughter. I couldn't afford to visit her, wasn't going to see her for a whole year.

We were constantly fighting with one another.

In our kitchen there's a center work station. We'd get on opposite ends making dinner and just carp at each other.

We came to the day before she left. I was sitting there with my afternoon cup of coffee in the breakfast nook, and Marty came in. Marty quietly poured herself a cup of coffee and sat down next to me. We were on the same side of the table, not confrontational like at the work station. I asked her if she needed anything before she left. Then we started talking about the past two weeks.

"I'm sorry I've been so crabby," I said.

That really started things off. "Me too," she replied. It wasn't argumentative.

I told Marty that I felt both sad and excited about her going. She was astonished, "You do?!"

All of that had been hidden away from her underneath the tension. I told her how frantic I had felt, and awkward. I told her I didn't want to be fighting.

"You don't?! I don't either!"

It really took only the first few words of apology and reconciliation to get us both bawling, and we cried so hard that afternoon that we were both sick afterward. We spoke many words at that table, but the important part was the final clarity of feeling and loving and sadness and real grieving.

Marty played a song for me by Peter Cetera with the lyrics "You are the man who would fight for my honor, you are the hero that I have been dreaming of." It has made me cry every damn time I listen to it. And both my daughters play it now on the piano! It has such an important message: that although they can't come right out and say it sometimes, they admire me, and the things they do, like bravely going to far-off lands, are in the spirit I have shown to them in my actions.

That evening, after the tears, when the tension had been broken, we were sitting on Marty's bed. It was getting late, and the Cetera song was on. Suddenly I felt clearly the love and need that we so often mask. I just wanted to crawl into bed that night with Marty and hold her close, to sleep together in that bed once more, before everything changed as I knew it would. The important thing about children's growing up is that we fear we will lose them. I had the urge to hug Marty close, to crawl in close, but I didn't—some taboos are just too strong. I sensed too that just as it was important to let her leave the next day, it was equally significant to leave her room that night, to leave her to her own thoughts on that "last night."

I did, though, make a tape of the Cetera song, and I played it every now and then in my car on the way to work when I missed her.

Fighting in a family often masks sorrow. Monica's simple apology opened both mother and daughter to the tears each felt about the departure and their deep love for each other. The directness of the feeling of sorrow can open us to recognize too what we love. When we can't talk about a loss or change—due to our pride or the depth of sadness or embarrassment we feel—then lashing out at the other person is a way to stay connected even as we battle with them.

Connie: "I felt like a typical mother hanging on to her son."

Connie is the administrator of a large nonprofit agency in New York City. She's used to dressing well and to being in charge. Her dark eyes caught the light in the meeting room as she talked, contributing to her air of confidence, a trait that made all the more poignant the uncertainty she related in her story about saying good-bye to her college-bound son.

This weekend Nate left for college down South. His father and I are divorced, so earlier this summer his father took him to freshman orientation. A few weeks later, I got some registration materials and there was a brochure saying there was a preorientation for parents who had missed the July orientation. I figured that was great, a chance for me to see what was going on.

I drove Nate down to school, made a reservation in a hotel for Saturday night, and planned on the parent's orientation on Sunday as the brochure said. But when we got to the school no one seemed to know anything about the orientation. I could not get a straight answer from anyone. So I dropped Nate off at his dorm and went to my hotel. He immediately started hanging out with his new friends.

After awhile that afternoon I went over to his dorm and kept asking about this parents meeting to no avail. Nate meanwhile had gone off with his friends. I was alone in his room and I started doing "the Mom thing"—putting his laundry away, folding his underwear.

All the students had congregated in the lounge and were sitting there talking and laughing, and I didn't want to show my face anywhere! Most of the parents had left, and there I was, Nate's *Mom.* I didn't want to walk out there and sit with him in the lounge, and I didn't want anyone seeing me in his room doing his laundry. Where did I fit in?

Finally, someone told me that there was a parents meeting just finishing at the student union. I hurried over there and talked with some of the administration people. They weren't all that nice and helpful, and that was that. By then it was 5 p.m. and I was wondering what was I doing there. I felt like a typical mother hanging on to her son. He should be out doing just what he is doing, without his mother still hovering around!

I didn't know what to do. Should I get into the car and drive two hours to the airport and fly home? I was very tired. So I went back to my hotel room. I considered just leaving him a note and being off. Nate was out doing stuff and had told me he'd be back at 8 p.m. So I figured it would be up to him.

I called him up at 8 and asked him what he wanted to do, get together or take care of things himself. He replied, "Come over and help me hang some posters. I need your help."

His directness and clarity really helped me. I had been doing a number on myself, telling myself I was overinvolved, when actually I was simply taking some time to say good-bye to my son.

So after we worked awhile I told Nate the situation: "Okay, Nate, there's no meeting tomorrow; it's already happened. What would you like to do, say good-bye tonight or tomorrow?"

He said, "Maybe I'd like you to take me out to breakfast and maybe I'd like to sleep late. How about if I give you a call if I get up early?"

So we left it that he'd call me if he wanted to get together in the morning. Then we went out to get something to eat. He had dessert while I had my dinner.

All through dinner I kept thinking that *this was advice time.* I felt there was some advice I *should* be able to give him about being on his own for the first time. The first semester in college is such a scary time for the child and the parent. The night before we left to drive down together I had this awful dream: He was putting an LSD-laced mushroom into the toaster in our kitchen and was telling me, "It's got to be toasted just right. Then it tastes so great!" And earlier that day we had a bit of a tiff over his car. He had saved up from working summers and contributed to buying a new car. But now it needed some repairs, and the insurance was due, and he didn't have all the money necessary. He was asking his father and me for the money. At the campus registration office, Nate didn't have the registration papers and didn't know where they were. Finally I said, "If the car is too much to handle you can always leave it at home."

He got angry. He said he needed it to go into town for things or to go to the mountains skiing. He said, "Don't get all in my face about this. Chill out, Mom, it's okay."

He was right, it was old parent-child stuff.

So in the restaurant, I looked at him across the table. He was so happy and excited. I thought about how this was the start of his adulthood really. I knew he didn't need any words of wisdom from me.

I *did* think about my own experience going to college. And I told him one thing, which I wasn't sure about whether to do or not. I remembered how depressed I and my friends were our freshman year, wondering about life—*Who am I? What's life about?* So I said, "Remember that some people get really depressed when they go away to school. You might or might not, but you can always call me."

It was interesting. He didn't have all that much of a response. But he didn't seem to mind my saying that. None of the "oh Mom" or rolling his eyes. Nate just looked up at me from the pie he was eating and said, "Okay. Thanks."

So we said good-bye that night.

Sunday morning he didn't call, and I wanted to call him so much, but I didn't. I just got into the car and left.

What am I most proud of from the weekend? I was proud that I didn't just drop him off that first night and scoot out of there and that I didn't overstay too long either. I said good-bye to him in the way that I needed to, and in a way that was attentive to his cues as well.

We can say good-bye without a lot words. And even awkward moments can be heartfelt and well done. Mothers remain important figures for their teenage sons; sometimes they are more important to each other than either can say. Connie was particularly mindful of her own vulnerability, which helped her take cues from her son—letting him help her see how best to say good-bye.

Selena: "Everything that came out of my mouth was wrong, and I knew it!"

Thick dark hair frames the face of Selena, a 55-year-old grandmother. She and her husband Ramon have a lovely small home in a rural area near town, a short drive from the Santa Fe businesses where they work. Selena and Ramon raised their children in their modest home and welcomed their daughter Sara and her husband and their two small children into the house when they had difficulty making ends meet. Then Selena and Ramon's teenage daughter Serena got pregnant.

I'm 55 and now a grandmother. We have three generations all living in our three-bedroom house. My daughter Sara is 25. She and her husband have two children, ages 3 and 5. Serena is 19 and has a 6-month-old. She never really wanted to have a kid.

Her life changed and so did mine. I didn't expect to have my children living with me when I became a grandparent. We had expected to have a little bit of peace and some money.

Yet it's quite wonderful in many ways. Ramon takes the 3- and 5-year-old kids to preschool, because their parents both work the early shift. Ramon also picks them up and brings them home in the afternoon. These wintry days they come home and want to make the fire. The little ones come in with kindling. "Helping, helping!" they say.

I never had that warmth as a kid myself. My grandparents were the coldest people, as were my parents. So in a wonderful way our grandchildren really warm up our lives, even if sometimes it drives us crazy. We have no privacy. Ramon and I have rigged up a little sitting area in the garage, with chairs and a stereo, where we can read in quiet. But, you know, little kids will follow you right in there, bring their books with them, and ask you to read to them!

Serena is a really good mother, but still it's so problematic. She's very playful with the kids, but she's so young herself, only 19. Becoming a mother was a major transformation in terms of her ability to accept responsibility, but she still is struggling to make it through college. She wants to be an RN.

Serena first got pregnant at 17 and had an abortion. Then she got pregnant again and had Pablo. That pregnancy was very hard for all of us.

I've had five abortions, all in the early 60s before my first child was born. Two of the abortions were horrible: It turned out I was much more pregnant than I thought I was. In those days, you went for abortions wherever you could get them. For one of them, I saw some guy out in the country who was like a witch doctor. It was a dark place; I was alone. I remember crying hysterically afterward.

Serena didn't want an abortion, then she agreed. I thought that because it was now legal, there wouldn't be a lot of feeling. Plus, it was early in the pregnancy. She held my hand throughout it, and she was crying. It felt like she was a grown-up and a child. It was a trauma for her. I was crying too. It was very painful. I sat there remembering my own abortions, how scared and empty I felt.

Then Serena got pregnant again, and I flipped out. She had talked to her older sister first and they said they both wanted to talk to me. My heart was in my stomach. Here were two sisters sitting me down and telling me that Serena is pregnant again. It was like watching a movie of yourself at a previous stage, your past going by right in front of your eyes.

I yelled at Serena, "I can't handle your having a baby!"

Well, that just didn't compute for an adolescent. She yelled back, "It doesn't have anything to do with you!"

"You have to have another abortion; you have no choice!"

I can't believe I said that! Everything that came out of my mouth was wrong, and I knew it. But I had to get it out. I couldn't stop it.

My husband handled it better. Serena has a different relationship with her father. He's less reactive.

Ramon got me to calm down. When he and I talked, I let it out—that I couldn't handle one more child in our house. Ramon got me to see that I was putting up a wall between me and my kids. I went back and told Serena that it was her choice and that we would stand beside her no matter what. She decided she wanted the baby.

After she decided to have her child, I talked with Serena about my own experiences with pregnancy. I had shared some of my life after Sarah's kids were born. Now I told them much more.

I'm most proud of the kind of mother I am. No matter how upset I am, how annoying I may be, I'm always there for them. And they know that. When Serena had Pablo I was there the whole time, thirty-five hours, a really long labor. I watched her grow up during those hours, me too. I watched her turn into a woman. There was no way to walk away from what was happening to her, as she had done before. There's a kind of vulnerability that happens when the labor is long enough, and I think that was good for her. Some high school kids have two-hour labors, and it's so easy. I'm sorry for them.

Serena at first was on an IV, pushing for a few hours. "I can do this. I can do this," she kept saying. But after twenty hours, she was forced to confront her vulnerability and her fears.

She came home and went through so many changes—hormonal, emotional. She wanted to breastfeed. It turned out to be very hard for her, and at times she wanted to give up. But she didn't. She told me how much she needed me.

It meant a lot because I never had a person there for me. My father was a very cold person, not very affectionate. He spent all his life running his hat factory and didn't give very much to his wife or to me. My mother was very manic, always upset about something. She had a hard start to life. Her mother died of a stroke right next to her in the car when she was 5 years old.

She told me once that she just expected me to be born and to love her. It doesn't work that way. Only if you love them do they love you. My parents may have loved me, but they didn't really show it. I was always the one who made the bad choices, fucked up. But with my daughters, I never—except when I went crazy about Serena's pregnancy—made them feel unloved.

If you have grandchildren living with you or if your grown kids are doing something interesting with their lives, people always want to hear. But if you tell people your grown children live with you, they ask, "Why don't you throw them out?"—as if kids are leeches when not living on their own. I don't share a lot about all this with my friends or at work because it's hard for others to understand. But I know I've been there for my kids.

We need each other in difficult moments in our families. Selena grew up along with her daughters, through the pregnancies. Being there for her daughter nourished Selena's self-esteem and filled a hole from her own childhood. Even though at times she was almost out of control, she could lean on her husband and her daughters to find her way through her panic and agony to support her daughter when she needed her.

Robert: "His wallet fell out . . . and rolling papers dropped out."

Robert is the director of an art museum in the Pacific Northwest. At 52 years old, he's a soft-spoken man who's been through a difficult time with drugs and alcohol in his own adolescence. He speaks with some irony about dealing now with a college-age son making choices.

My son's just begun college, which makes him actually closer to me. We're in the same city for the first time since his mom and I were divorced years ago. It's new ground for all of us, with him here in college, living in the dorms and so grown up. I know who he is, and I don't know. When I picked him up at the airport, his wallet fell out of his pocket and some rolling papers dropped out of it. He just brushed them aside but I froze. I couldn't believe it. I freaked out and got very shut down. It took me about two hours to bring it up. You don't carry around rolling papers to take class notes on. So I finally said, "What's with the rolling papers? What are they about? I know about rolling papers."

Basically I think James lied to me. He's been to probably a thousand AA meetings with me over the years, so he's heard my story about my drug use. He said that he's tried it and doesn't like it and that he was carrying the papers for friends to use at clubs. I want to believe it but basically I think he's lying. I've had the talk with him about drugs; he knows about the genetic link of alcohol and drug addiction. There's not much else I can do at this point. The outside of his life seems to be flourishing, though then again it wouldn't surprise me if he was an alcoholic, though I don't think he is. He doesn't have that sense of angst, not fitting in, that hole inside of him that so many alcoholics feel.

When we were arguing over the rolling papers he said to me, "You want me still to be the good little boy."

He's never had time to get really angry at me, because our times together were so special after the divorce. He'd spend July and August with me. Sometimes. I'd get angry at him and we wouldn't talk for hours because he didn't take the garbage out or because after I'd spend money on him I'd realize that no matter how much money I spent, he wasn't going to be living with me, that no amount of money would make everything okay. A lot of my anger just came out of the pain of him growing up really separate from me.

For some families, the late adolescence of their children is a time of confrontation and truth telling about the family's experience. While hard, these times can result in a deeper connection rather than separation. For Richard and James the rolling papers may be symbolic of a much deeper sorting out that needs to happen—about the divorce perhaps and its effect on the relationship and self-esteem of father and son. Father and son may wonder whether their relationship can tolerate the anger and sorrow that accompanies speaking honestly to each other about the disappointments and sorrows of having been separate and now together. What looks like a separation (going to college) actually means, for James and Richard, the chance to move closer and to share time together that is not just "special" but may be more "real."

THE PARENT-TEEN PROCESS OF HOLDING ON AND LETTING GO

Trying to come to terms with her son Bobby's desire to live with his father, Rachel observed that "I began to see that Bobby also wanted to try his wings, that he had an adventurous streak and wanted to try something new, and that it was not *my fault somehow.*" She recognized that the decision was about her son, and not about her. Rachel knew then that she had some grieving to do.

Many parents of teens may connect with the struggle to hold on to their children even as we are letting go of them emotionally. This is true whether our children live with us or apart. We come to see our adolescents as partly separate from us. We mourn the loss of the idealized, adored preteen that we knew and open ourselves to the growing near-adult who is different and separate from us in some ways.

The parent-adolescent process of holding on and letting go involves hurt and pain as well as love for both parties. A teenager's difficult behavior often is in the service of letting the teenager really be different from his or her parents. Words and behavior that cause us pain also allow them and us to break the bubble of adoration and merger between a parent and young child. When they're still very physically and emotionally dependent on us, as every preteen is, we can imagine our children are *just like us*, reflecting our deepest wishes and values and needs.

When puberty hits, and a son or daughter struggles with sexuality, with the seemingly limitless possibilities of adolescence, with the questioning and philosophizing they're capable of, we begin to realize too that they also are different from us. Sometimes our children have to disappoint us, normally and unavoidably, to let us know that they are not going to conform to some of our deepest needs and wishes. Bobby, for instance, may be saying to his loving mother that they are not going to live their lives in a primordial mother-son soup of being just like each other. He is not going to simply become an extension of her. Rachel had to "own" her anger at her husband and to separate Bobby from his father in her mind.

This process of psychologically separating from our teens is true, of course, for fathers as well as mothers. One of the tasks is to sort out, tolerate, grieve the disappointment when we realize, to paraphrase Rachel, that their job as children is not to live for us but to live their own lives. A teenager's being able to do this means, paradoxically, that they disappoint, scare, and sadden us in some ways.

On the other hand, we can overestimate our children's need for distance during the turbulence of the teen years. Amidst the teen body piercing, hair coloring, experimentation with drugs and sexuality, is also a child who very much wants to remain connected to his or her parents.

The language of separation and connection may be a "coded" one, as in Bobby's sudden desire to renovate the very room he appears to be leaving. In a coded way he's saying, "Part of me is not leaving; I *am* coming back." Rituals such as construction projects, tapes of favorite songs, or dinners together can express messages of hope and reconciliation hard for teens or adults to say in words.

Teens try to connect even as they look like they're disconnecting. The challenge for us as parents can be how to make a direct and honest emotional connection rather than turning away. Andrea found the difficult moment of confronting her suddenly eyebrow-less son to be an opportunity for her family to find a new and more honest way of speaking directly to each other.

A basic truth emerges: Adversity can help families become closer. Chloe, who felt so isolated in her Philadelphia town of perfect children, ended the story about her son Michael's struggle with addiction with a detail that illustrates this window of opportunity.

At the focus group Chloe explained that the worst of the struggle with her teenage son's addictions happened the very year that her husband was away most often. In fact, Benson had spent a large part of that year reviving a corporation in the South.

"We were talking, last Thanksgiving, about the difficulties in our family that year, ten years ago. Michael said, 'You know Mom and Dad, that was the year Dad was away.' During that year my husband was spending huge amounts of time down South getting the corporation he had bought back on its feet. He commuted back to our house on weekends.

"We reminisced about that year and I replied to Michael, 'That was the year I went back to graduate school, and you were in Jefferson Hall.'"

"Michael pursued it: 'Yeah. *And* the year Dad was in Alabama.'"

"I had never realized how away Benson was because he and I talked on the phone all the time, *but it was different for Mike.*

Part of the struggle for Michael that year was to find a way to connect with his father, to find some manageable way to live with such a successful father who was not there for his own son. The son's struggle with addictions brought together a family that was exploding outward—into the father's work and mother's graduate school plans—and needed to find a way to reconnect with each other. There was nothing wrong with the parent's commitments and excitement about their future plans. The son, however, may have been reminding the parents that the home fires also needed some tending. The mother and father were connected to each other via the phone and their commitments to career and school success; the son was lost and needed to bring together the parents who were lost to him (and maybe themselves) in their extra-familial commitments.

Might Chloe and Benson have been oriented too far toward letting go of Michael—relying too much on the broad shoulders of their son to bear up to the burdens he was under? It can be as problematic for parents to let go too quickly as it can be for them to hold on too tightly to their children. Neither needed to give up their plans to listen to the load of expectation and vulnerability the son felt on his shoulders. Jefferson Hall, the treatment center, became that opportunity.

The launching of a child is a tender time in a family, and the same moment may be experienced very differently by the adolescent and each parent. Sometimes the adolescent is oriented outward—to college, the army, Los Angeles, all the possibilities they are going to—while the parents are focused on being left behind. Sometimes it is the opposite, with the adolescent holding on and the parent moving forward. There is a lovely haiku poem by the great Japanese master Buson that captures the difference in separations, depending on whether you're parting or remaining: "For me who go, for you who stay—two autumns."[5]

Both parents and teens feel tugged at by competing feelings: the excitement of holding on and resignation of it, the need to let go and the joy of it. We can better understand the way our kids are torn as

---

[5] From Henderson, H.G. *An Introduction to Haiku*, NY: Doubleday, 1958.

teens if we can acknowledge the contradictory pulls within us. It can help to see how we as parents may be struggling, how *our* demons can be stirred up by our children's struggles. Monica's story of letting her daughter go to New Zealand, for example, points to the ancient terrors that our kids' leaving home can generate for us—returning us to our human loneliness and an awareness of how much we've come to depend on them. Parents can be caught off guard by the primal way that launching our kids can leave us questioning the familiar framework of our world. One father described longingly the "family walks" and dinners together that marked the preteen years with his children. He compared his family back then to the Olympic Rings, an interconnected image of togetherness and union. Now that the children were off in college, his family felt to him like "the Olympic Rings are coming apart," an image of separation and scatter.

It can be important for a mother or father to recognize their own worries, even terrors, of being alone, as we lose a primary job: that of being our children's mom or dad. That means exploring a new sense of self in the world, just as our teens and young adult children are. Rituals marking these family events can help us all.

We truly are on a parallel journey with our teens. No matter what changes we experience, though, no matter how "displaced" we may feel as parents, as our kids grow, we never lose the job of being their mom or dad.

Hidden Wisdom You Can Use

- Keep the lines of communication open—keep talking and exploring with your teen. If your 16-year-old son or daughter informs you that he or she hopes to move to LA or Boston next month to pursue a recording career, use this as an invitation to explore reality in a curious and friendly way. How will they get there? How will they go about finding an apartment? What about money? How will they get their music heard by record studios? Such dialogues are a good way to get you and them thinking about the consequences of actions.

- Be aware of your own stereotypes and misleading assumptions about teens and what they're up to. Try to be as specific and precise about the kinds of information you need to assure you that what your child proposes is safe and appropriate.
- Teens want to know some but not all of your history. It helps them to know you've struggled with similar dilemmas and are not just reflexively laying down rules from on high. They want to know where your value statements are coming from; they don't want to hear long-winded monologues about "the old days."
- There's a normal and natural terror to having teenage children. You are vulnerable to a lot of fears as a parent. It can help to network with the parents of your child's friends. Get to know them. You don't have to become friends, but it can help to know where they're coming from and what their expectations are for their kids.
- It is also a good time to draw on your own friends for advice—those who are parents and those who remember their own adolescence.
- Talk to older teens and young adults. Your friends may have older children. Without violating the privacy of your own children, ask their advice. Often older teens welcome an opportunity to feel their perspective is valued by older adults.
- A new language of authority develops when you have adolescents. It means acknowledging their views and values and separate perspective perhaps more than you did when they were younger.
- Acknowledge when you've been off base because of your own irrational (or rational) fears.
- Don't hesitate to apologize, if that seems called for.
- Try not to take testing behavior and experimentation too personally. Sometimes it has nothing to do with you and feeling that it's because you've failed can only muddy the waters for your child. Making teen behaviors into personal accusations ("You're doing this because I've failed!") doesn't help.

- Recognize your own struggles with love. You and your adolescent are coming from different places. Having a child grow up and leave home can rekindle old struggles for you from your adolescence or earlier.
- You always have your own teen experience to fall back on. What did you want and need from parents? What do you wish your parents had done and said? What was the adolescent passage like for you? Did you get through it safely? Did you wish for or find other adults who can help you?
- Do your own grieving; separate from your child. Think about what's lost, what's gained, and what you want from your own life post-teens.
- Rituals help to let go, to move on, and to hold on. You can create your own and find ones with your children as well.
- A sense of humor always helps, and your teens may respond to it.

chapter   seven

Fathers with Daughters

W e're sitting in the cozy oak-lined conference room of a church in a suburb of Boston, a group of ten men and women meeting to tell stories about parenting. It was a pleasant late summer's early evening—you could hear the cicadas through the open window—and after a while the talk turned to our own parents. What could we remember about being parented by our own parents?

Gloria: "I wish I had been able to appreciate him when he was alive."

Gloria, a 78-year-old grandmother, wanted to tell a story about her father. She began by apologizing; she wasn't sure she had much to say, because, in some ways, she didn't know him all that well.

I'll always think of him as Father, not Daddy, because he was older, 51, when I was born, and rather formal. I didn't appreciate him for a long time. I knew he loved me, though. He smoked a pipe, and I loved the smell of his tobacco. He always gave me the empty cans of pipe tobacco, and I used to play with them. Even now when I smell the strong aroma of a pipe, I'll think of him.

One special evening, just after my younger sister was born, he gave me a bath and read me a bedtime story. I was 6 years old. My mother must have been busy with the newborn, so on this one evening, he took care of me. How wonderfully warm and soapy the bath was! He was still in his business suit from work, but he rolled up his shirtsleeves and sat by the side of the tub with me. I remember being toweled off and then held by him. It felt so cozy!

Otherwise he didn't really participate in my care. Every Sunday he'd get ready to go to church. I'd help him make his breakfast, then walk up to church and back with him.

When I was engaged to be married, in college, he wrote me a letter telling me how much he loved me and his wishes for me. I didn't keep it.

The tears I feel now are because I wish I had kept it. I didn't know how to appreciate and love him. I always wished I had. I wish I knew him better. My tenderness came through him. He never raised his voice, and my mother did a lot. I didn't really know how to appreciate him and love him until I was much older. I wish I had been able to when he was alive. He died in 1953, soon after my third child was born.

That evening, Gloria's longing was palpable to the rest of us—her wish to have gotten more from her father and the wish that she had been more able to recognize what she did get. Most of all she missed him still, forty-five years after his death. Gloria that evening had surfaced deep feelings for her father that had been buried until invited to talk about him to the focus group. Her openness allowed the whole group to talk about the depth of longing, love, gratitude, and disappointment fathers and daughters may experience between each other.

There is a special connection between fathers and daughters, as there is between mothers and sons. It comes from the delicious flirtatious energy and deep bond that unites parents with their opposite-sex children.

The very vitality and frisson of the connection can leave us feeling awkward and uncomfortable. Mothers may want to be more involved with their sons, fathers with their daughters, but feel off balance, unsure, particularly as their children begin puberty and beyond. Can a mother continue to hug her teenage son without embarrassing him? How close can a father be to his teenage daughter without one (or both) of them feeling uncomfortable?

We love our children, of course, regardless of their gender. Personality, character, and temperament may be more important in shaping who we are. Yet gender is a fundamental duality that helps us see and organize the world. For fathers, daughters bring with them a sense of "otherness," as sons do for mothers. We reach across a distance of experiences that we don't share, even as we are united by being the same flesh and blood or same family.

Our children—and we ourselves as parents—will benefit if we can get into focus the extraordinary rhythms of flirtation, loss, separation, distance, and reconnection that describe the father-daughter, mother-son relationship. Moments of affection, deep insight, and support—true silver linings—come when we consciously or unexpectedly—sometimes miraculously—connect with a child who is both "like us" and also is "the other."

THE TREASURE GAME

The Treasure Game is a writing exercise we often play in focus groups or workshops for fathers and grown daughters. We usually start with the daughters. I hand out 3-by 5-inch index cards and invite the daughters to write down a memory with their fathers that they particularly treasure. This could be a moment together, something you or he said or did—a song, a phrase, a picture, an object. It could have happened as recently as today or as far back as you can recall. It may be something that you've never told anyone else. My invitation is to take as much of the card as needed to tell the story but to try and be direct and to the point. "Don't shortchange yourself," I'll urge, "*Include as much of the detail as you can.*"

We'll all write for ten minutes or so—we do this exercise fast, without worrying about revisions or grammar or getting it "just right"—and then read aloud what we've written. Usually we go right around our circle and read without comment, saving discussion until after we've heard all the treasures on the cards. It takes some trust to do this exercise, and often people will read their cards with a look that suggests to me, "Treat this story with respect. I don't have many of these memories to give you."

The effect of reading such memories while seated in a circle is cumulative and powerful. We get a picture of how much goes on between fathers and daughters that is overlooked in daily life and that we may forget or not notice at the time. It's a portrait of the gifts that fathers offer their daughters.

THE GIFTS FATHERS CAN GIVE DAUGHTERS

One thing that fathers offer daughters is welcome access to the touch and feel and safety of their bodies, as in this memory from Audrey, a mother herself remembering back to a treasured moment over six decades ago.

Audrey: This is silly but I remember from my teenage years, and even before, Daddy used some kind of brilliantine on his hair, and I used to go around and behind him and make little peeks and horns out of his hair, and he'd very absentmindedly brush it back. And that was a sort of a happy memory.

Simply being included in Dad's world can boost a daughter's self-esteem and leave her feeling beloved of this man who means so much to her. Fathers are the ambassador and guide to a magical world, the world of masculinity, as revealed by these stories from grown daughters from three different families.

Alissa: My father took my younger brother and me fishing a few times a year. He loved fishing. I remember rowing out on the lake, having him teach me to bait the hook with a worm, cast, watch, reel it in, take the fish off, throw it back or keep it, then clean it, cook it, and have it for dinner at a campfire.

I was petite and a Goody Two-Shoes type of girl, but I loved being included in this activity. It symbolized some kind of acceptance and inclusion in my father's world. He was a patient and gentle teacher. It was also wonderful to be out of the city in nature together.

Jesse: Every fall, beginning when I was about 8 years old, my father would take me hunting with him and his boss and his boss's sons. The sons were teenagers, so I was the youngest. We never caught anything, but that didn't matter. It felt great to be able to be with him on those crisp autumn days, decked out in our bright hunting sweaters and orange caps. Even though I was a girl, I was allowed into that man's world.

Sometimes fathers offer support and love in a way that only fathers can. Perhaps in special moments they can see their daughters more clearly simply from being outside the intensity of the mother-daughter bond. In the following story, Ada remembers back seven decades to a moment when her father was especially able to see her needs and respond, without words.

Ada: When I think about a happy memory with my father, this isn't a particularly *gay* one, but it was very important to me. My father and I loved each other, although we never talked about anything particularly important. To illustrate the way I felt about him—he took me to an eye doctor for glasses when I was in third grade, which I didn't want to wear because my mother had been shocked when I told her the school had wanted me to wear them. My mother was always concerned with my appearance, how I looked. So I felt the glasses would make me look ugly.

Well, the doctor said to my father "I don't think she wants to wear glasses at all!"

And I controlled myself until we came out on the steps of the brownstone, and then I just burst into tears. My father just put his arms around me and held me. Nothing was said. He just understood.

The length that fathers will go to try and break through their masculine reserve or discomfort with words—the awkwardness they're willing to endure—often carries in itself a powerful message of love for the daughter.

Vanessa: When I was 10, I was sitting on the couch with my father one afternoon watching TV. He wasn't a particularly articulate man, and he wasn't particularly comfortable with emotion or expressing himself. But this particular afternoon I was sitting beside him and he awkwardly but warmly put his arm around me and pulled me close to him. He just expressed his love for me and his affection. I knew he was uncomfortable doing that, but I knew it was important for him to say that to me and that's something I really treasure. It really held me in good stead for many years when there were rough times—because of the security and anchor of knowing that he really loved me and valued me. So that's a precious memory.

The magic that fathers offer their daughters can feel like a special present just for them. In the story that follows, Marion's father taught her a new mastery, an invitation to be less afraid of the wildness of the world. It was a gift she carried with her past his tragic, untimely death.

Marion: My father died when I was 9 years old in an automobile accident, but he's been an important presence in my life. One visceral, kinesthetic memory I have is of his teaching me how to bodysurf. I grew up in southern California, where there was great bodysurfing. We'd often go to the beach, the whole family, particularly on the weekends. And I'd always be intimidated by the waves. I was the youngest, and I'd *always* be getting crunched by the waves. For years and years and years the waves would come thundering in and pounding over me. I'd go under and get sand in my bathing suit and swallow saltwater, and I'd always come up and feel so proud of myself that I had made it. That's what I thought bodysurfing was: getting pummeled by the waves. I thought that's what playing in the ocean was! I didn't know you could play in the ocean without getting tussled in the waves, until one day standing together in the surf, my father said to me, "You know, you can dive underneath the waves."

I was shocked. "No, no, daddy! You can't dive *underneath* the waves. It's too scary,"

So he took my hand. There was one of those *huge* waves coming right at us, and he gently tugged me and we dove under. I remember this sensation of the wave moving, passing over my head, and knowing that it was safe to come up again with him. This was such a magical moment. I felt like my father had this secret knowledge that only he knew and that he was teaching to me. He took away my fear in this very loving way—mastery of the wave. It was different from my mother. My mother taught me many things, but it's a whole different quality of feeling. There was something very, very special in those moments, and it must have something to do with the father-daughter relationship, like his teaching me the secret of the waves was only for me—a little jewel that he was giving just to me. It was wonderful.

When things go well fathers offer vital protection to their daughters by teaching them mastery and skills to make the world safe by giving them straight answers to painful questions, as Nancy's father did when she was a 10-year-old on the edge of adult awareness:

Nancy: "I was with my father in the car, alone. Out of the blue I asked him a question that had been on my mind for a long time: "Is there truly a Santa Claus?" Some of my older friends had been teasing me about Santa, and I couldn't get a straight answer. I had asked my mother, my grandparents, and my teacher. They'd smile and hem and haw. I'm not sure I *wanted* to know either; I loved old Santa so much.

I hadn't asked my father, though. There we were driving to the grocery store together. He was looking out the windshield, thinking about something, when I blurted out my scary question.

My father turned to look right at me, and he replied in the most gentle, kind, and strong voice: "No, there's not." He responded so forthrightly, so honestly—no bullshit—that I felt safe with him. At that moment I believed that my father would tell me the truth forever, whatever the situation.

Nancy's father protected her from feeling overly confused and out of it and from being a target for mocking by giving her an honest answer when she needed it. Fathers can sometimes protect their daughters even when the father doesn't know what to do or the situation seems especially delicate, as Maria's memory from her days as a child in Puerto Rico indicates.

Maria: In terms of my sexual development, when I was 12 years old, my first period, the beginning of menstruation, happened late at night. I felt something strange happening to me. So I ran to the bathroom to see what was going on. And of course I saw bleeding. And I got so scared. I knew from before, but it was the first time. And I thought, "I'm not going to talk to my mother, I'm going to talk to my father." He just calmed me down and said, "Well, go with your mother. She will explain to you what to do." He calmed me by hugging me. I felt more protected. If anything bad happened to me, any physically painful situation, I would rather have my father by my side. I'd feel more protected.

Even the wild enthusiasm that fathers display for their daughters, the hopeless romanticism that may make a teenager cringe, can be remembered years later with great joy and appreciation. Daughters need to feel that their fathers are hopelessly in love with them and support their normal struggle to nurture the active, assertive, physical part of themselves. Rebecca's father found a way that his daughter ultimately treasured.

Rebecca: I tried all sorts of sports as a kid, T-ball, Little League, girls' basketball, and was never very good at any of them. When I stumbled on to women's volleyball in high school, I loved it. My dad knew nothing about volleyball but saw how much I enjoyed the game and learned all about it. He helped me with positioning and how to spike the ball and pass off. He was at most every game—I could hear him yelling over everyone else. "JUMP!" he'd shout when I'd go up for the ball. One time I remember he gave the whole team a pep talk about how to work together as a team. If he missed a game, the whole place seemed much quieter. Before I'd see him, I'd hear him, yelling encouragement to me. At first I was embarrassed, but over time I grew to love it.

There is a normal and healthy flirtation between father and daughter. Daughters need to have their femininity appreciated and validated by their fathers and, in fact, want to see a spark ignited in their fathers eyes as they parade in front of them. It need be a safe and contained spark, but it means so much for a daughter to feel that her father thinks she is something special. Often fathers and adolescent daughters are doing a shy dance about her growing femininity, yet it matters a lot for fathers, as awkward as they may feel, to somehow communicate to their daughters that they are wonderful, lovely young girls growing into womanhood. Not all fathers can say that exactly in words, but many of us try to communicate it as best we can. Sometimes we succeed in a special, shared way, as Mary-Alice found with her dad.

Mary-Alice: Shopping for a prom dress with my father. During my senior year, my father must have suddenly realized that I'd be graduating soon and leaving home. There were many teary moments those months. Anyway, he decided he wanted to pick out a prom dress with me that spring. We went downtown to Saks, Neiman-Marcus,

Dayton-Hudson. Some dresses I thought were too expensive, but he insisted I try them all on. I'd ask my father what he thought, and he'd be very truthful—Dads are truthful all the time. I remember coming out of the dressing room with a very low-cut one. He said, "Oh! Gosh! That's a little revealing." But he wouldn't say no if I really wanted it. Finally we found the perfect dress. He said, "That's it! That's it!" I agreed. It was simple and elegant, a long dress, ivory, with straps on the top. I loved wearing it at the prom.

Stories of father-treasures continue past adolescence to the end of life. For many daughters and fathers, the teen or young adult years can be difficult. "My father was so supportive of me as a young kid, until I got into boys in my teens—he just didn't know what to do with me as his daughter and a sexual being," lamented one daughter at age 30. Another woman, a successful professional and mother of several grown children, recalled at age 60 that "my dad made sure I got the kind of education that left me feeling smart and capable, until I graduated college and went to medical school. He had the hardest time with my wanting a career and not rushing into marriage. When I was in my 20s, things were rough between us. It's like he got confused: He wanted me to be a strong and capable woman—really the son he never had— but also to marry and be a traditional homemaker/mother kind of daughter."

Yet, as we age, there is always a possibility of remaking the past. The process of disconnection, connection, and reconciliation of course ebbs and flows, as the following story of a grown daughter and father in sud- denly unfamiliar territory reminds us.

Karen: When I was 25 years old my father took me for a drive in his car to get some ice cream. When we were alone driving along, he tried to talk to me about my plans to get married to the man who is now my husband. He was very hesitant bringing the subject up and kept looking out the window. Then he said, "About Tom, I have nothing against the guy . . . " I realized that he was trying to talk me out of our plans to get married!—or at least to slow me down. This was a special time because he was trying—in his way—to protect me. I remember his talking about how young he felt getting married and about how much he loves my mother—but he didn't want me to rush into things.

He sounded very awkward and apologized, saying that he didn't want to intrude but that sometimes it's better to wait awhile before making a commitment like that. I knew he was trying to let me know how much he cared about me. I felt how difficult this was for him to do, but that he loved me and waded into this unfamiliar territory—talking about love and life and feelings—despite his apprehensions. It was the type of talk we should have had years before that!

Sometimes as our families change, so does the relationship with a father. For example, after a mother's death, a grown daughter may find herself thinking more about her father, as Nanette reports. Nanette is a professor of sociology at an Ivy League college, and after a distinguished career is thinking about retirement. One recent semester she found herself connecting to the course material in a new way, as she rediscovered the role of her 92-year-old father in her life.

Nanette: Fathers and daughters? Oh goodness! I didn't realize how important he was to me until teaching a course on ethnicity last year. We were all—the students and I—talking about our stories about ethnic heritages, trying to connect to various theories and concepts, and I was talking more about my father than my mother! That was very unusual. I'm used to thinking more about my mother's influence on me. But I was thinking then about where he came from, how he had lived.

He had a much greater influence on me than I realized. He was more lower class than my mother, and a very interesting man. A sort of Walter Mitty type—he wrote poetry, songs, plays, was constantly making things—the sort of person who fantasizes himself in other places, but he carried it through. I didn't realize until we started talking more that he had worked in hayfields out West, wandered more than I thought. Certainly he wandered far in his mind.

I see his can-do attitude in me—the persistence, optimism. "Never had a headache in my life," he says! It's a change to realize the impact he's had on me. I've always felt closer emotionally to my mother. I could talk with my mother. He was more removed. Growing up, I'd play math games with him and talk about life with my mother.

After my daughter was born, I'd be at work and I'd come home and she'd be in his lap doing crossword puzzles with him. Watching my daughter and how close they were I remembered how I'd sit in his lap the same way.

I have an early picture on my desk—he and I looking at a watch—sitting in his lap but doing something. It's odd—he didn't know what to do with me a lot of the time. Having him in my house recently was hard—I couldn't talk to him and I felt bad. *I* didn't know what to do with *him*. He lives in his head. But his attitude about work, risk, wandering—he encouraged all that in me. He's always been willing to talk about ideas, plans, theories.

What would I like to say to him? To tell him in some way he means more to me than he may realize. I tended to ignore him. My mother and I were so tight—I think he felt peripheral, and he may not realize how central he was to me.

We've got a chance to connect, but he is so difficult!

Even as "grown up" as we feel, it may still be hard to say what we want to say to our fathers and to feel truly heard. Opportunities for reconciliation can take many different forms and occur at unexpected times and places. A grown daughter (or a young one) often needs to feel that she can give back *a gift of love to her father, that she has something of value to give back to this man she loves.*

Joan: When I was in the fourth grade, my father experienced an unfortunate turn of events in his career. He was laid off and became quite depressed. He went through a very difficult time. He lost his hair, was sad and withdrawn, had low energy, felt isolated, and so on. He never sought treatment or got help. Those few years following were very difficult, as my mother supported our family (I am an only child). The underground tensions and disappointments between them continued along at a low simmer. My mother has remained pleasantly bitter.

Many years ago, after I had finished up my studies in graduate school, my father and I were waxing my car in their driveway during a visit home. My father and I got into a talk about those days when he was so depressed and stuck. We often have good talks while doing something together. I recall vividly that at one point my father growled at me, "I wish you'd just forget about all that. My problems with my job are my business. They have nothing to do with you, or your mother.

They should have no impact on you. Just stop worrying about me and live your life. It's not your concern."

I got deeply sad, and angry. Of course those events had a tremendous impact on me! I care about the man. What hurt the most was his notion that his problem was his alone. In my family, it feels that the family members view their problems as theirs alone, and we can't help each other. I have always had to lick my own wounds, because my well-intentioned, loving, doting parents, didn't really know how much of the time I was hurting.

I couldn't stand it any more, so I yelled back, "You're full of shit if you let yourself believe that you and your life have no impact on me. I love you and I care what happens to you. So how could your job loss and depression be something I just wall off?"

He almost dropped his wax cloth. But he was listening. I told him that what hurt me the most is not that things happened that were painful but that he was not able to acknowledge that these things happened and that they had an impact. He was able to listen to me. I felt that I was able to tell him how much he mattered to me and that we didn't need to deny anymore that his difficulties did indeed have an impact on me.

A daughter wants to hear that she has value to her father, that whatever difficulties and alienation existed between them, she at least matters to him. Sometimes a simple word can do the trick—an apology, an acknowledgment of wishing things were different even if unsure of how to make them so.

These women's treasured memories echo the many impacts fathers can have on their daughters' self-esteem, sexual identity, and exploration of the world, not just with young daughters but with the grown woman as well. There's the magical father who can teach his daughter a trick for taking away her fear of the large waves; the father who really roots for you at volleyball or wherever; the father who welcomes his daughter into the world of masculinity, showing her that she is welcome in a man's world of hunting, fishing, the boardroom, or wherever; the man who is passionately convinced that you are the greatest and who by the power of his commitment maybe makes you feel that way too; the father who accepts and admires your developing femininity, who allows you to pirouette in front of him in your prom dress and tells you that it is wonderful, your developing femininity, that in his eyes you are a beautiful woman who can go out into the world—a sharing of the sexuality of everyday life between father and daughter; the father who tells it to you straight, who can soften the sting of learning that there is no Santa Claus; and the father who awkwardly—like so many of us— manages to communicate with a gesture or few words the extent of his love for his daughter.

The lesson for fathers is to take the time to explore this world of a daughter, expect it to be an awkward and at times unsettling experience, but know too that there are great rewards both for fathers and their daughters. And for mothers: Sometimes it's helpful to get out of the way of your husband. Mothers are sometimes unsure whether their husbands can bear the awkwardness or will really come through with what their daughters need. It can be hard for a mother to give her husband the space he needs to find his voice with his daughter. One mother once told her husband, half-jokingly, when their daughter turned 12, that "our son is yours, and our daughter is mine!" In fact, daughters, like sons, need to have emotional access to *both* parents. And as the stories in the next section indicate, it's clear that fathers also need their daughters.

THE GIFTS DAUGHTERS OFFER TO FATHERS

What do fathers report if asked for a most treasured moment with their daughters? The Treasure Game is a powerful and instructive exercise to play just with fathers. Again we use 3 by 5-inch index cards, same directions as with grown daughters, except this time the invitation is to write down a memory *as a father with your daughter* that you particularly treasure and hold dear to your heart. This exercise gives voice to what we love and cherish about being with our daughters. It's not easy for dads to talk about what they *get*; one father once blurted out before doing this exercise, "I'm not supposed to have needs. I'm a father!" Yet when given the chance, it's clear that fathers can be enormously filled up by their daughters' love. Here are treasured moments from four fathers:

Ted: At dinner when my daughter Carla was about 2 years old, she said to me, "I love you Dad." I responded, "I love you too." Where upon she replied, "I love you six!" When else has a female said *that* to me?

Dennis: My 13-year-old daughter was asked by her teacher to construct a poster that depicts one of her heroes, and she drew a picture of me.

Henry: I remember the first time my daughter made fun of me. I can't recall the exact substance, but the sense that my 40-pound daughter was comfortable enough with her 250-pound father was/is vivid and extraordinarily gratifying. She was self-confident and unintimidated and separate from me.

Jim: My daughter is 45, and has had a hard time of it in her marriage. Last month she came from across the country to visit with her mother and me and spend a few days with us. Things have never been great between her and me, my poor "lost daughter." I spent much more time with her brothers. But one day on this visit we sat on the swings out back, just the two of us swinging together like kids, and I told her how much I regretted what I had missed with her. She turned to me and said, "Dad, I love you."

We may underestimate how important daughters are for fathers. Daughters can grow us up, just as we help them grow. Our self-esteem, confidence, and feelings of being beloved can be boosted by the relationship with our daughters. For fathers, our struggles with the feminine aspects of our own personalities, with our tenderness, our curiosity and fascination, and our fear of the feminine world, can be tempered and soothed by what happens between us and our daughters.

DANCING WITH LOVE AND LOSS

The central dilemma for fathers with daughters is how to tolerate the dance with love and loss embedded in the relationship. As fathers we experience our daughters' adoration and love, an experience that is also tinged with some loss as our daughters age.

On the one hand, as a father you try to live up to a self-image of someone in control, someone whose job is to protect and defend those you love. You want to look like you have the answers and know what's going on. In general, parenting undermines our sense of knowing what is going on, but, in particular, parenting a daughter undermines our male self-image, because what we confront as fathers is adoration and flirtation that can undermine our male investment in control and independence.

When things work out right, the father-daughter relationship is essentially a romance. We're not lovers sexually, of course. Alas, this must be repeated: I'm not referring to sexual acting out, seductiveness, and the loss of boundaries between parents and children. In our current cultural climate—replete with stories of abuse and boundary violations—it's hard to know how to talk about the healthy, normal passionate relationship between father and daughter. This silence is part of the dilemma for fathers, because the flirtatious energy between father and child is so important to the healthy growth of both parties. We may be so appropriately aware of fathers and daughters who violate boundaries that we have lost sight of the more common situation of fathers who succeed in communicating a sense of self-regard and confidence to their daughters.

The ability to ignite the gleam of love in a father's eyes is crucial to a daughter's self-esteem. A father is the first man in his daughter's life and can help solidify the sense of being loved and lovable by men. For the father, a daughter's love can help him work out ancient fears and uncertainties about women, and deepen his own identifications with the feminine part of himself.

I feel fortunate to be the father of a daughter as well as a son. In one sense, of course, what's important is the love and bonding between parent and child. It matters not what gender your child is. Yet, too, I've been able to observe firsthand my struggles and my daughter's to connect. Sons are such magnets for fathers. You can see yourself in your son. It can be much harder to see yourself in your daughter. The ferocity of a daughter's wish not to be overlooked in favor of the son can also be intimidating.

As the father of a daughter, you are constantly being asked to explore a feminine world—dolls, dresses, a female body. Our own feminine identifications can be touched, those parts of ourselves that enjoyed holding on to mother, playing with her jewelry, feeling the softness of her clothes, thinking about having babies—thoughts and feelings that may have been pushed aside in the rush to become a man. You're also the object of intense idealization as a father. There is a wonderful flirtatious, passionate energy that comes from a cross-sex family relationship. I heard such adoration in my daughter's words the first time she found out I had a boss.

I was to spend a long week away from home, across the country, teaching at a Ph.D. program where I am on the faculty. As I was packing my bags to leave my then 6-year-old daughter, Emily was clearly not pleased. With eminent wisdom, she suggested I simply cancel my classes and not go. Part of me liked that idea, as I was not so eager to spend a long week away from my young family. I told her that it was a fine idea, but that my students would be disappointed, and worse, the Dean would not be amused.

"What's a dean?" Emily asked.

Striving for simplicity I told her that the Dean was my boss. Emily was astounded and aghast, and hurried to correct me: "No, daddy, no! Other daddies have bosses, but you don't!"

It was simply unbelievable to my Emily that anyone might have power over her daddy, and so I had to be wrong. And indeed hearing her words, part of me wanted to puff up, to always be her hero, her daddy-without-a-boss. Now, of course, my son might have said the same thing when he was younger, in a fit of 6-year-old parental idealizing. And I do want always to be his hero too, but my hunch is that the father-daughter spark gives this moment a particular heartbeat of its own. Yet another part of me knows that she needs to learn that I do have feet of clay. In her coming to see me as a "real person," with my own strengths, weaknesses, and idiosyncrasies, comes the opportunity for healthy separation and growth, for her to become also a "real person."

Our daughters will benefit, as will we, if we can pay attention to the heartbeat of the father-daughter relationship.

Alex: "We wound up talking about penises and vaginas."

Alex is a 50-year-old married father.

When my daughter Jane was 8 years old, I unexpectedly wound up having a sex talk with her. When the children were younger, my wife and I had agreed that we would listen carefully to their questions about sexuality and try to answer any that came up naturally, taking our cues from them. We didn't want to push them.

One winter's night my daughter was taking a bath, and I was sitting on the edge of the bathtub talking to her. My wife was still at the office, working late, and this was my night to get the kids to bed. Her younger sister was already asleep in her crib. My daughter has always loved the water, and it was wonderful to watch her take a bath, the way she would float and turn and dunk herself, clearly enjoying every moment. In a quiet moment, playing with the bubbles with her hands, Janey asked me about how babies were made. I was at first flustered and wished my wife were there, but I also felt that Janey had been asking questions like this before and I didn't want to duck it. So I told her in a general way about the birds and the bees.

My daughter is a very down-to-earth person, a no-bullshit type. She wanted specifics. "Well, Daddy, then how exactly do mommies and daddies make babies?"

We wound up talking about penises and vaginas, sperm and uteruses and eggs and what happens.

Janey's first reaction was disbelief: "No, daddy! You're joking! The penis goes inside the vagina!"

But she was clearly really interested, not scared, more amused than anything else. And she trusted me, wanting me to tell her about this fascinating new development. We wound up having a straightforward, direct conversation about how babies are made.

Finally my daughter had heard enough. She splashed some water against the side of the tub. "Okay, Daddy, that's enough."

Then she changed the conversation. For me it was a wonderful experience in which I felt my daughter's trust of me, her openness to what I had to say. It was so different from my feelings around most women, in which I feel like I'm being looked at with distrust as a man, someone who is the opposite species from women. My daughter's innocent trust felt so loving and accepting of me as a partner in the conversation.

Fathers can be a guide and helper to their daughters, even if their experience seems so different from ours. A chance talk about sexuality with his preteen daughter led Alex to feel less cut off from women, to see that he could be someone a female can depend on.

Stan: "I love that she'll still pee in front of me."

Stan is a father in his 40s, married with several children.

My daughter is 11 years old and has recently begun to develop. She now routinely wears a bra, and her body is more closed off to me. She yells "don't come in" if she's getting dressed for school in the morning, and I respect her modesty of course.

One piece of all this I treasure though is that my daughter has somehow still forgotten to be modest in the bathroom. Sometimes we'll be talking or brushing our teeth at night, and she'll walk over to the toilet and just sit down and pee in front of me, still talking about whatever we were up to.

I love that she will still pee in front of me, the openness and trust that she displays when she does that. I've often felt like sexuality has been such a division in my life, that I've looked on women as sexual beings. I can sometimes feel like a predator when I'm around women, and with my daughter it feels very different. I feel that here is a female who loves and trusts me and depends on me, one whom I can nurture and take care of in a way very different from how I've related to women before in my life.

The kindness and generosity of our time with our daughters can feel very different from the harsh sense of masculinity that we feel growing up

*male. The unselfconscious trust of his 11-year-old daughter helped Stan
identify part of himself that felt he had much to give to a woman and that
he could do the task of being a helpmate to his growing daughter.*

Mike: "She outplayed a lot of the boys."

*Mike is an athletic father who was a star basketball player in college and
still plays in a "Never Too Old" basketball league at age 46. He played
point guard in college—the guy who drives the ball up court for the
team. All of us in the focus group understood when he spoke about his
attitude of "going right at people" when he feels they are in the wrong.*

I have a negotiating story, with my daughter Amy. It happened
back when she was playing in Little League with boys. During her first
and second years of minors, she was not such a hot baseball player, but
between her second and third years, she had a growth spurt and
became quite good. She was 11 years old and had an excellent season.
So the question arose whether she should go out for the majors, and
she decided she wanted to try it.

At the tryouts that fall, she did great, but no coach took her for
his team, though she was clearly good enough. She hit several home
runs and hit one ball that practically took off the pitcher's head, and
he was the coach. I can still remember him going *whoa*! and
jumping out of the way as it sizzled past him! In the field she did
fine, nailed a few grounders okay. I don't mean to imply she was the
second coming of Babe Ruth, but she outplayed a lot of the boys
who were taken.

She got the news when they posted the teams on the bulletin
board outside our school. As we drove over, she was so excited. Then
we got to where the list of teams was posted and saw that her name
was not on any of the teams. She hadn't been selected for any of
them! I saw the names of at least six other kids who hadn't hit the ball
out of the infield at those tryouts and who were taken for teams. Amy
didn't say much looking at the lists, but she started to cry in the car
on the way home. Well, I went ballistic! (At least I didn't do anything
really stupid. Five years ago I might have shot the president of the
league or at least burned down his house!) To see my daughter

crying, to have such pain inflicted on her for no reason was very painful to me. I just felt this sense of injustice. My feeling was that these men are pigs; let's off them. I had never been so angry in all my life. For someone to make my daughter cry felt like an attack on me, and I wanted to go get the jerks.

My wife didn't seem to care. When we got home after checking the lists, Amy told her. She was good with Amy—she *"tsk, tsked"* about it, but she's not into sports very much and told me later that she didn't think it was such a big deal. She sort of adopted an attitude of "Well, the heck with them. Just don't play."

The problem was Amy *did* want to play. Maybe it's good that my wife didn't get too involved because I was enraged enough for the whole family.

Amy and I had to negotiate, and this is what I am really proud of. We had to do a lot of talking together. On my own I probably would simply have gone out and gotten a lawyer and sued the league. It was a clearcut case of gender bias, a no-brainer. But Amy wouldn't allow me to do that. I had to negotiate what she would allow me to do and what not. I had called up the president of the league and made an appointment to go see him.

Amy would not allow me to *force* them to put her on a team. I couldn't go in there and start pounding on the table and threatening to sue. All I could do, she told me, was to go in there and say, "I don't understand how this happened. She played so well, and she performed better than some of the kids put on the teams. How can we work this out?"

So at the meeting I checked my pistols at the door, so to speak, which wasn't easy for me, dealing with those jerks. I hinted around at legal action but didn't really threaten. Instead I laid out the facts and expressed my desire to work something out. The president agreed that this was a problem but said that he had no control—that the coaches made individual decisions and that each one picked via a draft system without consulting the others.

The president suggested that we go to the spring tryouts, right before the season begins, when some kids have dropped out from the fall and there is another draft to fill out the teams. We did that, and Amy made a fine performance. This time someone took her. I think that everyone knew that if she was not taken, someone would pay. And she did great in the majors!

For me, what I'm particularly proud of is that I had to listen and respect her opinion and go with her feelings a lot. I didn't go and impulsively do something way inappropriate. It was very rewarding to realize that we were *partners* in this deal.

Fathers and daughters can protect each other, without realizing it. Mike found a way to protect Amy without violating her trust, just as Amy at the same time was able to protect her father from his own tendency toward escalating aggression.

Marv: "I just wanted to give her a hug, but couldn't."

Marv's booming, infectious laugh punctuated our focus group whenever a parent story revealed some of the absurdity or irony of our lives. He's a large man, over 6 feet tall, very passionate and involved with life. He runs an outward bound consulting program for schools. So Marv understood some of the irony of his becoming nonplussed by his 12-year-old daughter's sexual development.

Touching Evelyn when she grew up and out—really *out* and developed—has been very difficult. Yesterday we were in the TV room, just the two of us. She looked so sad, she's been having some troubles with boys and wasn't saying much. I just wanted to give her a hug, but couldn't. I didn't feel comfortable. So I started talking to her, "I'm having a hard time with hugging you and all like we used to. I wanted you to know that."

Somehow touching my daughter felt too loaded. But I didn't want Evelyn to just feel ignored or like I didn't still love her. The TV was on, but she listened. She took it in. Nothing came back, but I know she heard what I was saying because she didn't start protesting, saying *no, no, no, Dad. I don't want to talk about this!* That's sometimes what I get. Instead she listened to me.

Then a little later my wife encouraged Evelyn to call some friends and make some dates. Boy, when she called some girlfriends up and made some dates she seemed so much better! I learned a lesson there: You don't always have to deal with it head on. A hug to Evelyn would have been better than all the words I could have used. Because of my wife's encouragement Evelyn forgot about her "boy troubles."

That left me wondering how come *I* didn't hug her and help her forget the pain.

As our daughters develop into puberty, we can become unsure how to respond to their becoming sexual beings. We may struggle with confusing, mixed impulses of attraction, love, and protectiveness and become more remote than we wish, merely as a way of handling the morass of feelings. In fact, a simple acknowledgment of our daughter's growing womanhood can help defuse the situation. Sometimes remarking how pretty a 12- or 15- or 18-year-old (or older) daughter looks in her new dress, how great it is that she is becoming a woman, can communicate a father's love in simple, direct terms. A lot of a teenage daughter's provocative behavior can be merely attempts to get a response from her father. A teenage daughter going out to the dance, the prom, wherever, may need to have her father simply say, "Wow!" She needs to know both that she can ignite the spark of love and excitement in her father's eyes, and that she can leave her father, let him go.

It's the letting go that can be so painful. A mother's perspective helps us understand the delicate dance of love and separation fathers and daughters go through, a dance that really involves the whole family.

Sarah: "Would it help if you could fluff my pillow?"

Sarah is in her late 40s, a teacher in the public school system, married for many years to Kevin, a professor of anthropology.

My husband Kevin is almost 50, a rugged man who has always been tenderly concerned about his daughter's well-being and safety. I can still see him carrying her on his forearm, gazing in his eyes when she was a newborn, lovingly giving her a bath or changing her diapers. He's been an involved father—tucking her in at night, reading bed-times stories, and fluffing her pillow before she went to sleep and he turned out the lights.

Our daughter Annie is 17 now, petite and pretty, smart and tal-ented. Last summer she was full of excitement about going off in July and August to an international camp across the country to be with other smart, talented kids from all over the world. Best of all, her boyfriend, the first boy she had shown any real "romantic" interest in, had also been admitted to the camp. Together they would drive there alone and share the whole adventure, a young couple in love. When she informed us of this part of the camp plan, Kevin said quite firmly, "No!" I went along with him, feeling torn, wanting her to have a wonderful experience and to learn how to be a free young woman, careful but not repressed about her sexual needs. I wanted her to explore, slowly, and with care and attention, what was going on for her and the person she was with. Young girls in love can get hurt so easily and quickly.

When we had first agreed to this camp idea, my husband and I had imagined we would drive her there together as a family outing, settle her in and wish her well as we had always done before when camp time came. We were very aware that this was the year before she would be leaving for college and that it would be "the last time." It then turned out that I had to go to a conference that particular weekend, so my hus-band felt it would be wonderful to take his daughter by himself, to share this trip with her as a father-daughter bonding opportunity.

Needless to say, Annie didn't want his "caring" company. She wanted to bond with her new companion and yelled at us about how we could possibly be so possessive: "Billy is a wonderful driver. He treats me very respectfully. I've looked forward to this drive for so long. What do you mean you want to come along?!"

Over the course of many mealtimes, my husband told her that dri-ving with Bobby was out of the question. I began to have second thoughts. Bobby was a good driver, and he did indeed seem to treat

Annie with great respect. I wondered why he assumed all boys were inevitably going to take advantage of our daughter.

I talked with Annie many evenings, trying to explain her daddy's behavior toward her, about how protective he felt of her and how much he relishes her company. I tried to explain that it must be especially hard for daddies to see their daughters turn to other men for protection. It makes them feel older, no longer needed, maybe even a bit jealous of all their young promise and vigor. It reminds them of their own youthfulness and early adventures, a time irrevocably gone. Remember, dear Annie, I said, there used to be a time when you couldn't go to sleep without one of us tucking you in and fluffing your pillow before a good night kiss. Driving you to the camp is the closest he can come now to tucking you in!

I also had several long talks with Kevin, trying to get him to express what made him so reluctant to let her go. After several days of all this, Annie was finishing breakfast about to leave for school. She was pleading with him to relent. He had been coming down the stairs in his bathrobe and she implored him to please, please let her and Bobby go alone. Kevin loomed on top of the stairs, while Annie stood in the door ready to leave for school. Finally, he threw his hands up in the air and groaned, looking frustrated and hurt, "Oh, all right!"

Annie looked up at him and asked, "Would it help if you could fluff my pillow?"

I'll never forget my husband's face. His expression spoke volumes, his brain furiously in action. It was one of those delicious moments when a person's face goes through a whole set of emotions in an instant, from hurt to sheer delight. He laughed out loud.

"Yes, I guess that would be okay."

When the day came and the two youngsters were ready to leave for camp, Annie with sleeping bag and pillow under her arm, her companion Bobby helping with her bags, Ken did give that pillow a final pat and shake, a symbol of his love and need to see her safe.

The pillow became a kind of shared transitional object. Now even the mention of it has the singular effect of asserting both the continued connection and new separateness of our family.

CONTINUED CONNECTION AND NEW SEPARATENESS

Being the father of a daughter means a shift in your very sense of what it means to be a man—as it was for the father who wrote of how wonderful it felt to see his early adolescent daughter pee in front of him, or the father who found himself unexpectedly comfortable and appropriate when giving his daughter information about sexuality—no longer a predator, no longer split off from women, but now experiencing being a man as one who can nurture and take care of a daughter. The daughter's love mirrors his own love for his daughter, a self-esteem boost as a man who can feel beloved of this female that he so loves. So too we may become more comfortable with the feminine parts of ourselves—enjoying the cooking, prom dresses, femininity that we can explore with this daughter-guide. As is so true of parenting, part of the challenge is not to abandon your daughter by withdrawing at a stress point that feels too intense for you—her developing sexuality, her testing authority, her becoming competent and able to stand on her own. Yet, another way to abandon your daughter is by ignoring her needs in a way that makes her overly a caretaker of you. Sometimes a father's needs for his daughter's companionship is so vast that the father cannot let the daughter rebel and go off to find the other man who will ultimately replace and honor him. John Updike has described the adolescent daughter from the father's point of view as "a pageant that would leave him behind."[6]

A daughter's growing can help us as men learn, once again, about loss and letting go. As a daughter graduates high school, goes to college or otherwise off on her own, there is a loss for her in giving up the familiar bonds with parents. For the father/husband, though, there is a loss that is not so easily healed, since he has not the potential replacements the daughter has. A daughter can replace a wife as a source of intimacy, as a father cooks dinner with his daughter while his wife works, or she listens to his struggles in a way that his wife doesn't have time, or interest, for. The loss of the "idealized daughter" underlies some of the sadness that fathers exhibit as their daughters grow up.

---

[6] J. Updike, "Man and Daughter in the Cold," Fathers and Daughters: Portraits in Fiction, T. Eicher and J. Geller (eds.), NY: Penguin, 1990, p.168.

And that reminds us that, after all, our primary relationship is with our wife. A "silver lining" of some father-daughter conflict during adolescence and beyond is that it turns him, effectively, back toward his wife, loosening the grip of the father-daughter idealization.

The depth of this loss often goes unacknowledged, both by the father and our culture. An observant wife or mother, though, may see her husband's struggle and offer some help, as Sarah did for Kevin.

So, fathering a daughter means growing and changing oneself, finding new opportunities for that passionate father-daughter attachment as you both mature and make real in the world those parts of yourself gifted to you by your daughter.

Hidden Wisdom You Can Use

- There's a special connection between fathers and daughters.
- Fathers have a big impact on their daughters' self-esteem, identity, and values.
- It's important to include daughters in our activities. Have you ever assumed your daughter "wouldn't be interested" in what you're doing, so didn't ask her? Try asking.
- Fathers sometimes assume that mothers are the "experts" on daughters. However, there are times when a father knows just what needs to be said or done. In what ways do you withdraw from your daughter, assuming your wife "can handle things"?
- Daughters need to know that their fathers love their femininity and also affirm their aggressive, masculine sides. They need to know from their fathers that it's okay to love sports even as they become teenagers, and to be smart and have the right answer in class. It can be hard for a father to let go of his "little girl," but it's important for daughters to know that their dads support all their aspirations.
- You don't have to have all the answers—it's okay to feel awkward and unsure around your daughter. What's important is simply to make time for her and to communicate your love in whatever way you're comfortable.

- Mothers too may need to examine their assumptions about fathers and daughters. In what ways do you assume husbands don't know about daughters?
- Daughters need to learn about life and love from fathers as well as mothers. What do you hope your daughter learns most from you?
- What are your hesitations in dealing with your daughter? Talking to your partner, friend, minister or rabbi, or counselor can help.
- Fathers get a boost to their self-esteem in feeling beloved by their daughters.
- As fathers and daughters age, their relationship changes. Difficulties that occur during the teen years or young adulthood can lead to reconciliation and renewal in later years.
- Fathers must be careful not to turn their relationship with their daughters into a substitute for their relationship with their wives. We need to make sure that the energy for maintaining the marriage is there.

chapter eight

Mothers with Sons

Mothers and sons are vital to each other's development. As with fathers and daughters, there can be many taboos about understanding the intensity of the mother-son relationship. Sons often feel enormous loyalty, love, and gratitude toward their mothers, as well as considerable fear of them. As sons, we can fear our mothers because of their power over us—their ability to remind us of our debt to them and the invitation to return to what many of us lose in our rush toward manhood—a childhood playfulness, timelessness, not feeling so pressured and armored. As one savvy man, a 45-year-old CEO of a large company, exclaimed at a focus group, "When I visit my mother, I can't get away from this feeling that suddenly wells up inside me that she is more than my mom, that she is the Great Mother, able to calm me down, soothe me, just make life easier!" Most of us knew what he meant, and it seemed like a gift to us all that night for a man to give voice to his childhood longings about mother. Through our lives, perhaps, we carry around a cartoon image of our mothers as The Great Mother.

Mothers confront a similar challenge raising sons. Sons can be a magnet for many of the mother's lost dreams and wishes. If she had to give up her wish to be "successful" in the world in order to be a "good wife" or a "good daughter," if she wants another chance to combine aggression and caring in her own sense of self, if she feels resentful of male privilege, if she wants to remain a good girl for daddy, sons offer another chance at a resolution of these matters. Mothers may long for sons to be Prince Charming, the idealized one who will restore her lost dreams.

We may see in our children an idealized version of a beloved lost figure from our past. Julia, a 77-year-old mother of several grown men, looked back on her relationship with one son in this way: "My eldest son seemed a reincarnation of my father's brother, who died when I was 13. I loved my uncle so much! I can remember him sitting on a couch with me reading ghost stories. He smelled of cigarettes, which made me very happy. I loved the smell. He went on business trips and would bring me back wonderful presents—a little beaded purse on a chain, a doll-sized wooden buffet for china with doors that opened and green glass windows.

My eldest son had the same golden halo I saw with my uncle. Now, looking back, I wonder if adoring a son as a replacement for a lost family member, is felt by, maybe resented by, the husband. But I was unaware of that at the time."

Mothers, too, experience the challenge with sons (like fathers with daughters) of confronting "the other": a child of your own flesh who is of the opposite gender. So sons may be partly a mystery. They are also objects of flirtation and enchantment, and a good mother walks a line between enlivening and vitalizing her son and overly binding him to her. Mothers, fathers, sons, and daughters—the task is often the same for thoughtful and well-meaning parents. How can we be close to our children without asking them to overly fulfill *our* needs, to make up for disappointments in our marriage, career, or sense of self?

If fathers need to confront issues about their "internal femininity" with their daughters, then mothers have a chance to heal the "wounded masculinity" inside themselves: the sense of maleness as predatory, evil, woman hating, that is based in their painful experiences as a female growing up.

For a mother to become aware of her fears of and expectations about her son can be helpful to herself as well as her son. There are many wonderful, healing, joyous moments of connection—silver linings through difficulties—that happen between mothers and sons across the bridge and divide of gender.

Judith: "The biggest surprise was having a son."

A secretary in a dental office, married, Judith's story began in response to the writing prompt "when I see my son/daughter naked . . . " She prefaced her story with "Before having a child, I figured the mother-daughter relationship was harder than that of mother-son because of all those same sex issues. It wasn't all that easy for my mother and me; she was on my case a lot, to look and act appropriate.

I was sure we were going to have a daughter. We went to a psychic, and all through the pregnancy we talked of having a girl.

The biggest surprise was having a son! When I saw him in the delivery room, I thought, *what am I going to do with him?*

Even now, months later, when I give him a bath, I'll wonder.

When I see my son naked, I can't believe he is a boy. It's first of all still a kind of shock. Secondly, I get the urge to kiss him all over—his soft, round body with the baby powder smell. I could eat him up! His little body looks just like his father's. It's so funny how a little baby boy can have the same fanny as his 34-year-old dad!

When I think of his body, I think of him growing big and strong. I tease my son by telling him that he is always going to be with me, that no girl is going to be good enough.

I can't imagine him grown and moving away to college. I told my husband that it would be okay if George was gay, so that I would always be the number one girl in his life. He could sit at home with Mommy and listen to Barbra Streisand albums. My husband, bless him, humors me. He just nods and says that however George grows up—as long as he's healthy and happy—is okay with him.

His 6-month-old's hands are the most beautiful sight. George places both hands on each cheek when I say "Oh Ma Ma Ma Mee Ah" to him in my best Italian slang. He laughs and claps his hands. His thumb helps to calm him at night to sleep.

I have watched his hands develop since he was born, well, actually before that—since I saw them on my first ultrasound. When he was first born, I thought it was amazing that there could actually be blood and bone inside those hands, because each tiny finger was so small.

Now at 6 months he looks at his hands almost in amazement of them. It's funny because they look just like his dad's hands. My husband Jack has strong hands. He is a mechanic for an elevator company. He can fix or build anything. He built a beautiful nursery for our baby! I wonder if George will work with his hands, learn to play the piano, or plant a garden. There seems to be so much potential in his hands.

Judith's exuberant essay contains many of the ambivalences mothers feel: He'll grow big and strong but always be my little boy, he won't really be sexual, he'll stay a little kid. He'll always stay momma's little boy, even while Judith's son reminds her of her husband—the acorn at the foot of the oak. Judith wants to merge with her son ("I could eat him up!") yet conceives of him in the model of her husband, not herself.

Alma: "I pray he maintains a positive self-image."

A housewife in her late 30s, Alma plans to volunteer in the elementary school that her son Raymond will be attending in a few years.

When I see my son naked it makes me so happy. He is just so happy and proud when he strips off that diaper—so free. I pray he maintains a positive self-image. He's not even 2 yet, and he has the exact same body as his father—same love handles and little pot belly. His skin is so soft, so pure. I slowly tickle his skin; he loves it. I'll do that when I change his diaper, and he'll roll over on his side, putting his back toward me so I can do his entire body. It's so relaxing for me, and I know how much he loves it. Last night he fell asleep that way.

I want him to feel proud of his body because I've struggled with that in my life. In our house, once when I was about 10, my mother walked around with her slip on and my father had a fit, yelling at her not to do that. I didn't get it. *"Who cares?"* I thought.

My father, though, taught me how to wipe and use toilet paper. We were in the bathroom and he showed me, without looking at me, how to wipe. His head was turned toward the wall the whole time. I'm free about going to the bathroom; I never close the door. My son wipes like I wipe. It's so funny, he's so free. The other day he asked, "Mommy, where's your penis?"

I want him to feel comfortable asking about those things. "I don't have one. You and daddy do," I told him.

My friend told me she had a talk with her mother about the facts of life. I didn't know who to talk to. My mother had died, so I turned to my father. He said, "I'll tell you." We went in my bedroom that day and he sat down and explained about what happens when a man gets an erection and what you do with it.

In mothering a son, we may draw on our own masculine identifications. For Alma, Raymond brings back images and memories of her father, exploring the world of male anatomy, being someone who can teach her son about his body in the way her father taught her. In caring for her son, she experiences a hopeful version of her own father. In giving to her son she feels the parts of her father that encouraged her. And, too, Raymond's simple question ("Mommy, where's your penis?") carries with it an early differentiation—the recognition that mother and son are different.

Sara: "I look at him from the viewpoint of what I think girls do."

Sara is divorced and has primary custody of her son Max. She works as a stockbroker in a large firm.

Among the single-parent moms I know, we all have a goal: to raise a nurturing male. That's a major topic of conversation: How can you help a boy be gentle and strong?

I've always had trouble with my son's competitiveness and assertiveness. I look at him from the viewpoint of what I think girls do. I think girls are more accepting of others' feelings and needs, for example. I'd be sitting on the playground bench watching Max, he'd push little girls off the slide to get his turn. I'd want him to take turns and to share play things. When a little girl would push back, I'd say to myself: *Yes! go for it!* I'd root for little girls to stand up to him, and I'd spend a lot time talking to him about being gentler, more caring.

When he was 6 years old, we were in a toy store and saw a display of Strawberry Shortcake dolls and accessories. He saw the pink Strawberry Shortcake stroller and ran up to it, saying, "Mom, I want that!" *Great!* I thought; *it's working!* So I bought it for him.

As soon as we got it home, Max started pushing it around the living room, running into furniture and smashing through his toys with it. "Boom! Boom!" he yelled.

"What are you doing?!" I asked, stunned.

He replied, breathlessly, "Look, Mom, it makes a great tank!"

At that point, I felt I had to accept his maleness.

Now that he's 11, I get worried when he seems too soft. He's still very competitive and aggressive, but he will also cry when he's sad or hurt. Is he too attached to me? I'm a single mom, and no one told him not to cry. I've always accepted that part of him, without making a big deal of it. His Uncles tell him to just buck up and suck it in. But if he's upset, he'll cry in school. I think as a single mom you always worry whether you've hurt your son by being close to him. I know it's crazy, but sometimes I wonder whether a mom can raise a son okay by herself?

What do we do with our sons' aggression? Boys are inherently more active, motile, and, as they grow up, very curious about power, strength, and aggression. In this story, Sara—a savvy, thoughtful single mom—gives voice to the ambivalence mothers may feel about their son's potency and helps us understand that there's a place for a mother to honor and accept her son's constant play with weapons and love of superheroes.

Sara tried to suppress her son's aggressiveness when he was young. Now that he's a preteen her impulse is to suppress his gentleness. Both these sides of our sons can press buttons for a mom. It's important to look carefully at our sons and at our expectations about what "girls" are and should be like. A mother's own aggression may be overlooked by her. She may not see the need to comes to terms with the power that a boy has. She may want to think about what girls lose when they are so encouraged to lose their aggression.

A mother may also feel some disappointment in having a son and not a daughter. While, of course, we love our children regardless of their gender, there may be parts of the mother not expressed in having only a son or sons. One thoughtful mother, deeply in love with her son, commented that "there is a wonderful old antique doll, Scandinavian, that I got from my grandmother. One of my first thoughts when I knew I was having a son was "He won't love the doll like I did." She went on: "He didn't get into dolls and I knew I couldn't look forward to showing him how to do the laundry, the dishes, all those things passed on from mother to daughter."

The answer to Sara's question about mothering a son is that yes, single moms can do fine raising sons. They need to have multiple opportunities for connection outside the family, and to be aware of the limits of their single perspective. But that's true for married couples as well. Raising a son today —with so many of our expectations shifting—can be inherently confusing for a mother or father. It can be helpful to talk to friends, and married couples, and to involve men with your child. There is an inherent aloneness as a parent—single or married—but there are steps you can take. As a single mom, you are going it alone, but you don't have to do it all completely alone.

Alexandra: "How much do I want him exposed to the stuff out there?"

Happily married, Alexandra came to a focus group without her husband, who stayed home to take care of their young son.

My husband comes from a family where he was the only boy; he had five sisters. I have two sisters, and they both have daughters! So neither of us, or our families, have had a lot of experience raising boys. It's a weird thing for all of my family for us to have a boy, and I struggle so much with him being a boy because I want him to be Mr. Sensitive Man of the '90s. The struggle for me is allowing his natural boy-ness to be there . . . his play. He's not a real rough kid, such a gentle soul, which makes me feel so good. My daughter is completely the opposite. She like to be rough and tumble and really stands up to boys on the playground; she refuses to go to the end of the line for the slide and just be a cute little girl, which is the way I'd like it if I could call it!

But all these guns and action hero figures and war stuff appeal to my son. He is a boy! We've had a lot of discussions around TV shows. There are some things I won't allow him to watch. I've lost a lot of ground over the past two years. My husband Alex and I have had a lot of conversations. Tommy says that "my mommy doesn't like me to watch too many fighting shows."

How much do I want him exposed to the stuff out there at such an early age? We negotiate with him about what shows he can watch. It's a constant struggle. He keeps finding new shows. He's a great negotiator. *Sailor Moon* was a classic struggle for us. It's a scary kid show.

"I want to watch it," he kept saying. So we all sat around and watched it. Then he wanted to watch it the next day, and after that. I said to him, "Tommy, it's no fun for you to be scared by the show, or for me. You come into our room because you can't sleep at night and wake us up." He kind of agrees, and so we decide we're not going to watch *Sailor Moon* anymore. Okay. Then two weeks later he says he wants to try *Sailor Moon* again. It makes me sad.

As Alexandra told her story that night, a dialogue emerged between her and another parent—Jim, a father of a son. Their interplay illustrates the different perspectives that we need to pay attention to in raising a son.

Jim: It would make me happy that he wanted to try again.

Alexandra: Well, it made my husband happy that he wanted to overcome his fears. I just wanted him to forget about it. I knew it was going to scare him, and I just wanted to protect him.

Jim: I would have been happy just that he thought it through and that he wanted to master that stuff that made him scared. It's good for him.

Alexandra: I let him watch it. The conversation with my husband made the difference. Charley said, "He's struggling with some issue and trying to work it through." He watched, and I think he turned the show off. But I'm not sure. I don't want him interested in that stuff. I want him interested in the stuff I think he should be interested in—music and art, you know, those nongender specific things.

Jim: If you forbid him, it makes it more attractive.

Alexandra: I try not to forbid anything. His friend has been to see *The Lost World*, but I wouldn't let him go. We've said, "No toy guns in the house." Then suddenly he's buying figures that come with guns. So now it's life-size guns. It feels like an endless and losing battle. And I'm not sure what I believe.

Both of the parents in this dialogue are representing an important truth about raising sons. Even mothers in intact families, of course, struggle with their son's aggression. We're all jumpy these days about signs of violence or hostility in our children. What's important is to engage in a dialogue with your son, rather than seeing him engaged in "bad behavior." What may be antisocial in an adult is simply part of a child's coming to terms with the world. Watching a frightening TV show over and over is one way that children master their fears. So too with guns: You don't have to love his weapons play to realize that a boy is struggling with issues of size, power, potency, and fear in the world.

What well-meaning parent of a son hasn't had the experience of banning toy weapons from the house and then having their 6-, 7-, 10-year-old convert a block of wood into a gun? In our household, we knew we had to rethink our attitudes when our then-young son sat nibbling thoughtfully on an edge of his slice of bread at dinner, only to put the bread in his hand and exclaim, "It's a gun!" spraying whole-wheat bullets around the room.

Aggressive play is an important way that sons make sense of their place in the world. Sword play, fantasy wars, computer battles, even chess and board games are ways in which children—girls yes, and particularly boys—come to terms with their little-ness and desires to feel powerful in the larger world. It can be helpful for a mother to think about her own attitudes and fears about her *aggression and impulses to dominate. How supported or quashed were they when you were young?*

Stacey: "Am I being seductive?"

Stacy and her husband are the parents of a teenage son and a younger daughter. Together they run an ice cream store in a small town.

In his swim trunks, he still looks like a small boy. Just yesterday he mentioned getting the hair on his legs caught in his soccer shin pads. I commiserated with him and told him that, well, we women have other parts of our bodies that get in our way—like my bosom when I cook! Am I being seductive? Was such a reference to my femaleness inappropriate, too erotically laden for him? Or am I just giving him a realistic appreciation of men's and women's special and different experience?

For the mother of a son, there's not just aggression to play with, but also sensuous, flirtatious impulses. As sons grow older, there can be a sense of loss for the mother, who no longer has access to this person whose body was once part of her body. Adolescent boys still very much need their mothers, and want to stay in contact even as they seem to distance themselves. The secret, closed off places of the teenager can leave a mother feeling like she no longer has a role. Yet she does.

Compare Judith's meditation, as the mother of a young son, to that of Stacey with a 14-year-old. Stacey gives voice to the wonderful early merger and then the having to let go, feeling excluded from this body that had once been almost her own body. There is the awkward trying to reach across the chasm of gender as Stacey tries to connect to her son's hair stuck in his soccer guards with a reference to her bosom! Is there a more vivid picture of the awkwardness of parent and child trying to connect across gender?

Mom's need to know not to withdraw. We may feel awkward connecting with our adolescents, but a 14-, 18-, 20-year-old boy still needs to feel that his mother is there even if he acts indifferent. It's when things start to get erotic and mixed in with flirtation that many moms withdraw from their sons, as fathers do from their daughters.

Rhonda: "I didn't want to just come down on him like a ton of bricks."

A single parent, Rhonda lives in Albany, New York, where she works as a hairdresser and raises her teenage son, Ned.

It's tough being divorced and having a son. Certain things Ned does remind me of his dad, like his teasing me. I feel sometimes that my boy is being trained in sexism and how to treat women badly. We were visiting my sister recently, and Ned was with me. She watched us together and came down hard on me: "I don't like the way he treats you. Why don't you put your foot down?"

My sister is a lesbian and stands up for herself. She'll tell me how much she doesn't like my ex-husband. I think she's hypersensitive to how men treat women. But still, she has a point.

She pointed out to me that whenever my son is scared or upset, I become the safe place on which to dump all his upset. Sometimes that feels appropriate, for him to come to me with his frustrations, but it's a hard line to negotiate. I didn't want to just come down on him like a ton of bricks and say, "You SHALL respect me." I can read what he's doing. When you've had a hard day at work and come home and slam the door, you're communicating something. You don't say, "Excuse me, I've had a hard day, and now I'm going to slam the door." You just slam it. But it did feel as though he slammed me verbally too much.

After we got home from visiting my sister, I was more aware of what was going on. He was leaving for college in a few days, and we were home packing up his stuff. It was an anxious time, and he was bitching at me. We were trying to get some CDs made into tapes on our stereo system for him to take with him, and he kept telling me I wasn't doing it right. Finally, I stepped away from the stereo and said, "Ned, I don't want you putting that stuff out on me. That is very hard on me."

He replied, grumpily, "No one else treats me this way. You're always correcting me."

"Of course! I'm your mother, the only mother you have. No one else treats you like I do."

We each wound up doing some packing and cleaning separately. After breakfast I came into the kitchen and said,

"I'm wondering about how you said you don't have these reactions to anyone else. I wonder if this is about feelings you have toward women in general that come out on me."

Well, that stopped him in his tracks.

He looked at me and replied, "Hmmm. I'm thinking about that. Maybe."

I suggested to him that we make a list of feelings he had about women, all the things that upset him. He wrote down that they're stupid, they're constantly changing their minds, and can't deal with machines.

It went on. We sat there and made the list. I told him that it was fine for him to say all those things to me, get his complaints off his chest, but that it was not okay for him to dump them on me.

We did some arm wrestling then at the table, we played around. It was light. I joked, "What do you mean that women aren't very strong?!"

I put my arm up there, and we were actually pretty evenly matched. Something happened there that Ned got that he was treating me in a way that was not related to me.

Sometimes the tension we feel with our children can be connected to the disappointment or upset we feel toward our spouse. As a single mom, one of the tasks is to keep your son separate from your disappointment in your former husband. A reality of being a single mom is that your son may take some of the heat for your ex. Rhonda is experiencing, too, the struggle of a mother without a father in the house. It's difficult to be without a father there to back her up or to do some of the nagging instead. In adolescence, a boy may be ready to wrestle with his father in a way that feels humiliating to do with his mother. However, Rhonda's honest, direct persistence and her use of humor show us that you don't have to be a male to wrestle productively with your son.

Mothering a son "is a process of being close to someone who is leaving you," as one mother of a teen remarked. "I was my son's baseball coach when he was in little league," she told the focus group, "and now

he's a teen in the school league and a better player than I am, and I feel left out. I can't attend practice with him and help him at the batting cage or in the field because often I don't know what he's doing wrong. He's at a whole different skill level. And it's a level where most mothers have dropped out and the fathers have taken over."

Sons need to differentiate from and to hold on to their mothers. We often only see the push to independence of sons, not their wish too to hold on to their mothers, whom they treasure so much. Sometimes mothers find creative ways to connect with their sons' "male" interests and preoccupations.

Teresa: "Here I am a teacher, and I'm being told my son is underachieving."

Teresa is a 50-year-old teacher in a school for academically talented high school students in the Midwest. She is a single mother.

My son Charles is 12 years old; he struggles a lot in school, with attention problems, fidgetiness. Here I am a teacher, and I'm being told my son is underachieving—it's very embarrassing!

In my childhood, my parents really kind of pooped out on me when I became an adolescent. I was supposed to be a "good girl," which I was. But I could tell they thought my intellectual gifts made me "unsafe" in society—I needed a man to take care of me, to keep me "normal." This was common in the '60s. Maybe that is why I teach teenagers now. I am trying to help adolescents believe that it's okay to be smart and adventuresome, that they can take on the world. Gifted kids, like my son Charles, are bursting with competencies—it's confidence and self-belief that the rest of the world will accept their talents that is lacking.

Charles is a computer whiz. And I know nothing about them—I marvel at his competency. One of the things I've felt is that my son plays computer games when he should be doing his homework. But he does love a fantasy adventure game called *Lords of the Realm* and he has been interested in the Middle Ages for about two years. One day last year I got an announcement at school that the state had a program of new educational initiatives for academically advanced students. So I suggested to him that we apply together to set up a one-week summer program for talented fifth and sixth graders on Medieval times. My son has a garage full of knights and figures that he paints meticulously, and he is always down at our local Game Shoppe where the owner runs *War Hammer* games and battles. In fact, I went down there once to check it all out and make sure that it was all on the up-and-up, given how much time Charles spent there. It was fine, and I was satisfied.

Charles was delighted from the very beginning with the idea of helping teach a course, and he was bursting with pride when he realized that I would be relying on him for ideas and expertise. We decided together that the course would be an interdisciplinary, multimedia interaction with the Middle Ages, using a program like *Lords of the Realm* to stimulate discussions of history and reading, sharing learning, role-playing, castlebuilding, and even cooking.

We wrote up the proposal together, and it was accepted! Charles spent the next month coming up with ideas, and he took a lot of responsibility for getting me to plan ahead. He cotaught, and, if truth be told, he was the more important partner.

I made sure his name was listed as teacher on the door to the classroom, as mine was. I even split the teaching fee with him. He put a chunk of money in the bank and used part of it to buy some computer stuff.

You know, being a single mother of a son is not easy, but there are some payoffs. I don't know if this kind of opportunity would have happened for Charles if he and I hadn't been so close, as only a single mother and her one remaining child at home can be.

Sometimes a boy's technical interest and ability can lead to a partnership with his mother and become a source of shared competency. Mothers may feel at times like visitors in a foreign world. Finding a bridge to the strange new land of boys and men can benefit both mother and son. Teresa was able to link up with her son's talents in a way that created a true shared "play space" for the two of them and reinforced her talented boy's self-esteem and confidence at a time when he really needed to have such experiences.

Working around machinery is a time-honored and fundamental way for boys and men to connect. Sometimes when you have something out *there to focus on, it can be much easier to be intimate. Mothers may want to talk, and focus on the relationship and "process" while their sons may want to tinker, fidget, and* do *something. Mothers can become pilgrims in an unfamiliar mechanical or technical world and find unexpected, rewarding connections with their sons, as Theresa did.*

In the following story, Alice gives voice to the way that a son can become the embodiment of Prince Charming for a mother, the man who will restore what she lost in the process of growing up.

Alice: "Remember the story of *Brigadoon*?"

Alice is married, the mother of two sons and a daughter. Her eldest, Edward, is now 15.

When I was 7 years old, we sold my childhood home and moved to the Midwest. I think I never really got over that move in some ways. My father grew up in the same house that I spent those first seven years in. My grandmother lived on the property too—seventy acres of land with black-eyed Susans and a little pony and a pond with ducks on it in the summer. It always meant a lot to me—the wildlife, the trees, the house, and the gardens. I loved my grandmother very much and loved my family; it was a very wonderful time.

This suburb of Hartford, over time, has become very developed and populated. But when I was growing up, it was really rural. A large shopping mall now occupies the site of what was once a large gravel pit with earthmoving equipment that never seemed to move.

When I was 7, my grandmother sold the property to a large corporation that was developing the area. Both my grandmother and my father went downhill from there; they were both dead within eight years of selling the house.

Last week I went back. I had never shown my children that property. My husband was at work, so I took the kids down there with me alone for the day. We live in a rural community in Vermont that in many ways is like what the childhood homestead near Hartford used to be.

Now, though, it is owned by a large international corporation, and there is barbed wire all around it. It was like we had gone back in time. The property hadn't changed. There was our old house, now all boarded up. The corporate headquarters were out of sight at the center of the property. Our old house was like a scene out of sleeping beauty, with the vines growing over it. We were looking around, and all of a sudden the security guard came screeching up and told us we couldn't stay on the property. My son started talking to him. He told him that we could tell the company lots of stories about the property, things about its history. Can you imagine? My 14-year-old was trying to get the guard to let us stay! The guard says, "I'm not permitted to discuss anything about this property with you."

Before we left, I took the kids over to see this oak tree on the property that I've always loved. I told them about the rock we always used to sit on. When I was 7, I sat under the oak tree when they told us we would be moving, and I told myself, "I am going to become a famous person, very rich, and when I am I will return and buy this property back. It doesn't matter what they do to change it. I will be wealthy enough to restore it to exactly what it is now."

My son came over to me when the guard was hassling us and we knew we had to leave. He said the most amazing thing: "Mom, don't worry. When I grow up I'm going to be an actor. And I'm going to be really wealthy, and I'm going to buy this property for you. So it'll be yours once again." It so touched me. I had never told him I had once had the same thought, and now he had it too. He went over and got me an oak tree sapling to take back to our farm. It died, but we brought back oak acorns, which I will plant and germinate.

You never know. Remember the story of *Brigadoon* where once every hundred years the town comes to life? Well, it's been forty years now. When my son is 45, it'll be one hundred years. Maybe he can bring it back to life.

Sons are powerful magnets for their mother's hopes and dreams. One of the joys and burdens of being a beloved son is inheriting the task of trying to make true your mother's unfulfilled hopes and desires in the world. It's normal and natural for parents to hope their children will be able to live out what they were not able to; good parents try to be aware of putting too many of our needs on to our kids.

Suzanne: "Have you two done the deed yet?"

In her late 30s, Suzanne is a single mother whose son Nate is now in college.

Sex education? With a boy it feels different. When he started to date and have girlfriends, he told me it felt too weird to talk with his Mom about what was going on. "You just don't talk to your mother about that stuff!" he said. I know he talks to his father, from whom I've been divorced for about 5 years. Recently, though, we did have this conversation over the phone when Nate called from college, and I told him that I was dating this man and that we had gotten pretty serious:

"Well, Mom, have you two done the deed yet?"

"What are you talking about?"

"Have you guys had sex?"

Well I didn't know what to say! I simply blurted out "no." And then I asked, "Have you?"

"Yes."

And that was that, but it meant a lot to me that we could say that to each other.

It can be wonderful for a mother and son to become "real" to each other, to get past the silences and taboos that mark the relationship. Nate's quick question traversed a huge distance and allowed mother and son to know something important about each of them. Sometimes honesty and a direct answer are what's called for.

Mary-Anne: "I had to say something."

Divorced and now remarried, Mary-Anne is in her late 50s and lives in Chicago, as does her 35-year-old son Stuart, now married with a family of his own.

Stuart and I have always been very interactive. He's a wonderful man, warm and caring, in a good marriage, and a great father. He's a tall, good-looking man, a lawyer in town, and I'm very proud of him.

I do have an awkward story, though. When he was in college, Stuart would come home on weekends after his father had moved out and gone to Boston. There I was, a single mother in Albany that he was coming back to. He had just had a heartbreak with this girl he had been going out with back in school, and he began talking about intimacies that I really didn't feel as a mother that I wanted to be privy to—why she left him, sexual difficulties between them, how pained he felt. This was a first, for him, for me, for us.

In ninth grade he had talked about a girl who had broken his heart, but this was different, more grown up. I felt like I was talking almost to a peer, except it was *my son*. I said, "This feels very private." Did he really want to be talking to his mother about these sexual matters with his girlfriend?

I tried not to get between Stuart and his father, but I wished his father was more available for his son to talk to. It was a time, though, when Stuart's father was a mess as well. So I heard all this guy stuff: How could this girl be so intimate with me, sleep with me, and then go to a party and go off with someone else? I was feeling the absence of his father. Maybe, too, I was feeling abandoned by Stuart's father, and here was Stuart—a guy—telling me about feeling abandoned by a girl. It was almost too much for me to hear; it was too loaded and close to home. But I was the only one there; his father was not there for him, and he was coming to me. So there I was sitting in our living room with my son—a senior at college—so upset, near tears. I had to say something. Having my son talk about intimacy with another woman felt like crossing a taboo, a boundary. He didn't talk about the sex part very much, but he did talk about his feelings. And he said, "I have to talk to someone about this and you're my mother."

So we talked. I said things like "Well, sounds like she was more interested in herself than in you."

That was right out of my own experience of the breakdown of my marriage! I tried to be consoling. I could tell his heart was broken. He showed me pictures of her, and she was beautiful in the pictures. I said so. And I told him, "You'll find somebody else who really loves and appreciates you."

Stuart did move on, and he found a wonderful wife. But he suffered so. It was important I heard him back then. In fact, he continued for a while to lean on me. He called me once about a fight he had with his wife before they got married; he was all upset and scared about whether he could trust in the relationship. I tried to be calming and said, "Stuart, take it easy, what you're going through normal. You two are in a stage of growing in your relationship. It doesn't mean something's wrong with the relationship."

Even growing up he'd come to me and say, "This friend is so two-faced. What happened?" and we'd share things. Or "So and so stole something, and I really like him." And I'd reply, "Look, you're choosing your own friends. Just know what the consequences are of hanging around people who are doing bad things. You might sometime be caught in it. But that's your choice. You need to make the choice."

I'd always say an opinion and put a little value in there and try to be calming. But I'd also express my faith in Stuart that he would know what to do and could do the right thing.

Mothers remain vital, important figures in their sons' lives as both age as adults. Mothers can struggle with awkwardness, wondering how close to be to their sons. The mother of a grown son may feel ambivalent about how much intimacy is right to share with her son. The parent's marriage impacts, of course, on the mother-son relationship. A wife's disappointments in her husband may lead her to look for a more ideal male in her son.

Mary-Alice is aware that Stuart needs to find another woman in his life, yet she is also his mother. She may feel envious of this new woman in his life, yet she also know she has to let him go. And through it all, mothers and sons need to know that they are there for each other, even if they can't lean on each other quite like in the old days.

A VERY PRIVATE FEELING

The love between mother and son is tender and may feel very private between the two, so private that sons may not be able to speak of it at all, and mothers may feel awkward doing so as well. Like all love, it's ambivalent. Sons may feel burdened by their mothers' expectations of them, or, if their fathers were emotionally or physically absent, they may feel that mothers are *too* important—our major lifelines to the world of emotional nourishment. If fathers were physically or emotionally unavailable, a son may have the shameful feeling of being nagged to death by his mother growing up. Not all mothers, of course, are experienced by their sons as nurturing or helpful, nor do all sons come through for their mothers. Yet in my experience listening to grown sons, most feel a profound debt to their mothers and a deep love for them that can be very hard to put into words.

Mothers may feel loving of their sons yet also awkward and unsure. Sons may be the "better husband" that they wished they had, someone to make up for the disappointments and failures of the real husband, the real relationship that needs to be mourned and come to terms with. Just as fathers cannot fall *too much* in love with their daughters—expecting the *frisson* of the father-daughter relationship, with its playfulness and excitement, to fulfill what the marriage should—so too for mothers, who must realize at some point that they need to let their sons go and turn to their husbands to satisfy their needs for love and empathy and excitement.

Yet too mothers and sons are vital to each other, and finding the way to say "I love you" between the generations is an important marker, as is the need to forgive each other for the debt we owe each other: the mother's longing for a Prince Charming and the son longing for a Great Mother who will take away the loneliness and responsibility of being an adult.

Hidden Wisdom You Can Use

- Mothers and sons have a special bond and energy between them; it comes from an opposite-sex family relationship. They project some of their hopes and dreams and conflicts on to each other.
- It can be helpful for mothers to consider what their own internal sense of "wounded masculinity" is. What messages did you get

growing up about what boys are like? Does that fit your experience of your son? How is he also different from stereotypes and images?

- Mothers want to "civilize" their sons and teach them values, self-control, and empathy with others. However, sometimes a boy's playful, aggressive behavior is misunderstood as antisocial. Sometimes boys are being connected and social by being aggressive and provocative. Think about your own wishes to be big, strong, in charge, dominant. It can help you empathize with your son!
- Often how a mother relates to her son is connected to her relationship with her own father growing up.
- It can be helpful for mothers and fathers to talk about their mixed expectations and concerns about their sons. When raising a son, both parents need each other and what they each bring to the relationship.
- Adolescent boys still very much need their mothers. Although there is an important role for fathers at this point, boys still need to feel that they have a strong connection with their mothers.
- Just spending time with a son is important. You don't have to have long, heart-to-heart talks with a son. Focusing on activities and things "out there" (perhaps a ball game or playing around with tools) can often help foster a sense of connection with boys.
- The relationship between mothers and sons continues all through our lives, and it is possible for mothers and sons to become friends and confidantes—certainly to heal some of the rifts of the past—as they age. Even a grown son can be afraid of his mother's anger or disapproval. And mothers as they age are often worried about the same thing: accusations from their sons of not having been a "good enough mother," of having failed at motherhood in some way. The key is to forgive and to find a way to talk about the disappointments and joys of the past.

c h a p t e r   n i n e

Parenting and Grown Children

P arents with children who are grown into their 20s, 30s, 40s, and older have a "long view" of the parenting process. They have much to teach those of us who are parenting young children and teens. We may think of parenting as being over when children are "launched" into college, a job, the army, or marriage. However, parenting is never really over. Children and grown parents return to each other throughout their lives for "refueling" and nourishment.

Self-esteem and healthy aging are tied to a parent's ability to connect with their grown children. And there's a lot at stake for the younger generation as well. The possibilities for reconciliation and transformation are present throughout our lives: A difficult time at one point doesn't have to darken the relationship forever.

The key lies in our ability as parents and grown children to see each other in a new light, freed from the cartoon images, idealized or demonized, that are a normal feature of growing up. Parents are larger-than-life figures for their children; children in turn are lightening rods for powerful parental passions, anxieties, and hopes. As we grow older, there are transformational opportunities to see each other more clearly.

Grown children and their parents are often searching unknowingly for a new language and way of connecting, one that involves friendship and forgiveness as well as disappointment and grieving. We search for a recognition of what is lost *and* what is gained as the generations age, power and memory shifts, and death comes closer. Once again we find parents and children striving sometimes clumsily, sometimes gracefully—often unconsciously—to acknowledge change, to forgive past disappointments, omissions, and betrayals, to hold on to each other as they intuit the preciousness and precariousness of their time together.

Grateful parents may first be *surprised* as they find themselves becoming friends with grown kids. Consider my friend Nora's story, in which a simple lunch and shopping trip with her 25-year-old daughter, Jane, brings joy and relief and reflection with it.

Nora: "I was too impatient with her."

Nora is a tall, well-dressed woman, a respected and well-known writer and linguist, known for her commitment to the Latin literary tradition. Her husband is a historian at an urban university. We talked in their crowded apartment in Philadelphia, surrounded by books and CDs. Professional journals vied with glossy magazines for space on the coffee table, and a stack of student papers lay piled on her desk, a leaning tower of student effort awaiting her judgment.

Like many parents of older children, Nora's story about her daughter starts back at the beginning, with the retrospective musing that accompanies the desire of midlife and older parents to sort out how they got from there to here:

I remember so vividly a Fourth of July party when Jane was very young. There were at least a dozen children there, and they were all building forts out of the lawn chairs. It was very hot, and some of them were throwing cups of water on each other, laughing and playing and running around . . . all of them except for Jane. She stayed with me, holding on to my leg the whole time. I was trying to talk to the other mothers, and I kept urging Jane to go off and play. I didn't want her clutching me.

She was an only child and I worried about her. My husband and I are voluble and social—I march right into a group and make a place for myself—but Jane hung quietly on the edges of crowds. When she was a teenager, she often chose not to go to parties or, worse, wasn't invited. She said she didn't care, that friendships and being in the "in group" weren't terribly important to her. But it broke my heart.

I always had some suggestions for her. Why don't you expand your friendship group? Have a sleepover party? She'd simply say no.

And yet she had friends, often exuberant ones, hysterical, noisy, colorful girls—the kind I was when I was young. I remember a beautiful *lush* girl—Amanda. In middle school, Jane would sit quietly on the floor with a game, and Amanda would sit next to me on the couch, knitting, telling us jokes—wry jokes. But when they were younger, the two of them would spend hours together creating imaginary women—drawing them, cutting them out, giving them types, cheerleader, doctor, secretary—inventing whole imaginary worlds for them. Jane had a lot going on inside that she kept to herself.

What I am realizing now is that all the while that I was pushing her, academically as well as socially, she was calmly holding her own—in school, with her excitable girlfriends, with me and my husband, with our friends, too, when they came to our house for parties—parties full of laughter and debate during which Jane said almost nothing. But she enjoyed those parties, she tells me. She was not suffering as I imagined she was.

When it came time for college, she chose City College of New York. And I worried again—I felt sick—because it was such a big, non-coddling institution. But she made friends there, too, and found a passion—poverty law. When she was ready to apply for jobs and graduate school, she would not use any of our contacts, would not let us open doors for her. She was carving out her own territory, becoming valuable on her own terms to her colleagues. Now she's a major figure in her department.

I had lunch with her today. We teased each other and laughed—about silly things, our hair—and she told me about some books she's read that have quoted me. She said she was grateful she had listened to me about some course choices she made in college. We had such a fun, easy time.

If I could do it differently, I think I'd be less anxious about having a child who grows up differently than you expect. I felt such urgency in my wish that she be out there. What was I saying? That I wish you were a different kind of person than you are? She's developing her own way of coping with things. I was too impatient with her. With a second child, maybe I would have been wiser, but there was no second child.

I think back to that Fourth of July party, and I wish I had been more patient with her wish to hold on, more patient with her reticence. I'm so thankful now that she does come back, does hold on to me!

Our gratitude may lie in the fact that we are simply able to spend enjoyable time together with our grown children. When kids are young we are so caught in the intensity of the moment, so pressed by their need for us and often so overwhelmed by the demands on us that we wonder if we'll ever get any peace and quiet, time to be our adult selves separate from them, away from their inevitable "clutching" of us.

When we parent young children and teens, perhaps too we are more inflexible. We worry about every detail, feel so in control and so important. Whatever they do seems to flow out of us, is a reflection on our values, our choices, our skill at parenting. When your kids are grown, it's possible to see more how they are similar and different from you.

So Nora—the mother of a young child—could barely tolerate the ways her daughter was different from her—more observant, more on the edge of social groups, unwilling perhaps to compete with her mother for the social spotlight. Nora's bemusement at her daughter's choice of "out there" friends may be just the point: It was in this way that Jane found some identity separate from her mother. She wanted to make it on her own and not rely too much on her parents, and it was just this exasperating part of Jane that years later became a source of pride for Nora as she watched her thoughtful, confident 25-year-old daughter make it in the world as her own person. "She was not suffering as I thought she was." Nora mixed Jane up with herself: *Nora* would have suffered being on the edge, *Jane* was comfortable there.

How do you negotiate a changed relationship? The core of the process is seeing the way that you each are different while also honoring the connection between you. For Nora, it means being able to see her daughter's strength and to hear Jane's love, her daughter's desire to tell her mother how much she means to her, to thank her for helping her in college even as she seemed to be pushing her mother away.

Parents need to acknowledge a new dependency. In the case of Nora and Jane, the daughter who used to clutch at her mother's leg now has a mother who wants to clutch at her daughter, to hold her close. Nora in a good-natured way is grateful for the time they spend together. She's lucky she can open herself to her own need for her daughter. Sometimes parents push their children away because they can't tolerate needing their kids so much.

There's a task of recognizing and responding to change for the grown child as well. Jane needs to acknowledge the new power that her ability to be separate from her mother gives her. A new sense of responsibility and opportunity can come from the recognition that your parents, who are growing older, need you in a new and different way than when you were young and they seemed to hold up the world. Here's a silver lining amidst the turmoil: Both generations can leverage some relative freedom from the "cartoon images" of each other that are a normal and natural part of growing up, and from which we are never entirely free.

In the stories that follow, mothers and fathers and sons and daughters try to find a new language of reconnection. As in so much of parenting, there is no single "right way." There are many ways to speak this language. What we often find is a letting go of judgments, a willingness to embrace forgiveness, and sometimes a grateful recognition that you're a kind of friend as well as a relative. Many of the stories begin with memories of the early years of family life as the parents trace a journey toward a deepening of the relationship. Perhaps in reading, you too will feel an opening of doors, a welcome home.

Bonnie: "It's a different idea of 'parent.'"

Bonnie, at age 63, has been widowed for five years. She works as a librarian in a town near Baltimore, where she now makes her home. She raised her family far from the little town in the Pacific Northwest where she grew up.

I thought I would always be the parent. I never anticipated that my children would be my friends. That's one of the most blessed things about us all getting older. I didn't have that with my mother. She was The Mother; then suddenly she was elderly, and I was her advisor. My sister and my mother didn't get along, and I was always the mediator.

After I moved to the East Coast with my husband, at age 20, our contact was mainly over the phone and by mail. It was mother-daughter contact—she respected me. As she aged, she did okay, until at age 78, she was mowed down by a car in a pedestrian crossing in Seattle. I had to take over long distance. She depended on me for everything except finances. I advised her long distance on who would take care of her, do what—things like that.

Now my children are in their 30s. I can still remember the difficulties of mothering them as young children. I felt so proud of myself when I was able to almost assuage my youngest daughter Olivia's hunger as an infant. She developed thrush, which affected her entire alimentary system. She was unable to suck or to swallow without pain. She was such a large baby that she needed a lot of milk. She had been a very easygoing, alert baby until the hunger pangs got to her. She would scream and become very angry. She developed a surge of anger as an everyday phenomenon. It took all my patience to allow her to express her anger. I was concerned not to squelch the anger, which seemed to be a part of her personality. She wanted to have things right away and that felt connected to her feeding. Being able to meet such a deep need was profoundly significant to me. She needed that fluid. It wasn't possible to give a baby like that a bottle. I had to squirt it directly into her mouth from my breast. That was very difficult. I enjoyed the quiet of the night, sitting with everyone asleep. At 3 months, she wouldn't go to anyone else, just wanted to have me. I gave her a lot of yogurt when her feeding improved. I accepted it all because she was physically well, and that was what counted.

My older children, of course, felt differently. It was quite a nuisance to her older brother and sister; they didn't consider Olivia human till she was about 6 years old. For Lilith, my firstborn, life had become quite horrible. She'd sit next to me in her white party dress because it was the closest she could find to being a baby. It was a very hard time.

It has turned out that Olivia, among all the children, is the best at communicating emotional content and feeling in her work. She's a scientist and does ecological modeling for communities and businesses. She has to get people really excited about things that need improvement in the environment. She gathers data at various levels about land/water usage, and then she has to really plug things, get people interested and willing to provide money to buy into it. It is quite a sight to see her at work with audiences and groups, this girl of mine who was such a difficult feeder thirty years ago. I'm glad I stuck with it.

We have a great relationship now as adults, because she is such a great communicator. It's surprising. It is a blessing to engage with your children as friends. It's a different idea of "parent." My children will treat me as though my concerns about friends are on a parallel with their concerns. They give advice about my dating. They'll make suggestions. Meeting someone? They want to know the details of how it went. My children quiz me as to what these guys are like. It feels fine. I've been checking in with them about their relationships. Last year two of them married. They check in to see if my life is in balance. My son heard I wanted a sound system. So he did some research on home entertainment systems and insisted on contributing four-hundred dollars because he felt it would be an opportunity to give a gift I'd like.

They have a desire to enjoy common interests. Lilith was totally disinterested in art when she was young. Now she decided we had to go to an exhibition at the art museum that I love. I've loved art since my teens. Lilith started engaging me in conversations about art, something she never would have done as a teen. She's the one who used to sit beside me in the party dress looking for some attention when I was so preoccupied with her younger sister, and now we are able to tour art museums together and enjoy each other's company!

How we negotiate the changed authority relationship with our children when they become adults is shaped—but not completely determined—by how we and our own parents managed this process. Bonnie and her elderly mother had not been able to find an adult relationship of anything other than a sort of distant, formal respect. Bonnie and her grown children create a different kind of relationship, a more "equal," open one, less formal and reserved, partly as a result of her ability to persevere with them through difficult times.

Kevin : "I no longer have to be his mentor."

Kevin is a federal judge, used to making judgments and decisions. He's a big man, sits upright in his seat, clearly used to positions of authority. He comes from a family where the fathers are teachers of sharp values. Now his 29-year-old son has become his equal, offering the father a way of seeing the world differently. Kevin's story began in response to the writing prompt "I laughed out loud when my son/daughter . . . "

When my son was 7 years old, he made me laugh out loud when I slipped on the ice while we were at a ski lodge in the mountains. I fell in front of a big restaurant window. The diners began laughing when they saw me take a tumble like the proverbial person slipping on a banana peel. I fell right on my backside, which fortunately is well padded, so I wasn't injured. I muttered an oath as I hit the ground. My son looked surprised, then very concerned, and then noticed the diners all laughing at my predicament.

He became very angry and shook his fist at them, scolding: "It's not funny; it's mean to laugh at people who fall down."

He was so serious that I began laughing, which startled him. I explained that it seemed almost instinctive to laugh at such a situation and that the people weren't really being mean, since I wasn't injured. I quickly reassured him that I wasn't laughing at him or his response, which was, I emphasized, a good and compassionate one, but just at the somewhat ridiculous situation.

I'd like to think that his mother and I inculcated in him the empathy with me that he displayed that day. The darker side of this is that the censorious attitude that showed, along with the empathy, is something I probably taught him. Like everyone in his generation, he grew up with a lot of TV, probably too much. I took it upon myself to be a critic of TV, and after every commercial, I'd tell him about how they were all lies and not to believe what he saw.

I've always tried to teach my son—to be his mentor. Now my son does computer work for an advertising agency. We have a good relationship. I'm surprised, and not surprised, that he's so outgoing and gregarious. I feel much less so. His view of the world is no longer something I regard as a child's. I no longer have to be his mentor. At age 29, he has valid, real perceptions. I marvel. Sometimes he seems much better than me—he has a knack for helping friends with emotional problems. Most of his energy is in his band; he really works to earn money so he can play music. He's the mediator in his band, a chip off the old block, in some ways. He has traits I see in me, but some all his own.

He'll be a great father. We'd love to see him with children. He not only is protective of his nieces and nephews but actively engages them in games and play and genuinely seems to enjoy being with them and interacting with them. He's such a gregarious person, who seems at ease in every situation he finds himself in, and as I ponder this, I am surprised because of my own introspective and solitary personality.

We don't really have heart-to-heart talks; those seem to happen more with his mother. Yet I feel totally connected to him to the extent I'm able to connect. It's great that he's become a peer of mine. I speak to him as I would to colleagues. It feels natural. We talk about current events, things on the news. I entertain his views as valid as anyone else's. I used to step in and try to educate his views. Now I just like to hear how he sees the world.

There is a shift in the affect balance as our children become adults. For Kevin, the father, used to being the teacher, now sees he has much to learn from his son, whom he so admires. In a way, Kevin is wrong—he'll always be his son's mentor, because grown sons look to their fathers for validation no matter how successful or different they seem. Yet the truth in Kevin's words lie in the fact that now the father looks to the son for some mentoring. Kevin seems to yearn for his son to show him how to connect, for the son to really see him, to understand him, to penetrate into his heart, hidden perhaps by his traditional role of The Father. Like many aging fathers, Kevin—so used to judging—may wonder how his son judges him. Older fathers can be caught in a formal sort of distance, solitude, and reserve—the traditional male role—and yearn to feel some companionship and connection with their grown sons or daughters.

Lorna: "The hate that poured out of him—it was awful!"

A housewife in Westchester County New York, Lorna also volunteers in a local Head Start program. Her determined tone in reading aloud her story underlined its importance for her, as she described the decade-long process by which she and her oldest son moved toward some reconciliation, both drawn back together finally by the arrival of grandchildren in the family.

My eldest son was one of the easiest to raise until he hit his teens. Then he became quite obnoxious and independent. I was holding him tight to the line. He had a job working at the local grille washing dishes the summer of his 16th year, saving money to buy a car. When the owners gave him the job, they asked for a guarantee that he would work through Labor Day, which he agreed to.

Jerry then became part of a teen crew in a new sailing/cruising regatta. The grille was very nice about it and gave him time off to compete in the sailing. Then they won, and his crew was invited to the teen nationals. Jerry came home one day and said that he was quitting his job and going off sailing. I replied, "No you're not!"

An explosion of anger followed, "What! I could be sailing in the nationals!"

I told him that it was better that he fulfill his commitment. Well, the hate that poured out of him—it was awful!—here I had clothed, fed, and loved him—I felt it was important that he not throw something over when it's not fun anymore. He had made a commitment, and I felt it was important he keep it. He washed dishes till Labor Day but our relationship was rocky for years after that.

After he became a father with a young son a few years ago, he came over and said he wanted to talk. He laid me out in lavender, saying I made Christmases miserable with all my demands and events. And here I thought I had made these Technicolor Christmases he'd always remember! Then he went home and told his wife, "I had a great talk with Mom."

I felt like a failure. Mothering is such an important part of me. So I wrote him a letter and said that I wanted to talk about these issues but that I had to have my therapist by my side. I was kind of joking, but I did talk about our relationship for quite awhile with my therapist.

My son agreed to my offer to talk, but I wasn't sure if he really wanted to. Some of the tension between us drained out, though, after the letter. My husband and I have really enjoyed the grandchildren— he'll drop them off for us to baby-sit from time to time, and we spend holidays all together.

Recently, after a lovely Thanksgiving together, I said, "I wonder if seeing me grandparent draws us closer."

He nodded agreement. Watching *him* parent makes me feel so much closer to him. He's so involved and loving—scooping up his two little girls, doing their hair up in ponytails, helping them dress. I expected to see that part of my daughters, but to see your son doing that is very unexpected. His first daughter is quite a character—she's very powerful. One day she was having a full-blown meltdown when I was visiting and there was Jerry, trying to calm her. "Use words, Emmy, use words," he pleaded. But she was in no mood for words. I must say, what goes around comes around!

The arrival of a new generation can thaw out ancient, frozen postures in a family. We begin to understand our own parents better when our children arrive. And watching us parent gives our parents a chance to see sides of us that may have been masked before. Both generations can focus on the grandchildren, allowing them to reconcile with each other. These changes don't come guaranteed. In Lorna's story, it took a brave, frightening effort on the part of both mother and son. Each experience things differently: A "great talk" for the son was a grueling experience for the mother. Often the content of the talk doesn't matter. What matters is that parents and children acknowledge that they want to talk, and make themselves available to do so. Usually it's the bitter silence into which anger and misunderstanding pours; a heartfelt invitation to talk in itself can start to drain the bitterness.

Dick: "You're always connected, even through a divorce."

An administrator at a small private university in New England, Dick has been through two painful divorces. He's successful in his career, but his many references to life back in California made clear his desire to move back to the small town near Los Angeles where he grew up and where his only son from his first marriage now lives. Dick is a wiry, athletic man who talks in bursts of words.

It's great to have a 28-year-old. He's living in California, and he called me last night, opened his heart. It was a great conversation, like back when he was 4 years old, before the divorce. It was wonderful between us back then. At age 4, a kid's vocabulary is developing, he has this great energy, interested in everything. And a kid at 4 years old thinks that his dad is the greatest guy on earth.

Then so many things happened. After the divorce, my ex-wife moved with Zeke across country. I didn't contest that, but it felt like I sealed off my heart to what happened, the loss was so great. For several years, Zeke was traveling back and forth to stay a few weeks a year with me.

You're always connected even through a divorce; it's never over. We talked several times a week on the phone, and he would visit several times a year. It was always good between us. When he was 13, he got his ear pierced one day. This was fifteen years ago, before body piercing was such a common thing. He walked downstairs to the kitchen for breakfast sporting this earring. I didn't miss a beat, just kept eating my eggs and said, "Oh yeah—when are you going to get the other ear pierced?" That stopped him in his tracks. It defused the whole issue, and I was proud that I had stumbled into the correct response. I didn't want him to get earrings, but I didn't want to make too much of an issue out of it.

But we've also had hard times. Through his teens he hated school, and he didn't get along with his stepmother. His mother had remarried and decided that Zeke would do better living with me. My new wife and I had a new baby in the house. I was concentrating on the baby and wasn't aware enough of what that was like for an adolescent and for my new wife. They both wound up angry at each other. So he spent several years with us and then went back out to California to live with his mother. We've always managed to stay in contact, though. Nothing magical—we just talked about what was on our minds.

Now I find I can *really* talk to him. It was 12:30 a.m. last night when he called, 9:30 West Coast time. He told me he knew I was up late most nights, and he just wanted to catch up. He still drives me crazy; he recently got a tattoo. He loves trucks and got a big V-8 insignia tattooed on his chest, same as on the dashboard of his truck. I told him he looks like an ad for vegetable juice. He says he likes it.

Even so, I can talk to Zeke in ways I never was able to. There's a big irony in my life right now. I've been offered this great job in California, nearer to him and to my parents and brothers, but I can't take it. I'm again divorced with joint custody of several young children, and when I remarried I wrote in the contract a clause that neither parent can move out of state without the approval of the other; I didn't want to go through the pain of what happened with Zeke. My dream job is available in California—heading the development office of a large, successful nonprofit agency in my home town in California, great salary, great job, great place to live—but it would mean leaving my kids and a girlfriend of three years, whom I love.

So on the phone he asked me, "How are you doing dad? What's happening?" I told Zeke about the job offer and my dilemma. He responded, "Doesn't sound like it's the right time, right place. It's just not right for you at this time, Dad."

That was such a reversal. I'm still, on one level, his father, and he's the 4-year-old, but on the other hand, *he's* the father—very wise, sensitive.

I recently came from a family reunion, and I can see how we are all aging. All my children were there, the three of them from both marriages. My parents are 76 and 77, and for the first time I had the feeling that some day these kids could be taking care of me. I wondered if the kids would put me in a nursing home,. It was a joke this past reunion: "Oh, Dad, we'll be pushing you around in a wheelchair!" In California the line is that nothing ever rusts or ages, people or cars. But how long can you pretend that's true?

What pleasure for a father to feel he can lean on his son! We work so hard to be heroes to our kids, and as we age, it can feel increasingly difficult to strap ourselves back into our armor each day. And Dick gives a gift back to Zeke in allowing his son to give him advice. In so doing, he confirms to his son that the boy has wisdom and caring he can offer to the world. Certainly a silver lining in the father's struggle with aging!

Susan: "I felt the weight of my mother's head, resting on my hand."

What of the grown child's perspective? Susan is 40 years old, married, without children. A physician, she has a busy practice in sports medicine. One recent Thanksgiving holiday she made a surprising discovery about her elderly mother Ruth and herself. Susan spoke in an animated fashion as she described the circumstances that led up to it. Her story began in response to the writing prompt "My mother's skin . . . "

My mother's skin is thin and thick at the same time. For the longest time, I thought my mother was pretty tough. She sure liked to make it look that way. I didn't see past that because I thought I knew so much and was so clear.

My relationship with her has been pretty conflicted all our lives. She had a horrible relationship with her mother, who died when I was 18. My mother can be pretty sharp and judgmental. She acknowledges that she felt closer to my brother, even though she loved us both equally. "You're like your father, and your brother is like me," she'd tell me as a child. When I was sick, which was not often, she was very nurturing. After a winter's cold she'd take me ice skating and for hot chocolate when I felt better. But my brother was sick for long periods with asthma and then she wouldn't be so nurturing to me.

I remember her telling me not to hold on to her hand so much when we shopped. She just didn't want to deal with this 5- or 6-year-old needy child. Later, when I was at summer camp, she'd sign her letters to me "Luv," without her name. And I'd be hurt—I'd wish for her to simply say "Love, Mom." I guess that captures a lot.

Several years ago, my brother and I asked our parents to tell us stories about their growing up. We wanted to record it for posterity. It was wonderful. We met in our summer cabin at the shore—my husband, my parents, brother, sister-in-law, and I. We heard lots of stories from my parents. Afterward, my brother and I were outside waxing my car, when my sister-in-law came outside and said,

"There's something else on the tape. You really should hear it. We were just talking some more."

My mother was tearfully saying how proud she was of me, that I had gone to medical school and was working and had accomplished what she couldn't. I thought, "What is this? Where is this coming from?" I couldn't connect with it and didn't talk to my mother about it. I stored it away, though.

Then, last fall, my father was ill, and we went home for Thanksgiving. He can really get on my nerves, and I was thinking of what I could do to not get so irritated. I pride myself on being nonjudgmental, but with my parents I'm very judgmental—I can get like a teenager complaining about how my father just doesn't listen, he's not thoughtful, very judgmental. But at some point you have to realize this is who they are instead of saying it has nothing to do with me.

Preparing for that visit I became aware of how I relate to my mother in the same way—she's very critical, and I get that same way. If there's a piece of clothing that I don't like, I'll just say it. Sometimes she'd try to impose that judgment on me, and I'd push her away.

So there we were on Thanksgiving day after the big meal at their house in Brooklyn, and we were cleaning out her medicine cabinet, just she and I. She's not a big makeup fan, but she asked me to help her put on some eye shadow. I'm taller than she is now, and she stood in front of me, her head tilted slightly up so I could see her face better. I was holding her head with one hand, putting on the dark eye shadow with the little brush, a foamy pad on a stick. Her eyelids were so crinkly, the skin wrinkled. She seemed nervous. She giggled and moved away slightly.

"Just relax!" I said. "I'm not going to hurt your eyes."

She calmed down, and laughed, apologized, then stood still. I felt the weight of my mother's head resting on my hand, under her chin. I put the powder across her eyelid. It was hard to put on smoothly because her skin was layered with wrinkles.

I realized that though her skin seemed thick to me, it was to cover up her softness. She liked having me put on the makeup, enjoying it just as I did, mother and daughter playing with cosmetics, in just the way I wished we had when I was young. I was acting toward her like I liked her, and she *liked* that.

How come I couldn't see the obvious before? If I am not defensive and instead act like I value her, as I do, then she acts differently to me. I wondered how afraid my mother had been of connecting with me all these years, afraid of the mother-daughter relationship, maybe—who knows?—because of how tough it had been with her own mother.

Susan was able to let go of her grudges and alienation and to see that she blocked opportunities for getting closer to her parents. We all have "cartoon images" of our parents—rooted in childhood—and at some point it helps to see that parents grow and change too. In doing so, Susan was able to see the vulnerability and desire for connection underneath her mother's seeming toughness.

Carl: "We're not touchy-feely."

Carl owns and operates a garage in rural North Carolina. He's known as the most reliable tow operator in the county. A jolly man, he is quick to smile and laugh, particularly when he talks about his young son.

I've always wanted to just feel "okay" with my father, not looked down on. I come from a family with lots of judgments—my grandfather was a minister, for starters. During the depression, he would drive around the Midwest holding revival meetings, haranguing people on street corners to go to his church. My grandmother went deaf, and that gives you some idea of what conversations were like with him. My father was also active in the ministry and became a church organist and musician. My father has lots of opinions too. I know I've disappointed him in not being more religious. We fought a lot in my teens about faith, and going to church, and the sultry women I dated.

Dad and I have never talked too much on the phone and have never been real good at sending letters to each other. Ever since my son was born, three years ago, though, I've wanted to talk with my dad, have him know me better. It's so hard to break through sometimes. I've thought of just shocking him with stories about my experiences with women and all. But really I just want him to know more about me. Soon after our son was born, my parents came down here to North Carolina to be with us. We both like carpentry, and I had it in mind that Dad and I would make Christmas gifts together for the family. I stocked up my shop with wood and supplies and waited until he got down here. He no sooner arrived than he announced that he was going to visit some church friends who live in a nearby town, and then he was gone for a couple of days, the very days that I wanted to spend time with him. I never said anything about it, but that was a big disappointment.

The other day I was visiting my parents. My dad's got a favorite spot in his living room—a sheepskin rug with a big beanbag pillow and another pillow on top of it set up against the big hearth of the fireplace. That's "Dad's Spot," and it's where he sits, right between the stereo speakers, watching TV. This night, after we had all had a lively dinner, I got there ahead of him and stretched out, feeling mighty relaxed, before he could turn on the TV. He came over and looked down, smiled at me lying there, then just leaned against the beanbag with me. The evening routines went on around us, my mom and my wife cleaning up the dishes, my sister sitting reading the paper, while my father and I sat there leaning against each other, talking.

We're not touchy-feely. We don't typically hug or kiss or sit close, but the feeling of being able to lean up against my father, to just be able to sit and be together, without TV, music, interruptions, felt wonderful.

Sometimes reconnections with aging parents are wordless, accomplished with a touch or a simple leaning into each other. They may be less grand moments—though no less important—than we hoped for, not intense conversations in front of the fireplace or long hours spent in the shop together. Sometimes simply leaning into each other on the living room floor will do the trick.

Joan: "At ages 56 and 33, we are just beginning to reconnect."

Joan is a 56-year-old legal secretary, and when she talks, it's hard not to notice her lovely dark black hair. She and her second husband, Al, came together to a focus group. She crafted a story of family fragmentation and reconnection across several generations and decades.

It's taken us thirty years, but now my son and I are starting to reconnect. When my son was born, he was so small I was absolutely terrified of this tiny creature. It was an absolutely normal delivery, but I hadn't a clue about being a mother. His skin was so wrinkly and pink and soft and warm, and I couldn't believe how loose his skin felt on his bones, how tiny and fragile they were. I thought, *Oh my god, how am I going to do this job?*

My mother paid absolutely no attention to me when I was young. And she forced me to marry the man who was to abuse us and whom I eventually divorced. I cried in my bedroom the night before my marriage, barely 20 years old, begging my mother not to make me marry this man. She told me she knew what was best.

So there I was at age 23, with no idea of motherhood, my husband not interested, my mother there every way but emotionally. I wriggled along, like a caterpillar, struggling to raise Jessie. When he was 16, I went back to school, to finish college.

I didn't want him connecting to me like my siblings and I had with my mother, to feel smothered, unable to get away. I went back to school to give him some freedom, but I also closed myself off to him without realizing it, worrying about term bills and course credits and passing those tests. He and I were too bonded. After my husband left, Jessie helped manage things, maybe too much, taking care of the house, the lawn. I didn't want him trapped in the nest. Now he is grown and competent and a father and a husband and successful businessman whom I find it hard to get close to; I feel sad for all the things about him I don't know how to relate to and yet grateful that I still have the opportunity to try and get to know him better. At ages 56 and 33, we are just beginning to reconnect.

When he was growing up, he loved the time he spent at my grandmother's house in the Adirondacks. We had an extraordinary relationship, fishing and boating. Jessie loved it. So, last year I asked Jessie if he would like to go to Montana for a family vacation together, fishing and boating. I was very nervous and didn't know how to ask. But finally I went ahead one day in the spring. Two weeks went by, and finally he called back to say yes. I was stunned and so grateful. He and his wife and two kids and myself and his stepfather all went together. Al has been a great stepfather for them. He has been a blessing to us all, his willingness to come into our family when the kids were just teenagers and love them and show them what love means.

When Jessie's child was born, he mentioned to me one day, "Al'll have to show him how to fish, because grandfathers do that sort of thing."

I realized that *fathers* do that sort of thing, but that Jessie didn't know that because his father was so abusive and then gone.

We spent a week on a ranch in the Rocky Mountains, near one of the top five fly-fishing rivers in the country, next to thousands of acres of wilderness preserve. We stayed in a little cabin with two bedrooms and a tiny living area, the six of us. I figured by the time we left we'd either be killing each other or much closer.

The first day we were there we went fishing, but Jesse didn't catch anything. Al was reluctant to intrude. I urged him, "You don't understand, Al; he's here because he wants you to teach him how to fish."

So Al went and showed Jessie the "Al wiggle," and Jessie caught fish every time they were out, beauties—trout, pike, bass. Jessie wound up following Al around all week like he was 5 years old. He had this delightful gleam in his eye for Al.

But he also had it for *me*, and that felt wonderful. Instead of smothering my son, I've found we can just be *soft* together. I feel it when I watch Jessie cook. He is a gourmet chef and has created some wonderful meals in the big lodge. I baby-sat while Al, Jessie, and his wife fished. After dinner I had Jessie to myself.

It was really the first time Jessie and I had time together without my mother or my ex-husband in the way. When we divorced, my ex-husband told me that if he couldn't have his daughter, then I wouldn't have my son, and he tried to poison our relationship. I had lived with this man for twenty-two years and been through years of family therapy. We did every conceivable thing to make it work, and it all failed because our marriage was over before it got started.

I'm not sure if anyone who is not divorced can understand divorce—it's worse than death because it's never finished, never over. It's not just that you feel like a failure in your family, but everyone in the culture looks at it as a failure.

Our time away was so powerful because we were blended, for two weeks there was the emotional protection of being a family in a way we hadn't been for years and likely wouldn't be again. And it gave my son and I a wonderful chance to reconnect like in the old days.

One night at 1 a.m. I was hungry. I got up and went down to the kitchen to have some peanut butter and jelly. I'm really not supposed to have any because of my elevated cholesterol, nor is my son who has a similar condition. There was nothing much else to eat though. Just as I opened the jar and had gotten out some crackers, I heard someone coming down the stairs. I left the PBJ on the counter and raced upstairs. When the coast was clear, I went back to bed. After they left I went back down to eat my snack.

Next morning, Jessie announced to the whole family over breakfast, "You'll never guess what happened last night!"

The kids were immediately all ears, "What? what?!"

In the most playful tone, Jessie informed them, "Well! Your grandmother ate a PBJ sandwich."

And I got into it.

"That's right. Your daddy caught me!"

All week Jessie was telling us he was looking for postcards because he couldn't wait to write to his brother and sister about the PBJ!

To me it was wonderful to play with Jessie again! I was so excited and happy and peaceful and content. He was so excited just like when he was little and we were pals. It was wonderful he could accept that I'm not perfect, that it was okay. There was some forgiveness there, my own as well as his.

When he was in high school, a counselor told me that "your son is a boy with twinkling eyes and a frozen body." I had always blamed the frozenness on his father, until recently I saw that I was the frozen one. I pushed him away when he was an adolescent, thinking that I was protecting him. I'm a person who doesn't often show people how I feel. I don't talk of myself a lot and tend to assume that other people are angry at or disinterested in me. As he and I are getting to know each other honestly, I've shed some major skin. I feel more like I did when I was young, before I married and then froze for twenty-four years.

Joan came to accept the imperfection in herself—her own frozenness and fear of intimacy—and so was able to play with her son, no longer a passive victim.

Al: "The judge went along with it—so I lost my kids."

Joan's husband Al is a professor in the business school of a large university. He was at the focus group, he explained, "because I drove my wife here." A tall, laconic man, Al at first offered to sit in the waiting room while the focus group met in the office next door but then welcomed an invitation to join the group of parents, "Just to listen," he advised. As we each wrote and told stories of parenting, though, his reserve faded. He was attentive, smiling and nodding. Like many husbands at the focus groups, Al had a lot to say once the members were willing to give him time to feel at home. After a while, Al offered a story of his own about a different fishing trip in which a grown stepchild helped heal some of the pain of a damaged relationship with his biological children.

I'm a stepfather and have been for fifteen years. It's a tough situation because I came into a family with three teenagers who basically had no father. It's a delicate situation to be in. It was clear from the start that I wasn't to come in like The Father, setting rules for them. They were angry that they hadn't had a father and made it clear that I had no right to tell them when to come in at night, when to go out. I managed to develop good relationships with all three kids, now adults, basically by spending time with them and being interested in them, and what they were doing.

When my stepdaughter got into a car accident and wrecked the front end of the car, I was more interested in whether she was okay than in the damage to the car. She was amazed that my first question over the phone was "Are you okay?" She expected I'd be mad about the dents and scrapes on the new car paint. She was so used to abuse and neglect from men that her being all right was totally irrelevant to her.

What was hard for me was feeling like the outsider. I had never changed their diapers, felt their skin as children. And I was alienated from my own children. My ex-wife brainwashed them into thinking I'm a terrible person. So I've had to live with no contact with my own sons.

I'm particularly proud of the fact that my oldest stepson—Jessie— asked me recently to go on a fishing trip with him. It's a group that goes every year to upstate New York to fish for salmon on a wonderful whitewater river. I wasn't sure how I'd fit in—all of the guys are younger than me. On the trip, they played a card game I didn't know, called Acey Ducey. We were in this beautiful old Adirondacks log cabin built early in the century, in the middle of nowhere, the seven of us. I kept an eye on how it was played, then the last night we were there a big game developed, and I joined in. People were dropping out all night after losing a lot of money. The pots were quite big! I was doing okay, and finally the game got down to just the three of us—myself, my stepson, and a guy from Canada. There was a rivalry between Jessie and this guy, who had won a lot of money over the weekend. We played into the night, and finally Jessie dropped out, leaving me and the Canadian gent. Finally on the last round, I won the pot—a lot of money! Jessie's reaction was so wonderful—he was delighted I had won. If he couldn't win, he was glad that I had. He didn't say anything to me, but his mother told me that the day after we returned the story was all over the family that I had won, that I had taken care of the Canadian.

It was special to me to be invited by Jessie. I was the oldest man there, most of the others were in their 30s. It was like Jessie was saying, "I'm willing to let you see me with my friends, let you be a part of my life." Maybe too, in winning that pot and having Jessie spread the word that I had done it, he was saying, "My dad is bigger than your dad." I was able to fit those shoes for him, to be a source of pride. It sweetens some of the sting that comes from not being able to see my own kids. Once in a while on that trip, I'd think, "Gee, it would be nice if I could go fishing with my biological son like this." But I'm grateful for what I have with my stepchildren.

Parenting someone who is not your biological child can take some of the sting from a family relationship that seems hopeless—so the value of being a stepparent, an aunt or uncle, a Big Brother or Big Sister, or even a mentor at work. Al feels worthwhile and valid with Jessie in a way that life has denied him with his biological sons. It doesn't replace what he's lost, but it does lighten the burden.

Gary: "I'm trying not to be the husband and father who holds everything in."

In his early 30s, Gary owns a kitchen supply and renovation business in the suburbs of Phoenix. Coming to terms with his elderly father's decline has helped him learn an important lesson about his family and himself.

I thought we were a pretty close family, but then I realized a few years ago that we didn't relate very well. My father's struggle with Alzheimer's disease has been very frustrating. He worked for twenty-five years as a salesman in a car dealership. Then he suddenly lost his job, and we couldn't understand why. He had always done a great job and was well liked.

My brother and I run a family kitchen remodeling business that involves sales, so we took our father in, at age 65, and he worked for us. Within a year, we were totally frustrated with him. Now I can see what was happening back then. He was completely forgetful, couldn't keep up with customers, sales, business orders, and back orders. At the time, it was a big mystery to all of us, and we wondered if he was depressed. So we went into therapy as a family, and that was great— it really opened us up to each other and how to be able to listen, as a parent, as a child, as a spouse. At first we had to drag my father along. But once he opened up, we learned a lot about each other. He's a very quiet man, hard to read. His disease has brought the whole family closer.

I had a very good upbringing. I can think of some things I do differently, but my parents tried very hard to let me be the person I wanted. But my dad was always the kind of person who kept things inside. He never wanted to burden anyone. Now his father is dying, and his mother is in a nursing home. My 90-year-old aunt came to visit recently, and my mother said to her sister, "David is forgetting things, he's not doing well, is he?" He doesn't want to burden her with these things, so he's not talking, but she knows. Even from the nursing home, she knows.

So one of the biggest gifts that I've gotten from these struggles is learning how to communicate, to listen. I'm trying not to be the husband and father who holds everything in. One example is back from when we took over the business in 1989. It was not a very good time for remodeling. In 1990 we came very close to losing the business. This was a family business my grandfather started in the 1940s, so there is a lot of sentimental value there. I didn't open up to my wife for a long time, but one day it just all came out. I told her that we were having a hard time in the business and that I didn't know if we'd make it. My fear was that she'd collapse. The opposite happened. She was really there for me. I could hardly believe it. She listened to me, rallied, said we'll make it through this, we're young, strong. She was working at the time and supported us for several years. She was wonderful that day when I let out all my fears and worries. She just let me let it out.

Many of us, as we age, seek to fashion a different version of our-selves as males, to be more open, able to lean on loved ones as well as let them lean on us, reveal what traditionally men have kept close to their vests. When a father opens up—as Gary's did in the family therapy meetings—it can help his sons and daughters learn how to do the same. We may feel we're being weak by showing our feelings and needs, when actually we're learning a new kind of strength—the courage to acknowl-edge limits and ask for help.

Christine: "Things changed from that explosive fight."

Christine is a legal secretary at a busy law office in Portland, Maine. Her husband is a school guidance counselor in the small community near Portland where they live, on the Maine coast. In her 50s, she is the mother of several children, and also a grandmother. Her brown hair is held tightly around her head with a silver barrette, giving her face a severe look. Yet Christine's voice is surprisingly soft and engaging as she tells the story of an explosive battle at the time of her mother's dying.

For years and years I hated my mother and felt indifferent to my father. I left home when I was 16 and had no relationship with them until my 30s. In between, I managed to almost kill myself. I went through drugs and a heroin addiction. It was a pretty bleak childhood. My mother's mother had died when she was very young, and she really didn't know how to mother. We had a big family. One of my earliest memories was the time we all went out for pizza to this joint, when I was about 7 years old, and in the rush to get home to watch some TV show, my parents got everyone into the car while I had wandered off to the bathroom. When I came back they were gone. They came hurrying back in a few minutes, but I still remember the shock of finding them gone, and my tears. That kind of sums it up. My father spent more time in a week at his construction company than he did my whole childhood with me, I'll bet.

Then about eight years ago, my mother got cancer—she died of ovarian cancer about five years ago. At first, we were a little bit in touch, nothing major though. She was in chemo, on a macrobiotic diet, doing everything. Then one weekend she really wasn't feeling very good, and she and my father came to stay with me and my husband. At the time, one of my cats, Down East, was dying. Her kidneys were shutting down. We really loved Down East. We had just brought the cat back from the vet, and she was on an IV and lying around on a special cat bed we had rigged up on the living room couch. My husband and I were very sad, very attentive to the cat, monitoring it, and we were basically paying no attention to my mother. Finally, my mother lost it and yelled at me,

"You're taking better care of that cat than of me!"

I got furious. We had one of the best, most open fights I ever had with my mother and father. I didn't allow myself to yell too much. I told them both, "Your job is to love me, not just to expect me to love you! Where was your love when I was growing up and needed it?"

"We thought you just *knew* how much we love you," they explained.

"How was I to know that!" I replied.

I told them how cheated and ignored I felt in my life with them. I actually *blamed* them for the first time in my life. I told my father how he just sat there like a bump on a log in our house. That he watched too much TV. That he loved his construction company more than me. I felt very guilty yelling at my father.

"What happens in this life has something to do with how you treat me, it's not like I'm just a lousy fuckup," I told them.

Well, we really went at it. They told me how hard they had worked, how rough it had been with five children, how they did love me, very much.

Things changed from that explosive fight, though not immediately. Thank god my mother lived several more years. Every visit, she and I would talk—we started with a lot more of the anger and blaming. But that siphoned out after a while, and I got to tell her about my life, about what had happened in those many years I had completely withdrawn from them. I told her about the drugs. Over those years I had to open myself up to the fact that I loved my mother very much and needed her. I always thought I just hated her, but I also loved her.

After my mother died, my father changed. Today he is 83 years old and the most incredibly warm and loving man. He sends cards to us and the grandchildren from his home in Arizona; he writes about how much he loves us. "I love you, Christine," he signed one card. He never once told that to me when I was young, and now he can. As my mother was dying, he needed to show his love to her and he did. He took wonderful care of her that last year. She died at home, and he comforted her in her bed, changed her, brought friends together. He found a way to express his love for people by being there for my mother when she was dying.

Many of us fear getting angry, of hurting or being hurt by those we love. Yet sometimes direct, honest—even "explosive"—confrontation can cut through layers of denial or misunderstanding. Many of our images of confrontation are of anger out of control and frightening; yet a "good fight"—honest feelings spoken and heard—can open up the congealed places in our relationship.

A DIFFERENT KIND OF PARENTHOOD

"It's such a different idea of a parent," exclaimed Barbara, whose daughter began life barely able to breastfeed—so dependent on her mother for nurturing—and now has become someone who can wow audiences and charm her mother. Barbara in turn now leans on her accomplished daughter.

"I thought I would always be the parent," she advised, and in fact she still is, but in a different way than we may at first think of "being the parent." Parenthood brings to mind images of hierarchy—authority, control, having power. The notion of a parent as a coequal, friend, interdependent with his or her children, can challenge our imagination. We can recognize our children's dependency on us. Can we also see how we depend on them?

What may be most compelling about these stories is the idea of *change*, that we don't have to stay stuck at a dark or difficult point that will then define who we and our family are through time. Families are not written in concrete.

Often the change starts within oneself. We may come to see that *we* are the ones who can't forgive or let go, or that *we* are invested in having our parents (or children) be as frustrating as we make them, or that *we* overreact to what others see as amusing character traits in our mother or father.

We may need to see what happened way back then as a sin of omission rather than commission, a result of circumstances or pressures on our mothers or fathers, a struggle that goes through the generations, rather than a symptom of pure intent to hurt or disappoint us. Depersonalizing the disappointment or betrayal can help us gain perspective. Our parents' choices or decisions may have had more to do with the pressures they struggled with than with our being "a fuckup," in Christine's words.

Seeing your parent, or your child, as simply a human being struggling with human flaws, pressures, hopes, and loyalties, rather than as an unrealistic hero or devil, can help. "At some point you have to realize that is who they are," advises Susan, after letting her mother rest her head in her daughter's hands for the first time. Susan, at the medicine cabinet with her mother, and Joan, with her son Jessie, show how important the change in our own perspective is, whether we are the parent or the child. We may be waiting for *them* to change, when it's *our* own way of seeing that needs to shift.

Judgments are very important in life, but they don't get us very far in families, and the early years of parenting are filled with judgments: Don't watch so much TV, or you'll never learn to read! Don't talk like that or you'll never get a job! Pay attention in class, or your SAT scores will go south and you'll never get into college! As parents we worry so much; then it turns out that our children *do* learn to read, *do* get jobs, *do* go to college. Part of the task as parents of grown children may be to get past judgments, to find some understanding and common ground. There needs to be some forgiveness there between the generations. To move toward reconciliation, we first need to forgive our children, and they need to forgive us.

Forgiveness may not come through profound moments of heartfelt outpourings between parents and grown children. We don't necessarily all sit down together in front of a roaring fire, look deep into each other's eyes and talk of ourselves, the past, and our future. Sometimes that does happen, but more often the forgiveness and grace can be found in the small moments—leaning together on a pillow in "Dad's spot" or putting eye makeup on together and laughing, or having lunch and shopping, not forgetting also to appreciate who each of you has become.

Parents may be shy around their grown children, fearing their judgment, feeling very vulnerable in the world, not wanting to open a can of worms, wanting everything settled. So a mother will say on a tape what she can't say directly to a daughter: I love you and am so proud of you, my beloved daughter. A father will come for a family stay to visit with his son but then immediately take off on a three-day visit to his church buddies down the road. We can imagine what it is like for a father filled with judgments from his own father, having been too busy to really be present when his boy was young, to spend time with his adult son, now a father himself. *Will my son accuse me? Will he spend time together with me? Is he a better father than I was? Am I as good a son to my father as he was to me?* The aged father may be struggling with mortality, wondering what his elder years hold in store for him, while his son is in the midst of his fecundity and creativity. How can the father who is used to being busy, a minister whom others turn to, actually look to his son for help? How can he talk of his own neediness? There is risk here, that of showing his vulnerability and need, in contrast to the ideal image of The Father as self-reliant, all-knowing, protecting everyone else even at great danger to himself.

We can imagine a similar theme between mother and daughter. Susan's mother, Ruth, who felt cursed by her own mother, now confronts the wrinkles in her face, her own aging, while also perhaps envying Susan's youth. Ruth may wonder if she *can* lean on her daughter. If she rests her head truly in Susan's hands, will her daughter treat her with the same anger she felt toward her own aging mother? Given the anger that had existed across the generations, Ruth may wonder, "Am I entitled to turn to my daughter?" To Ruth, anger and alienation may seem the natural course of events between daughters and mothers as they age. How wonderful then that Susan can find a way to hold her mother's weight, can see some of the thin-ness—the need and vulnerability—beneath the apparent thickness of her mother's skin.

Gary's story of his father's struggle to protect his family (and per-haps himself) from his Alzheimer's disease points to one source of family disconnection for fathers: the internal expectation we carry within that husbands and fathers are supposed to be strong and take care of others while not needing help themselves. It can feel very shameful to say that we have a problem or need or weakness.

Yet, in fact, one of the most important gifts we fathers can give our children is a realistic picture of what it means to be an adult man. We need to communicate this in ways appropriate to our children's age. It doesn't mean flooding the family with our sorrow or resentment or neediness in a way that leaves young children desperate to take care of us or get away from us. What is involved rather is to show a child that the full range of human need and emotion is part of the stuff of being a man, in the amount that can be managed within the family. A worthy goal for mothers as well is to get past narrow, stereotyped images of what it means to be a woman. Perhaps then our children can learn that you can be a mature adult without isolating yourself precariously from those you love.

Our children can become our confidantes, as Dick found with his grown son's late night career advice. It is a poignant shift, one in which the parent, so used to being in authority, finds herself or himself relying now on the wisdom of the child. We hear perhaps the first inklings of Dick's dealing with ultimate questions about his own aging when he muses and jokes about nursing homes. He may be wondering about how he and his children will manage his own aging and elder years together. Matters that parents and grown children may be shy to talk about are often part of their heart's deepest yearnings as they age. Does Dick want to be in a nursing home? Does he secretly hope to live with or near his children? What does he hope for from his aging, and what do his children hope for? These matters of immense consequence for families can become part of the process of decision making between parent and child about the elder years, if the generations can take the risk of talking openly together.

The impact of grandchildren on the older generations is another recurring theme. Jessie's having children sweetened some of the tension between him and his mother, Joan, as it did for Lorna, who now was able to observe her son's kindness and gentleness with his young daughter. Seeing a grandfather teach his eager grandson how to swing a tennis racket for the first time or a grandmother rummaging around through her jewelry collection with her entranced granddaughter sitting next to her can help us see the potentials and caring in parents who may not have had the time or presence of mind to do the same for us when we were children.

Stories of connection, disconnection, and reconciliation are hopeful ones. Every parent, in his or her heart, knows the oppressive strain of parenting. And we are equally oppressed by the powerful cultural myth that parents should be able to manage it all without wrinkling their shirtsleeves or mussing up their hair.

These stories, in contrast, point to the reality of parenting. They are antidotes to overly bleak or overly cheery views. They show us the possible gifts children of all ages bring with them, as well as the difficulties. Children can help heal wounds from one generation to another even as they may also strain and stretch us. When we give to them, we may comfort a part of us that didn't get enough when we were young.

Hidden Wisdom You Can Use

- It's never over as a parent. There are always possibilities for reconciliation and deepening of the relationship with your children.
- You're always connected, even through a divorce; it's never over.
- Adult children and their parents are in a whole new ball game, one different from the needs and pressures of having children or adolescents. Authority and power shifts—you're still the parent,

but more of a coequal. It can be helpful to think about your image of a parent. Is it hierarchical, in which parents are always "in charge"? Can you imagine or do you know of egalitarian relationships between parents and children?

- It's okay to be friends with a grown child; in fact, it can be very healthy for both of you!
- To understand more about what your grown children are experiencing, think about how things changed with your parents as you became an adult. What do you wish had happened differently between you and your parents? What would you like to happen similarly between you and your adult children?
- Grown children at some point may realize that they play an active role in how things go with their parents. Being an adult with your parents is different from being a young child.
- Remember that all parents succeed and all fail. How did yours do both?
- Sometimes hard times wipe out memories of happier times. Try to remember what was good between you long ago. Feel both the sadness, the joy, and the wish that things were better.
- Healing is not necessarily dominated by talking about "feelings" endlessly or rehashing each disappointment or miscommunication.
- Small overtures can mean all the difference—listening more attentively, a kind word or thought or action, a new place to meet, or an activity that changes familiar, frozen patterns of behavior.
- Don't expect enormous changes at the last moment from each other. As one grown son once commented, "Age 70 is not the best time for a parent to learn new psychological defenses." Sometimes small changes and connections can change years of neglect or distance.
- Remember that anger often masks feelings of sadness, hopelessness, and disappointment. Seeing through the provocative behavior to the wish for acknowledgment and connection can be the first step to approaching things in a new, playful or creative way.

- An elderly father once exclaimed at a focus group, "Our children don't realize that as you age the most important thing becomes forgiveness!" Some betrayals may feel unforgivable, but most are not. Often the sins of the past are ones of clumsiness, ignorance, or misfortune, not of intent. If we can truly mourn the lost opportunities of the past, we may find that we can "thaw out" ourselves and our parents.

part three

How We Grow as Parents

chapter ten

When Do I Really Become a Parent?

eing human means experiencing a tension between individuality
and connectedness. As parents we experience that struggle. We
may assume that parenting comes naturally and that all parents
just "bond" with their children, yet we fall in and out of love with them,
and back in love again as time goes on.

When we birth children, we also birth parts of ourselves, connecting or reconnecting with hopes, dreams, capacities for love and
care, as well as darker sides of ourselves—anger, envy, despair, and the
wish to get away from those we also love. Getting our own struggles as
parents into focus can help our children with the very human struggle
with attachment and connection that underlies so much of the conflict
and opportunity of life and can help us parent better.

Gary's story illustrates the way that we discover ourselves as we parent. He is a friendly, thoughtful father who runs a business in the suburbs of Washington, DC. He speaks carefully and hesitantly, as if exploring new territory in telling his story.

Gary: "I feel so proud of myself for having stuck with it."

Like many fathers in parent groups, Gary was quiet until finally one of the mothers asked him about his family. He produced a picture from his wallet. In it we see a red-haired, smiling 2-year-old, reaching for the camera as his father takes his picture. Looking at the picture, he almost apologized, saying he wasn't sure if he had a story, but bravely plunged on anyway.

When my son Eric was born, I knew I wanted to be different from my own father, but I wasn't really sure of how to do that. My father was a good father, but he traveled a lot. He was a salesman for a manufacturing company and spent long parts of every week on the road.

I work from nine to five, get home by dinnertime, and want to be there for my son. When he was first born, I was so ecstatic. Being in the birthing room was one of the greatest experiences of my life. My wife and I made a decision that she would be an at-home mom for our children for their first few years, but I wanted to be a bigger part of Eric's life than my father was in mine.

I started reading to him every night before bed, beginning when he was almost a year old. For the first three months, we didn't get very far into a story before he became bored. He'd start to twist and turn and want to play with the mobile above his bed, or else he'd just drift off to sleep. I wondered if it mattered if I was there or not.

But I stuck with it, and after three months, he started listening and enjoying whole stories. At times he'd try to read the stories himself, looking at the page just like I did. He made no sense at all, but he was very serious and jibbered and jabbered. I loved to watch him, and I also listened carefully to him, telling him how interesting that was, just as if he were really reading a story to me! Eric just turned 2 last month, and he loves to hear me read each night. He has memorized some of the nursery rhymes from *Mother Goose* and repeats them along with me when I read. I feel so proud of myself for having stuck with it.

Gary and his son Eric have to "find" each other and connect. The son's reaction vitalizes the father, helping him discover an ability to enchant his son that he wasn't sure he had, an ability he hadn't felt in his own father, who spent so much time at work that he missed the chance to read to his little boy. We are raised by our children as much as we raise them. Eric's mimicking of his father and his evident gradual enjoyment of Gary's reading to him encourages Gary to keep trying, and it vitalizes the part of him that wants to "father" his son in a different way than his own father did.

In forging these connections, Gary now finds an emotional life with Eric, opening himself up to the world of his child, able to influence and respond to his son. Think of the fathers and mothers who, for whatever reasons, don't discover this!

Gary's story reminds us that connecting with our children means connecting with ourselves and all that parenting stirs up within. Gary fears being too much like his father, yet also feels he was a good man. He fears he can't be different, yet feels hopeful love and fascination with his newborn son. Compared to parenting, what other activity is as lush with possibilities, merging past, present, and future, hope and despair, separation and connection, love and resentment? To truly be able to guide our children into a healthy sense of emotional connection with themselves and others means to be able to recognize without ourselves our own intimate struggles with connecting and staying separate, with the way the past and the future are brought right into the present.

We don't always bond immediately with our children, feeling at home as a parent the first time we hold our babies. Very loving parents can also feel ambivalence, uncertainty, even hostile feelings toward the very child they love so much. Mixed feelings are a reality that we don't talk much about in our culture. Becoming a parent is a scary experience and for some moms and dads feeling really connected with this new part of their lives can take some time. In the stories that follow, we'll find parents confronting their own ghosts from the past and hopes for the future, and finding in some special moments the discovery of a new part of themselves.

Junelle: "Could I really do this?"

A lively, warm woman, Junelle is now married and a full-time mom, with several children. She had been trained as a secretary/bookkeeper, working for a while in her husband's small business. In the focus group, Junelle would from time to time run her hands through her long blonde hair as she told this story about the arrival of her first child, Derek, several years ago.

Becoming a mother was not easy for me. My mother died when I was in my teens. Truly I was petrified of having a baby. I put it off. My husband wanted a child, and I didn't. When your own mother dies when you're still young, having children can be very scary. *Could I really do this?* I wondered.

I felt so proud of myself when I lived through the first weekend home after Derek was born. On the night before I came home for the first time with my baby from the hospital, one of the nurses came into my room in the middle of the night to have me feed my son. I was learning to breastfeed and she woke me about 3 a.m. and started yelling at me, telling me I was doing it all wrong. I was terrified, and felt completely inadequate. I wouldn't let my baby leave the room with her. I kept him beside me, terrified.

That morning I was to be released. My husband picked me up and we drove home and I could not stop crying. I walked into our house in a complete panic with no one to turn to, scared I'd not be able to breastfeed my son. I was engorged and everyone kept telling me to relax, but I couldn't. My baby went over twelve hours without eating. I ended up with him back in the hospital, where a lactation consultant helped me. That was very helpful, but then I had to go back home. Panic struck again. The lactation consultant was there off and on through the weekend and it finally started to go well. I was proud that I stuck with it despite how badly I allowed that nurse to make me feel. I did it! I could give my baby the healthiest start to life. I was still afraid but I made it through. I'm so glad I stuck with it! I really could be a mother despite the nurse who came in and terrorized me that morning. That's why I'm so proud of my decision to stay at home and be with my children. People think I'm not doing anything, but I'm working harder than I ever did in my life!

For Junelle, becoming a mother meant a confrontation with her own lost mother. The beginning of her feeling that she could indeed do it lay in discovering that she could nurture her newborn and that neither she nor her new baby was going to die.

Keith: "I had a list of four things fathers could do."

In his mid 30s, Keith teaches in an urban studies department at a major city university. The eager way he leaned forward in his seat makes clear that he loves to tell stories about his kids. He does so with a wry, ironic tone. Keith's story began in response to the writing prompt "My son's skin . . . " The story he ultimately crafted reminds us that real bonding with our children doesn't always take place right at the birth:

When my first son, Henry, was born, I was 25 and a graduate student. I felt that because I had grown up without a father, I didn't know how to be a father. Since my wife is white and I am black, I wondered a lot what his skin would look like, and I've thought a lot about his skin over the years.

Henry was a planned home birth with only a midwife present, a natural (and cheap) way to do it. When he started to crown and I saw the top of his head, an excitement filled my body. I was struck with wonder. Then his full head popped out, and the wonder filled with fear as the midwife said that the umbilical cord was wrapped twice around his head.

That's when I noticed that my son's skin was blue, a shade I was not expecting. As the cord was unwrapped and the delivery continued, the color slowly, very slowly, started coming in. He was a rich mocha brown color, a skin that was to endure the typical active boyhood marks and scars on his knees and elbows. But that day, when I called my mother to tell her she had a grandson, she asked, "So what color is he?"

I replied, so overwhelmed by it all, "He's blue, Ma."

"No, really, Keith, what color is he?"

"Really, Ma, he's blue!"

I went about becoming a father like a school exercise from my university: Here's a problem, now solve it. I couldn't breastfeed so I had a list of four things fathers could do: Give him a bottle, if hungry; blanket, if cold; put him in the crib, if tired; and if wet, change his diaper.

I kept that list in my mind and would go down it if Henry seemed grumpy. Then if nothing worked, I felt I had done all I could do and could give him to my wife. I was off the hook.

As I look back this all makes sense. My father left our family when I was 4 years old. I had an older sister who helped raise me. My mother became a supermom, she worked and raised us. I grew up in a tough South Side Chicago neighborhood, where there were hardly any dads around—it was all mothers and grandmothers. So, of course, I didn't know what to do. I had no model for fathering. I think my first model for Henry was a cat.

I was doing fine with the day-to-day chores, what I didn't know about was bonding with my child. Then, when Henry was 4 weeks old, he seemed to have a cold. But it wouldn't go away, and after a few days his temperature shot up to 103 degrees. Our pediatrician was on vacation, and I called the ER. When I told them his temperature, the doctor on call said "I'll meet you in the ER in five minutes."

Henry's body was burning up for two days. His temperature reached 104, and they admitted him to the pediatric ward. They gave him a spinal tap, and talked ominously of various possibilities. We lived in the pediatric ward for those two days. They could not get his temperature down, and I saw him with wires coming out of him. We lived right there with him in his hospital room. It was a huge room but very dark and shadowy, not a cheerful place. I felt so helpless. The hospital process was going on all around us all the time. I wondered, *what would happen if we lose him?*

In the middle of the night, I realized that I didn't know how to father, but I equally didn't know how *not* to father. It was awful, until finally after two days, the medication finally did bring his temperature down and the infection went away.

As we gathered our son up to take him home, I was near tears. I realized how much he mattered to me, how scared I had been for three days that he was going to die. At the time, we had no health insurance. Even as I worried about how we'd pay the bills for this, I realized how much I had bonded to Henry. It was a cheap home birth followed by a $5000 bonding experience.

One night I was holding Henry, rocking him to sleep while watching TV, sitting on our concrete floor in our cheap apartment. *American Playhouse* was on, with a version of Kurt Vonnegut's short story "Displaced Persons."

Vonnegut's story is about a black army division after World War II in this little town in Germany. A black sergeant is stationed near a village with an orphanage for displaced boys. One day a biracial boy comes down the road. He's the son of a black American soldier and a German mother, and he has been abandoned. The boy has heard about the black division and has run away to it, searching for his father. He asks the sergeant to take him to America. He believes his father is Joe Louis, a great hero. The sergeant has to take the boy back to the village orphanage, and on the way back they bond. Both of them are displaced and uprooted. The sergeant doesn't want to be in Germany.

Up to then I was kind of drawing a pattern as a father and coloring it in as I went, but I was wearing myself thin. I was holding in a tremendous amount of feeling about my son and my own father and didn't even know it.

I watched the man and the boy, and it was the first time since my father left that I cried about him. I cried about my father's absence. I cried for myself. I cried for *my* boy. There I was holding my boy in my arms wondering what the hell am I doing being a father.

And from that illness and those tears, I built myself as a father. I colored in the silhouette. And I think I've done a pretty good job by my boys and daughter.

Sara: "I felt a lot the fear of harming him."

A successful lawyer, Sara was reluctant at first to tell a story, saying that she'd rather listen to the other parents who had gathered in the small side room at the local YMCA to write and tell stories about parenting. As we went around the small group, though, she asked if she could tell about a moment that she was particularly proud of. She told us: "There are hundreds of moments when I've been proud of my son. It's much harder to be proud of myself as a parent. My mom could be scary in her anger, and I worry that I can be that way too. But I think I've handled limits well." Her eyes sparkled with an intensity as she spoke.

One day, when I was eleven I was playing at my best friend Ellen's house, across the street. She had such a nice mom, who never got out of control. People in the neighborhood knew how angry my mother could get, how she'd start yelling and push me around, even hit me. That day Ellen's mom came into the room and said,

"Your mother just called and wants you home." She knew. "Don't bother cleaning up, just go home," she said.

I walked across the street terrified. I can remember saying to myself: *I never, never want my children to feel as frightened of me as I feel of my own mother.* It was such a horrible way to feel. Remembering that feeling and that resolution has helped me get under control with Alex.

I felt a lot the fear of harming him when he tested limits or got provocative, because I got hit by my mother. She wasn't coherent at those times. "You know what I mean, you know what I mean," she'd say repetitively, and half the time I didn't know what she wanted. My father would try to calm her down, but he wasn't very effective.

One day, when Alex was a preschooler, he needed to have limits set. He had been yelling about wanting the toy of a friend, who had come over. When he kicked his friend I just had it. I sent him to his room, and sent the friend home. Alex needed a time-out in his room. He was very quiet for several minutes, which for preschoolers is half a lifetime. Then he asked if he could come out; he said he was scared. Clearly he had suffered enough and needed a hug. I was glad I could control my own anger to give him a hug and not act like my mother, whom I'd feel overwhelmed by when she got frustrated.

Perhaps we truly take possession of our own parenthood when we connect with our children in a new way, different from our childhood experience. We find we can be like our parents in some ways but also different. Sara really became Alex's mom the day she saw within herself that she could control her anger in a way that her own mother could not. In feeling different from the toxic parts of her own mother, Sarah came to trust herself as Alex's mother.

Ingrid: "I remember wanting to turn away from my first baby."

Ingrid still speaks with a trace of her Norwegian accent. She came over to America in her early 20s, not long after the death of her mother. She is a historian in a college and is married to a doctor. They have several grown children, and her story looks back on the early, difficult days with her newborn daughter (who is now completing high school), when Ingrid didn't want her baby. We talked in her book-lined home, the fireplace roaring in the middle of a snowy winter. Ingrid laughed and said she felt right at home, pointing to a picture of a snowy fjord near her childhood home in Norway.

My mother was a midwife, and I loved her very much. When I was a child, she let me occasionally be present right after a delivery to witness and share the miracle of birth. She died when I was barely 20, and I was devastated. But I never realized just how vital her advice and insight were to me till I was pregnant myself and ready to give birth. It was my husband who wanted to have children. I myself had doubts about bringing them into the world. Yet I loved him and respected that basic of human needs and thus agreed to have children with him.

However, I had a difficult first pregnancy. The birth was high risk, exhausting, and excruciatingly painful. Throughout I wondered why I had ever said yes to this. When the baby finally emerged, she looked beautiful and perfect. She had these enormous wide-open, blue eyes, ready to take me in. But I wasn't ready for her. I said to nobody in particular, "What shall I do with this *thing*?"

Yes, I said "thing," not even calling her a baby. Not wanting to hold her, not even really to look at her, I handed little Sharon over to my husband, who eagerly embraced her and marveled at her perfection. I was completely exhausted and just wanted to be alone. I felt such guilt and despair about my response to her. What if she heard me and was harmed for life because I couldn't love her like a mother is supposed to? Oh, what agony, what regret, what fearful anticipation!

I was a fine mother as far as taking physical care of her was concerned, nursing her, singing her to sleep, and so forth. I remembered how my mother did it. I had all the requisite skills, and I certainly was willing to give it my best effort. But I simply didn't feel any special love or connection to my child. And during all those early weeks, I ached to have my mother back to ask her for advice and insight and receive her comfort and assurance. How profoundly I missed her now that I was trying to be a mother myself.

Still worried about my attachment to little Sharon, I went to see a counselor at our health plan when she was about 4 months old. The woman doctor watched us for a while, then asked whether she could hold the baby. "Of course," I replied, and handed Sharon over to her.

"What a bright and responsive baby you have! Did you see how she first made eye contact with you before she let me take her? You have nothing to worry about. You have done a fine job of bonding with your daughter. Just give it time. Watch and savor how she looks to you for approval and how she trusts and loves you!"

Needless to say, I was immensely relieved and comforted. It was the kind of affirmation all mothers need to hear from more experienced women when they first start the incredible journey of mothering.

Now at 17, my blond-haired, blue-eyed Sharon has grown into a lovely young woman with whom I share a deep and abiding love. She's in her high school drama society, and when she steps out on to the stage with such conviction and pizzazz, I know I have done fine by her and by my mother.

Ingrid's birth as a mother meant living through her wish for her own lost mother. Perhaps we all experience in becoming a parent the yearning for our own parents. In some small way, perhaps, Ingrid was able to take

*from the counselor at her HMO the encouragement she yearned for from
her own mother.*

Mary: "Not only am I not sure I love this kid, I'm not sure she loves me."

*Mary and Karen, parents who are lesbian, are raising their children in a
suburb of Philadelphia. We talked, the three of us, in their lovely home,
which they slowly have had renovated over the years, as their finances
allowed. Mary is a schoolteacher, and Karen works as an administrator
in a HMO. They have adopted two Paraguayan children over the past
ten years, Erika and Meg. As we talked over their dinner table, Karen
often nodded her head in agreement as Mary described her disappointment and confusion, all part of her struggle to feel like one of the
mothers of her youngest daughter. Clearly Mary and Karen had talked
about these matters before. The story began with a shameful memory
that Mary worked to put into words.*

Just last night Meg brought home a writing assignment from her
fourth grade. She had been asked to write about an important event
in her life. She decided to write about coming from Paraguay to live
with us.

Meg started writing about the moment when she met me for the
first time in the orphanage. She started almost muttering under her
breath, "This person was my mom, but who was this person?" I can
remember the staff of the orphanage was yelling, "Meg, come meet your
mom!" She was doing her best to be excited, but inside she wondered,
"Who is this total stranger, so tall?" I must have looked like a giant.

I took Meg to look on the bathroom wall, where we keep a poster
of kids with all these expressions on their faces to match their feelings.
Meg said, "I don't know how I felt!" We looked at the wall, and I asked
if it was anger or surprise. Then she finally exclaimed, "I was confused!"

So we talked about that. But the bottom line is that *I was* confused.
I went down alone to Paraguay to get Meg, and I still remember
walking into the orphanage. I had seen one gray, slightly blown up
photo of her that had probably been taken a year earlier. I remember
walking into this classroom, which had about twenty-five kids in it, and

they were all playing some kind of singing and clapping game. I look in the classroom to see her, but no one looked like the picture I had. Then I saw one kid that I thought might be her and I focused on that kid, thinking, *"This is going to be my daughter!"* When the staff picked out another kid, I was totally disoriented. I thought, *"Wait, no, no; that's not it; that's not her!"*

In that moment of confusion in the orphanage, it was like I was expecting to get another Erika. Someone who was more like Erika—dark hair, dark skin. I was very disconcerted by what Meg looked like; I hadn't expected that. Also, it just felt easier to bond with Erika, who came to us as an infant. Meg was a fully formed little child, 3 years old.

This is very hard to admit, but for the first couple of years, I went through tremendous turmoil about this kid, as Meg was going through *her* turmoil. For the first three months, she was on her best behavior. But after that, she started to go through great turmoil and many hateful intense behaviors which made total sense.

She was very different from Erika. Meg was much tougher in school. The teachers wanted to put her in all kinds of special programs, which we resisted. When she was not throwing tantrums, she was bonding with Karen and shutting me out. I remember thinking, *"Not only am I not sure I love this kid, I'm not sure she loves me."*

In addition, Karen and I were fighting, fighting, fighting, rather than aligning with each other.

Finally, one day, I looked at Karen and Meg and said, "I don't want to have anything to do with either one of you anymore!" It felt so beyond a mother being angry; it felt like an unforgivable sin. I had this deep sense of *"Oops, I went beyond what I should."*

Fortunately, Karen didn't take it as forever, and we've talked a lot about those difficult months, gotten to a new place. She had, she's told me, an unwavering belief that we'd bond. Each child is difficult; they push us to find the depth in ourselves. The easier relationships just happen. With Meg, I've learned a lot about loyalty within myself. When Meg and I get along, there is this kind of joy. Everybody doesn't love everybody perfectly all the time.

Mary's journey toward her motherhood identity with Meg has been through disappointment and ambivalence. However, by sticking with it, she has been able to learn about new parts of herself—her ability to commit and be loyal even when she doesn't love her new daughter "perfectly."

THE MYTH OF PERFECT LOVE

"Everybody doesn't love everybody perfectly all the time," Mary reminds us. Maybe that's a load off our backs, not having to live up to a myth of "perfect love." If we don't have to be perfect, then we can find the space to play and experiment, as Gary did when he allowed himself to read and read to his son until finally his son was able to show how connected he was with him.

Parts of ourselves are being born along with our children. Sara, for instance, finds herself as a mother when she realizes she can set limits differently from her own mother. Mary finds she has the patience and commitment to be there for Meg and writes later to tell me how happy she was one recent morning to find that Meg decided to get up at 5 a.m. with Mary so "just the two us could go shopping together—no one else in this family would have done that! It was a special time for us."

So too, Junelle and Ingrid each are slowly "born" as mothers, finding that they can transform their fear and sorrow at the absence of their own mothers into the capacity to respond to what their children need. For Ingrid it helped to have the friendly, available support of a counselor at her health plan, who could say to her what her lost mother was not able to: "*You can do this. Look, your daughter loves you and needs you.*" The counselor's calming, reassuring words helped Ingrid to find the calm part of herself that knew very well how to mother, the part of herself nurtured perhaps at her own mother's side during midwife rounds. For Sara, the moment she heard her young son's plea for reassurance through his bedroom door helped her see that she is really separate from her own mother, a realization that we need to learn over and over.

These lessons are never learned once and for all. We are born and reborn throughout our parenting years. Sara manages to calm herself and not get lost in angry rage, like her mother who could not be calmed. Instead she finds she is different, even if her mother's explosive anger may live within her and does not go away—at least at that moment she calms herself and gives Alex what he needs. No one in that household is terrorized as she was as a child, and in that difference, a new part of Sara is strengthened to come into the world as a mother.

These moments of struggle are hopeful in themselves. Keith's story shows us how adversity can enrich your life, a theme that reappears through out this book. Born of the terror of losing his son, Keith became aware of how much his son meant to him. The shock of his son's fever jolted the man into taking the risk of forging a new sense of self as a father, different from what he knew from his own absent father.

There's an intergenerational connection here—having children means reconnecting with the parent within ourselves, the images of our mother and fathers that we carry around from our own childhoods. Connecting to his hidden tears at the absence of his own father helped Keith open up to his fatherhood. For Keith the tears at his father's absence are the beginning of his awareness of his son's need for him, just as for Sara the ability to remember her own fear of her mother as a child is the wellspring of her ability to return to Alex and sense his own need not just for limits but also for connection with his mom.

At some level, as parents, we are all "displaced persons." We explore new territory, sometimes far from our familiar childhood homes, in search of connection and hope, a path often—though not always—chosen voluntarily. We can partly rely on our native tongue of caring, the one we learned as children in our families, but as parents we also learn the language ourselves as our kids grow and change. Being able to hang in there and be present throughout our child's birth, seeing the look of love in our children's eyes, and hearing how much they love and need us bring into life those parts of ourselves that want to respond.

The emotional birth of our family may lie in our awareness as parents of how much *we* grow and change, new parts of ourselves come to life as our children grow and change. As the stories in the following chapters make clear, we continue to grow up right along with them. For some of us, the emotional birth of the family and our birth as truly pre-sent and available parents may take place months, even *years,* after the actual birth date of our children. And we aren't of course just "born" once as parents; we are reborn and need to rebirth and reinvent our-selves through the parenting years, as our children grow and change.

Hidden Wisdom You Can Use

- Be mindful that you're going through a transition as a new parent.
- Bonding is not perfect and doesn't always happen right in the birthing room or when you first adopt a child.
- Mixed feelings after the arrival of a child are common. You may love your child and also feel anger, fear, envy, and regret.
- Think about your own parents and what you most wanted from them, That's often a good guide to what your children need.
- Your child loves you despite your confusion and hesitation—and his or hers.
- Thinking "bad" thoughts is different from acting on them. Count to ten or leave the room for a moment before acting.
- It takes time to get a child's attention and interest. Keep trying, and it will pay off!
- Fathers are as important emotional providers as mothers.
- Parenthood is important to your own identity and develop-ment. You get love, touching, and hope from your kids. Make time for that.

chapter eleven

The Spiritual Journeys of Parents

A s parents, we are inevitably confronted with issues of spirituality and faith, both our own and our children's. Having children can raise anew unanswered questions about belief and meaning that may have been put aside when younger.

What parent doesn't wonder if it's okay to be unsure about faith and spirituality? Can we share our own uncertainties, or must we live up to the all-knowing and god-like images of parenthood that are still alive and well in our culture?

Parents and children are often on a spiritual journey together. Opening ourselves to our children's search to find meaning in the world can be a source of renewed wonder and understanding and can be helpful to our children as well. Certainly that has been true in my own family. My wife was raised Protestant and I Jewish. Our children's struggles with their religious heritages—particularly our decision to raise them Jewish—helped rekindle my own spiritual search and healed some of the painful alienation I felt from my own religious heritage. As they came of age spiritually, so did I.

Consider Paul's story, about the day that an ordinary errand with his 10-year-old daughter, Nancy, became an unexpected moment of spiritual dialogue between parent and child.

Paul: "She was feeling what *I* hoped to feel."

Paul is 54 years old and has been married for many years. He is the owner of a busy bowling alley complex in a suburb of Cleveland. He's an active, robust man, used to being around people, which made the shyness with which he talked about religion all the more poignant.

We're Jewish, which is not all that easy for me to say. I've felt very mixed about my religious background. I *feel* Jewish, but I grew up in the 1950s in a suburb of Cleveland. My parents were what you'd call "cultural Jews." They were very aware of Jewish culture but weren't interested in the Jewish religion, which they considered barely above superstition. When I was 3 years old, some kid called me a "dirty Jew," and I ran home and asked my mother what that meant. They sent me to Hebrew school so that I'd have some idea of how to deal with that.

But I wasn't supposed to really become a devout Jew—certainly not go regularly to synagogue. Oddly, we did light the Shabbot candles every Friday night. And I was bar mitzvahed at age 13. But I wasn't drawn to my religion. Many of the Jews I knew seemed so interested in possessions and accumulating things. Anyway, I married a woman who was raised Jewish, who is also not very religious.

After our daughter Nancy was born, we began to think about what we wanted for her in terms of values and religion.

We felt it would be important for Nancy to have some connection to religion. We wanted her to have a strong sense of values. So a few years ago, we started sending her to Hebrew school on Sundays, and she has been making a commitment slowly to her Judaism. She doesn't have a lot of Jewish classmates in her school or in our neighborhood, so she's constantly questioning and thinking about Judaism. She'll sometimes say, "How come I have to be Jewish?"

Her questions helped me realize how much I've turned against my own Jewishness. We've begun to light Shabbot candles on Friday nights to celebrate and acknowledge the beginning of the Sabbath, the time of rest and family connection. We all look forward to the candle lighting, and Nancy often will light the candles and say the prayers.

The other day we were in a craft store not too far from here, buying some supplies for her jewelry making. We were laughing, talking, joking. It was after we had gone out to lunch together; it was a fun time. I saw on the shelf beeswax in different colors for decorating candles. I had the idea we could make the Shabbot even more fun. I whispered softly, "Nancy! Look, we could use this beeswax to decorate the Shabbot candles."

Nancy looked right at me and said, "Why are you whispering?"

There were a few people in the store, but it was hardly as if I needed to keep quiet. Deep down, though, I knew why: It was because I was ashamed to make public that we were Jewish in this non-Jewish community. Nancy must have read my mind. She admonished me, *"We can be proud of our religious heritage, you know, Daddy!"*

I was dumbfounded and so grateful. She was willing to stand up for her religious heritage. She was feeling what *I* hoped to feel. I was so grateful that she didn't feel the pit of shame that I felt so much growing up and so happy that she was feeling more comfortable with her Jewishness.

We can imagine too what is going on here for parent and child. Nancy is growing into her sense of belief, based in part on her identifications with her father and mother. It's as if she is urging her father to stand up for what he believes so that she can believe too. And in doing so, she is leading her father toward a deeper reconciliation with his own religion and his childhood experience of it. Paul is finding in the Shabbot candles a reconnection to his own childhood awe. He is exploring a different kind of connection to his own history, owning parts of himself that he hasn't before. Even amidst their skepticism, his parents provided some warmth, a friendly family ritual that brought mother and father and children together on Friday nights, memories of candles flickering, gentle prayers, perhaps a cozy meal together.

The smells, sights, sounds of ritual and connection are often the deepest treasures we can give our children—candles burning brightly, warm bread, fragrant spices, voices happily lifted. These are the nutriments for feeling safe and at home in the world. They ground us. How wonderful when we and our children can return to them, even if only for moments out of a busy day or week.

The doors to faith are ours to find, and we each open them in our own way. It's not necessary to again embrace painful experiences of religion, to feel trapped in a church or synagogue or mosque or other faith community deaf to your experiences, listening to an oppressive sermon or prayers in an unintelligible language.

The stories in this chapter focus on two spiritual themes. The first has to do with awe, the second with creating ritual. Moments of awe happen when we as parents are renewed, astounded, and moved by our children and their appreciation of the world. Often in these moments, we hear echoes of the deepest issues of meaning and faith, life and death, love and commitment.

The theme of creating ritual occurs when we, with our children, are able to breathe life into old rituals or create new, meaningful ones that foster a sense of spiritual home in the world for our families. Sometimes, through our children, we can reinvent new forms of our old faith—luckily, astonishingly—making new pots out of broken clay, finding again moments that move us and remind us of specialness beyond ourselves.

These spiritual moments can come at times that we may think of as very "nonreligious." Spirituality and organized religion are not the same thing, and parents may find themselves spiritually renewed in the most unexpected moments and places.

Annette: "I don't want you to die!"

Raised Catholic, Annette is the chief of staff for the senior vice president of a large computer hardware company outside New York City. She's 35 years old and has been married for eight years to Jack, a reporter for a large metropolitan newspaper. Annette brought an ironic tone to the parents writing group the evening she participated. She knows she is a go-to person and describes herself as "good at making an agenda get done," a point illustrated by the unexpected call from her car phone to my office asking for alternative directions when she found herself stuck in traffic fifteen minutes before the start of the group. She made it on time. Annette's real-life ability to control events lends a poignant backdrop to the story she wrote.

I've been in a muddle about religion since I was a teenager. For twenty years I told myself that I didn't believe in God anymore. Now I'm not so sure. My husband and I were both raised Catholic, and when we became parents, we said there was no way that we would bring our son into the Church! There were just too many disappointments. My mother has always had faith, and I've envied her even as she enrages me. She would tell me when I was little to "be a good girl because God always answers your prayers."

When she and my father were yelling at each other in the living room, I used to pray to God at bedtime to make things right between them. But He didn't. "God looks out for His own," she used to say. When our cat—the stray we found one Thanksgiving years before—came down with leukemia, she told me to pray for him. I did and then cried and cried at the vet's office when they told me Pumpkin had died. I didn't get much of the straight scoop from my mother about a lot of things and certainly not from the Church either. Amidst all the Latin and incense and praying, there was not a lot of comfort for a little girl struggling with loss and death.

So I'd done absolutely nothing with my kids. Our eldest, Chris, is just starting to think about God. He's 6½. The biggest way it came up for me was last year when we were on Christmas vacation visiting my mother in Florida. One night in our hotel room, Chris was trying to figure out the family relationships. He said,

"Well, Nana, where's *your* mother?"

My mother didn't know what to do; her cheeks got all red, and she put her hands in her lap. Not liking to deal with questions about death, she said, "She's in heaven."

Chris asked her where that was. My mother started to stammer out that it was "up in the sky somewhere." Chris deserved a better answer. My mom never told me the truth, and goddamn it, I was going to tell Chris the truth! So I said to him, "Chris, Nana's mom is dead. She died."

It struck him like a thunderbolt. It's one of the most painful moments I can remember in parenting. In that second, he figured out that people die. He got very subdued, didn't want to talk anymore, and left his seat on the couch near his grandmother to play with his plastic car collection on the floor, very quietly, without a lot of the "va-rooms" that usually accompany his pretend racing.

After my mother left, while we were brushing our teeth for bed, Chris came over to me and his father. He said, "Mommy, are you going to die?"

"Yeah, honey I am . . . " Then I added, "Probably not for a really long time. That's what happens; it's part of nature."

He looked at me and said, "I don't want you to die!"

Well, oh my god, we were all in tears. He was crying. Jack was crying. We were all a mess. I had to recognize that I didn't want people to die either, and there was my 83-year-old mother in her cottage just down the road, getting old in Florida. How much time did we have left?

Then Chris asked, "Do children die?"

That really almost finished us all off. His pain was so palpable. He's been talking about when people die, when we die. It's like he's planning on what to do when his parents are gone.

Since he's made death a topic in our house, Jack and I have been talking a lot about it. I've begun to think about my parent's death, my own, the pain I felt way back then when my cat died, and how that was handled, about how alone I felt.

Chris didn't have anything to hold on to, anything to really give him hope, and I realized that I didn't either. I could talk to him about death as a natural part of life, but that's not the same as the grandeur of the sacraments, the whole community of worshipers around you. I wanted some comfort as well, and, in fact, it *was* wonderful to be able to speak to God, to turn to Him for some comfort.

I'm scared, though, because the disappointment when my prayers were not answered was so devastating when I was young. There were many nights when my parents were fighting that I'd cry into the pillow, wishing God would answer my prayers. But I can also remember how wonderful it was to hope and to believe—the relief I felt with my mother and father in church, the power of the music, and the wonderful way the priest looked with his colorful vestments and ornaments. And I can remember the sweet smell of the incense. There was something there for me.

I'm not sure how we'll sort it all out. The idea of going back into a church with a full heart touches a very tender place in myself. And I don't like much of the New Age stuff. We've been shopping around, going to different churches, not all of them Catholic. We'll see. But I am so grateful to my son for showing me his need and my own.

We're not all that different from our children—their needs may mirror our own. Chris raised questions that his mother Annette pushed aside growing up. His tears opened up his mother's. She thought about the difficulty of her parent's marriage, her own powerlessness, fears about death, even the death of her dear cat so long ago. As a child struggling with loss and uncertainty, Annette did not find much comfort from her parents or the Church. She is now valiantly trying to do better for her son and feels that he needs the organized frame of a religious tradition in order not to feel so alone in the world, a concern raised by many parents who want their children to have somewhere trustworthy to turn to rather than be isolated when struggling with the reality of adult life and choices. May we not also suspect that Annette is recognizing her own vulnerability in the world, not just her son's? Her mother is elderly and facing death more directly, and she can't protect her son from the reality of loss or herself from the fear of losing her child—a most basic fear of any parent. In Annette's sense of emotional and spiritual homelessness lie the roots of her spiritual journey at age 35.

Perhaps too as parents our spiritual uncertainty can help us understand our parent's limitations—we may feel that "the older generation got it wrong, and we as parents are going to do it right now." But then we too as parents confront the same human difficulty they did in offering support and consolation through life experiences without easy answers. An opportunity for forgiveness (of ourselves and of them) may lie in seeing that we're all in the same boat, rowing as best we can.

Lydia: "I saw his grace then and my own."

Lydia and her husband are Quakers. They run a dairy farm in upstate New York, along with the help of their large family, comprised of several older daughters and a teenage son. While (or perhaps because) she has raised several daughters, Lydia confessed to the writing group that "boys have always seemed like a mystery to me," which makes the spiritual connection she finds with her son all the more meaningful.

Although I've grown up around men, I don't always see them very clearly. I've never had brothers, and my husband and I had several daughters before our son Ricky was born. My own father was a very dominant and colorful man. He helped run a railroad company in upper New York State. He drank hard, lived hard, and died too young. When we were growing up back in the 1940s, he'd get pulled over for speeding after he drank too much. I remember my dad could argue and cajole the police officer into apologizing for disturbing us! I always felt that if a family was like a steam locomotive, then it's the men who get to toot the horn while the women have to shovel the coal.

Now I find myself the mother of a teenage son. My husband and I are Quakers. We attend the Sunday prayer vigils in the Village Meeting Hall, near our house. Ten to fifteen of us gather and sit in silence. It is really quite wonderful to be connected without words. There's magic to the circle; people only speak when called by the spirit to do so. Then there'll be more silence. It's very calm and serene.

When Ricky was 14, he would sometimes join us. This was a time when he was having a lot of difficulty. There were angry outbursts in school and at home too—particularly about assignments not completed. It was scary. He's a big, gangling kid—over six feet with long, solid arms. He has his father's thick, muscular, tightly packed body.

There were several Sundays when Ricky suddenly appeared at the meeting hall and tried to come in through the door. There is nothing noisier than Ricky trying to be quiet. We would hear the door creak open, then his feet scuffling across the wooden floor. People squirmed and moved and coughed to make a place. I was happy to see him, but it was always a noisy moment, though he was always very quiet. He would sit down next to his father, who would make some gesture to acknowledge him—pat him on the head, put his arm around his shoulder, touch his hand. Within about five minutes, we would all be back in our silence. Ricky would sit there, quietly. Here was this strapping adolescent in so much trouble in other parts of his life, sitting in silence with us all, so peaceful! He worked very hard to be quiet and together with us in silence; he was so respectful of what we were doing. Watching him, I felt my whole body relax and warm to him. I realized how gentle and caring he was, that this was not only an angry adolescent lumbering around but also my son who wanted to find a place for himself, a quiet and gentle one, who maybe had to squirm and twist to do it, but he wanted to. I saw his grace then and my own. I didn't feel like we were male and female, or mother and son, but rather that we were simply two loving human beings.

In a different context, we may see our children differently. The spiritual world can be a place where a son or daughter can express their gentler, more interconnected parts of self. Lydia, for example, found a moment of spiritual connection with her son that allowed her to see the deeper gentleness that had been masked for her by his size and masculinity.

Karen: "Watching her awakened a little girl inside of me."

An infectious laughter dots Karen's demeanor in our story writing group. Her story illuminates the second theme in the spiritual journey of parents: finding meaningful rituals as a family. As Karen struggles with a coming of age ceremony to mark her daughter Judy's 10th birthday, she finds that the girl leads her mother toward a new vision of faith and "sacred places."

I was raised Episcopalian. Religion was never very joyful in my house growing up. Mother is a rather proper woman and always referred to religion as "the foundation of your character." The Church *was* like the foundation of a house to me—heavy and concrete and gray. My parents dragged my brothers and me to church and religious instruction. I did lots of squirming, trying to stay still. The minister would stare down at us in our pew, not amused at my fidgeting. The music was great, and the singing, but what I most loved was to hang out at the swing set in the little playground next door when we were allowed to go outside.

I married a man who was raised Catholic but was basically agnostic. When Judy was born, I wanted at that time to baptize her. But he said no. A couple of years later, when we separated, he wanted to baptize her in the Catholic Church, and I felt very strongly against that. So Judy didn't have any baptism.

After the divorce, I felt my mother in my head saying, "Take her to church so that she has some foundation!" So for a couple of years, I sat in church, grinding my teeth, and took her to Sunday school, until one day in the car on the way home, Judy made the funniest comment.

She said "Mom, why are we doing this?"

"Because I want you to learn about this stuff."

Judy replied, "It's okay. But you know they're always talking about God, Our Lord, in there, and that's not how I think about God."

She made it really clear that she wasn't interested. So we stopped going. Then on her 10th birthday, several friends were talking about confirmation and baptism, and Judy was concerned that she hadn't been "named," that she hadn't gone through a ritual of naming. She was very clear that she didn't want the ceremony to be in a church or otherwise connected to organized religion. She decided to have a naming ceremony in honor of the Earth and the Sky.

We have a friend and neighbor who is very versed in Native American healing and celebratory rituals. So she went to Donna and talked with her about some options. I wanted to be a part of it, and she was okay with that but she was very clear that *she* was going to create it and decide who was going to be there. She invited four of us to a ceremony on a hilltop near our house at sunset one summer evening. She worked it all out, picked out the symbols for the four elements of earth and the seven directions of the spirit, and from her own mouth came this incredible wisdom about water, about feathers, and animals and trees and the Earth and masculine and feminine.

I just sat there and cried the whole time. For each direction, she was very thoughtful. "Here's water, and it means this . . . " And I knew they were not Donna's words because that's not how she works. It was the most astounding thing. She was 10 years old!

Watching her awakened a little girl inside of me who doesn't want to just be good and sit still but who can also be down and dirty, who loves dirt and water and the elements, who can play in the trees and breathe deeply and not just be a sweet little thing. Judy was making a place for that in her church, her sacred places, and I felt that maybe I could make a place for that too in the church inside me.

In giving to our children, we may free up a part of ourselves. Karen gave her daughter the freedom to create the ritual she needed; perhaps now she will be able to give herself the same gift.

Barbara: "I love the gentleness of the priest and the Mass these days."

Sometimes one generation can help free up another. Barbara's story reminds us of this, with a different twist. As a child, Barbara found Catholic school to be a refuge from a difficult home situation. The order and strictness of Catholicism helped her get into adulthood. Today she is a successful interior decorator, married with several small children. Now, when she is in the Mass with her young children, another hunger surfaces—not for rules and strictness but for a gentle and kind welcome from the Church. It's a welcome she's found only recently when in church with her children.

I went through Catholic school for twelve years, and yet I feel the way I was raised was weird. All my five brothers and sisters in front of me had alcohol and drug problems. I was the youngest, and I remember as a young kid making a decision that I was not going to wind up like that, that I was going to be different from all of them. What that meant was that I decided to listen to what my parents were saying, because I was the one not getting into trouble. I was going to do everything right.

So I went to Catholic school and listened to what all the nuns were saying. Don't do this; don't do that. They whacked everyone around. I took in all the abuse and the intensity. I made it through by praying to God. When I look back, my feelings about Catholic school are positive, but at the time, I was petrified every day. The nuns were mean. If someone talked in class or pulled a prank, bam! They were at the board or getting slammed across the knuckles or worse.

That didn't happen to me because I decided never to get into trouble, but it sure scared me, and I went around scared a lot. I used to think that Catholic schools were so brutal, but I wonder if I hadn't been there what my life would be like, because they told me what to do and I did it. Now here I am happily married and a mother myself.

Now when I go to church, I'm just a regular person going to 9 a.m. Mass. Yet there's not a time I don't cry. I embarrass my kids, particularly during the family masses. Everyone brings their kids, and the priest is always bringing kids up to the altar, relating the sermon to them. I love what he's trying to teach those kids. It's what I want them to know. I hope they're taking it in, and also I wish someone had treated me so nicely as a kid. The tears just flow, even as I try not to cry.

When I was a kid in Mass, it was always about sitting still and not talking. It was always "take that child outside; they're being rude." Now when kids cry and fidget, the priest smiles and says, "It's God talking through him." He doesn't mind their crying. The priest is so gentle and calm, inviting the child to stay, telling us that God speaks through the child's tears. I love the gentleness of the priest and the Mass these days. He's speaking to me as well as my kids!

Through our children, we can get back some of what we didn't get enough of ourselves as children. The Mass now calms Barbara, as it does her children; she finds in the gentle welcome of the priest some of the calming and soothing she sought as a child and didn't receive. For the young Barbara, the Church provided the structure and containment she needed, but not the sweetness. Now she finds just that missing ingredient as a Mom in church with her children.

Selena: "I realized how jumbled up all of this is in my mind."

Selena was raised Jewish in the Midwest, but she married a Catholic man whom she met while working in the Central Valley of California, where she now lives. She is 45 years old. Her dark hair and tanned skin, the slight Spanish accent after years of living in what she calls "a Mexican family here in California," seem a far cry from the Chicago of her youth. She is the mother of two daughters, ages 10 and 6.

My kids are Mexican, not half and half. And that's a good thing. Their grandmother is Catholic and Mexican. She's a classic Mexican grandmother—very loving, quite stern, but very involved with her grandchildren. Spanish is a very warm, passionate language, and she can speak to them very tenderly even when scolding them. She loves to make tortillas with them, to help them collect the firewood for the stove on chilly mornings.

For me, the loving part of my family has been the Mexican Catholic part, not the Jewish part that I brought along from growing up in Chicago. My parents, my aunts and uncles, have a hard time showing their love. It was always "don't leave the table till you've eaten your chicken liver." Yuck! So for me, for many years, there's been an unloving presence of Judaism.

Yet I can remember, even as a child, having a warm feeling walking past the synagogue and hearing the cantor singing. He was a kind man, and I loved the sound of the Hebrew being chanted. But I hadn't thought much about Judaism for many years, and our kids know nothing about it.

So the other day I walked into a pharmacy in town with my kids, to get some toothpaste and stuff. Near the cash register, three Mexican boys were playing on the floor, spinning around what looked like an odd sort of top. When I looked closer, I realized that it was a dreidel, the spinning top used to celebrate Chanukah! One of my kids asked the boys what it was, and they didn't know either. When you spun the dreidel it played a tune, and the kids wanted to know what that was.

As it spun, the dreidel caught the light beautifully. I got down on the floor with the kids. I had to play with it. I showed them how to spin it and told them about what it meant. I realized that this was the week of Chanukah, when you often play dreidel games. So I told the kids about Chanukah and how to play dreidel games. Then they all wanted to spin it. I told them about the song "Dayenu, Dayenu," which we used to sing when I was a kid in Hebrew school, and the song *"I have a little dreidel."* That's the tune that came from the dreidel when it spun around.

There we all were, on the floor of a pharmacy in the Mexican section of our town, playing dreidels. I had to buy it. And I took it home for us.

I realized how jumbled up all of this is in my mind. But I do know that playing dreidel with my children made me feel very good; it was something to share from my background, something warm that I loved from Judaism.

There is a real vulnerability of parents around spiritual matters. Many of us are still working out matters of faith, family heritage, and groundedness in the world, even while our kids are doing the same. Sometimes we may feel that we have to look or act as though we have it all together, but in fact children profit from the open sharing of our questions about god, meaning, and values.

Moments of spirituality involve deep connection with ourselves, and even a small interaction can mean a different kind of connection with our own history, with parts of ourselves we have put aside and that may yearn now to be re-acknowledged. If we can connect with these parts of ourselves, we can offer our children a chance to connect with different parts of themselves. We may offer a growing space to our children as we open ourselves up, even as they do the same for us.

Mary: "The spirit was audible because of the music."

Mary is a 42-year-old college professor married to a professor in the law school of a major university in the Northeast. She comes from a family of successful professionals and humorously mentioned in the parents writing group that "I guess I am driven and know only two speeds—fast and faster!"

I'll tell you about what was a deeply spiritual moment, although I can't explain exactly why. It happened when my daughters started to spontaneously dance in church one evening. You see, every summer we spend several weeks in a small cabin in the Pocono Mountains. It's the same place where my family has been going since I was a small child. The cabin is in a small town, where we got to know the people, and even though we were though we were thought of as the "summer people," I always felt very loved and accepted.

Going there with my children has a lot of resonance for me. As a kid, this was a special place for me. I remember the summer months in the country. My parents were pretty hard-driving types, both professionals, very committed to their work, but in the summer, I'd see them relax. I can remember the little sleeping cabin my sister and I slept in behind the bigger cabin that my parents used. So many nights we'd sit out under the stars in the triangle between the big cabin, our cabin, and a friend's house. I recall the warm summer air. We'd sing songs. I can still remember "By the Light of the Silvery Moon," all of us singing—my family, our neighbors, and their two sons, whom I thought were the most wonderful and handsome boys in the world. I remember my mother laughing and happy, enjoying my singing. She wasn't happy very often. That was so many years ago, but I remember it so vividly!

So there we were, about a month ago, in the little church in town. The local chamber music group was giving a concert with only four instruments. My daughters, ages 3 and 5 at the time, were dressed up in their finest duds for this event, these wonderful dresses my husband and I had bought for them. It was a very intimate setting. We were in the second row, and there were candles up on a table in the front, giving off this wonderful glow.

Allison and Jeannette stood up quietly, walked into the aisle and just started to dance, very slowly, gracefully. The quartet was playing a simple melody, Mozart maybe, and it was not really dance music. Who would think of dancing to chamber music?! But the girls got it just right and danced so beautifully—the whole spirit of it. That night with my daughters, the spirit was audible because of their waltzing around. Lots of times it's not audible, but my daughters felt it and danced to it. And I could see it and smile and appreciate them and their beautiful little girl-ness. There was just such grace to that moment.

Spirituality lives outside organized religion as well as within it. It's often there with our kids in ordinary, unexpected moments, if we can open ourselves to it, as the next story affirms as well.

Jackie: "Through the retelling of my game, he taught me so much about life."

Spiritual moments can take place anywhere, even on the golf course. Jackie is an EAP counselor for a health maintenance organization. She's divorced with several grown children. When invited to write about "a moment of real spirituality in my family growing up," Jackie said eagerly that she wanted to write about golfing!

I don't remember my father ever going to church. A lot of the values he taught us were through the game of golf, actually. He talked of being a good sports person, being honest, being on time, and not cheating.

I think a lot of the enjoyment came from being outside and loving the walking. He would say that his spiritual experience was walking down a fairway on a Sunday morning. There were a lot of things he taught us. Even though he wasn't there when I played golf, he'd insist I tell him all about my game when I returned home. We'd sit in the living room for hours and talk about wind speed, T shots, sand traps, the condition of putting greens and how to deal with them. Through the retelling of my game to him he taught me so much about life. He spoke of sportsmanlike behavior. He said that he expected me to keep my emotions in check no matter what, that you shouldn't get really angry that you made a bad shot or really happy that you made a good shot, that you should keep everything on an even keel all the time. Those have been important lessons that I have taken to heart in my life.

Parents don't have to take their kids every week to religious services in order to communicate a broad and meaningful frame of values. You can have a deeply spiritual connection with your children and the world without seeming "religious."

Elizabeth: "There was the freshness of the moment."

Family rituals can have a powerful "sensory" impact on us, both as parents and kids. What may seem everyday or ordinary to the parent can be treasured for years to come by the children, as Elizabeth's story reminds us. She remembers back many years to recall the true spirituality that went on in what looked like an ordinary walk to church.

Spirituality for me means connection. Walking to and from church on Sundays with my father was my favorite time when I was school age. It was a special time we got to spend together. He worked such long hours during the week and came home at our bedtime or even after. So my sister and I got to walk with him on Sundays, since he didn't drive. My stepmother stayed home to cook Sunday dinner. I didn't mind going to church because of those walks. They were usually the same route, occasionally a different one. He made up different games and songs to keep us occupied. One ritual was to look for money. We always used to find a nickel, dime, or quarter. I wonder now if he used to drop them for us to find—we were so excited! We'd talk about school or make up questions about sports or current events. My sister and I always wore hats to Church, usually with wide brims. On sunny days, the brims threw all sorts of shadows, and we made up names for ourselves to match the way our heads and hats looked on the pavement. She'd call me "pot head" when the brim looked like a pot handle and I'd call her "spoon head" in return.

It was a time of special closeness and happiness. On the way home, we'd always have a treat, especially in the cool lap of fall and winter. There was the freshness of the moment: birds singing, dew, fallen trees, the sweet perfume of my father's *Old Spice* aftershave, the stop at the drugstore lunch counter for a cup of hot cocoa. I've never smelled cocoa with the kind of aroma of that Sunday cocoa with dad after church, with its dollop of whipped cream.

For Elizabeth, much of the spirituality of her childhood took place before she even walked into the church!

Ariane: "Saying prayers with Rene brought back that wonderful feeling."

Rituals can be calming and soothing and can provide a sense of safety and order in a world that can seem chaotic and frightening, as during or after a bitter divorce. Ariane is a single mother who found a way to weave a helpful set of spiritual rituals that proved calming and supportive to her young daughter Rene and herself during a difficult time.

When my daughter was 8 years old, she had a lot of nightmares and was afraid of a lot of things. We did have troubles at the time. My husband and I were going through some tough times together. Rene would wake up scared, complaining about headaches and stomach pains. We took her to a doctor who also had some Buddhist training, and he wanted to help Rene learn how to be calm. He gave her a picture of his guru and also taught her a mantra. He said that whenever she was scared, she could say her mantra and good things would happen. Rene went home and put the picture of her guru up on the wall. Every night for years we would say that mantra together.

Eventually, the nightmares did go away and Rene kept that up. Rene's mantra got me thinking about my own childhood prayers. At one point I wondered why she was saying a Buddhist prayer rather than the prayer we used to say at night—"Oh Lord, please protect . . . " When I was Rene's age I had a pretty good relationship with Jesus. I thought of him a lot and prayed to him. But I didn't want him to manifest himself to me, that was too scary!

Saying prayers with Rene brought back that wonderful feeling. For a while, her bedtime got pretty strange. We'd say the mantra and the Lord's Prayer together, but it was pretty wonderful, full of feeling. So, in fact, good things did happen when she said that Buddhist prayer.

Calming rituals really helped her a lot then. We had a dream catcher on her wall; it's an American Indian device—yarn woven in and out of sticks to make a sort of net, decorated with stones and feathers and whatever. When Rene was really struggling with her bedtime, we made the dream catcher together; we decorated it and then put it over her bed. Then at night we emptied out all the bad dreams of the day— usually we'd shake it out the window.

The whole time gave me a great deal of satisfaction. I was at my wit's end and so glad that Rene was able to find a way through her somatic complaints and all. When I was a kid, I was also pretty scared at night, but I didn't find many ways to feel good about myself then. So it was great to be able to help my daughter. And, to tell you the truth, I found that saying those prayers together— Buddhist, Christian, American Indian—was healing and comforting for me as well!

What is more spiritually enriching than to find in comforting bedtime rituals a sort of "dream catcher" to calm our fears? Ariane provides a creative portrait of a parent drawing on all available resources to create a calming ritual.

Paul: "I was thrilled to think of her making a real connection."

Paul is a 50-year-old contractor with a charming smile. He flashed the smile in a focus group when I invited the parents to write about "a spiritual moment with my son/daughter . . . "—the exercise clearly gave him pleasure.

Last night the temple sponsored a youth night, with movies and pizza for the kids. Our daughter Evelyn has had a difficult relationship with the temple—she doesn't like the rabbi, struggles with learning Hebrew and getting to Sunday school on time, and so forth. But I've stuck with it with her, and so has she. I've been very touched that something is getting through about being Jewish. So I was astonished last week, and gratified, when she told me about a movie night that was coming up on this Saturday night and how she couldn't wait to go. I was thrilled to think of her making a real connection with the temple. All week I held my breath, waiting for her to change her mind, to tell me she wanted to make a sleepover with some friend or go somewhere else that night. But on Saturday she even asked me to call the rabbi to check on the time. That night she was dressed nicely and ready to go.

As we drove to the synagogue, Evelyn wondered where the movies would be shown. "Upstairs?" she asked, referring to the sanctuary on the top floor where we all worship, "Or else downstairs in the basement meeting rooms." She hoped it was upstairs because that was such a quiet, beautiful room with all the wood and the stained glass windows near the ceiling.

I realized that my daughter felt what I did in the synagogue— the calm and beauty of that room, despite all the imperfections of the place itself and even the religion. Then, as we walked through the concrete entryway, past the big wooden doors, she took a deep breath and said, "Oh, its so nice to smell the Temple without worrying about learning Hebrew."

I loved that comment. I loved that she was feeling good in this place that ultimately does matter to me, that maybe she is getting something out of our efforts, that perhaps she'll find a home somewhat in Judaism, that she'll have it to turn to in moments when she's hurting, to find comfort as I have. I realized how much I wanted my daughter— so perky and creative and different—to be able to find a home, and I hoped Judaism would help provide it.

With one exclamation, Evelyn was able to help Paul clarify his own struggle with his heritage, as well as provide the father a warm sense of being able to give a sense of home to his daughter even in the face of his own ambivalence about religion.

FINDING A HOME IN THE WORLD

"How nice to go into the Synagogue and not worry about learning the Hebrew," observed Paul's daughter. There are times as parents when we can free up our imagination and explore spirituality with our children in a new, heartening way. We may leave behind old rules and forms that constrict us, or hold on to familiar, reassuring traditions, or blend the new and the old.

Our search may come from recognizing in a new way the reality of death, as Annette did, or from worries about how to really instill a sense of value and meaning, as Paul described. What is most important is that the spiritual reach provides parents and children an opportunity to explore the deeper mysteries of life and to renew and reconnect, as Lydia did in seeing a new part of her son or Karen in discovering a shared desire with her 10-year-old daughter to no longer be the "good girl."

The points at which our kids struggle with meaning and faith may infuse our own sense of magic and wonder and awe in the world. We go right through it with them.

We all know you're not supposed to mix yourselves up with your children: mistaking what you need for what they need. Sometimes we insist our children participate in a certain religious ritual or event, when actually we have a need to reconnect with our faith. And we all as parents need to guard against the trap of trying to "undo" painful parts of our past by forcing our children to go through what we did in the blind hope it will somehow be different this time. If you can't make the spiritual journey enjoyable for your children or meaningful to them, it might be a time to back off and get some help or support from your partner, other parents, a trusted friend, a minister or rabbi or a counselor.

However, there naturally are times when our children struggle with faith, meaning, and connection, as we did, and as we still do. Helping them do it differently than it was done for us can be healing for parent and child. Sometimes we rework points of pain in our own childhoods through their resolutions of the same dilemmas we struggled with, in a different way, as Annette noted when she tells us that "I had to recognize that I didn't want people to die either."

Some bar mitzvahs or confirmations and other religious marker events seem to reflect what the parents had wished happened to them rather than the reality of who their children are. But it is also possible for there to be an intergenerational healing that comes from religious events that bring families together. We may feel the pride of seeing that we were able to help our child through a difficult childhood moment where we stumbled, realizing that we can be different as we help our children deal more effectively and happily with a moment that caused us pain.

One 50-year-old father, Stuart, wrote movingly of feeling incomplete about his lonely, unhappy bar mitzvah years earlier, until his son reached the precise age that had saddened him. By drawing on his memory of what he himself had wished for from his own father and not gotten (calm caring support), Stuart was able to respond to his son in a way that left both father and son feeling better about themselves and that may have been a gift for the entire extended family. He wrote, "It's clear that my son got bar-mitzvahed for himself, not for me, but in so doing, he allowed me to finish a job that I had not completed. "

Meeting your children where they are means seeing their needs and responding to the anticipation in their search. You may know you are doing that when you feel joy and if you're there with a playful, engaged manner rather than a driven, pressured set of expectations that likely has more to do with your unmet needs than theirs.

"Grace doesn't have to be found in a church," one parent pointed out telling his story. "Grace and spirituality can be found in a wonderful moment of connection with my children."

Regardless of whether you believe or not, how you approach and listen to your children's dance with faith shapes their own. You don't necessarily need to become devout yourself; you don't need to attend services regularly or advocate beliefs or values that don't really reflect you. In fact, if you don't really feel it, your kids will know. However, there may be places where you feel a deep connection with something beyond yourself, a sense of awe and gratefulness, a feeling that *this* is what really matters. It may be on the golf course as Jackie's father felt, or in your work, or in fishing. Spirituality is not the same as organized religion, and many of the moments children remember from their lives with parents take place *outside* of the church, temple, mosque, or meeting hall.

The specific form of ritual or religious pathway matters much less than that our children have an opportunity to see our passion about matters beyond the commonplace. It is this glimpse into what really moves us that children treasure. You can hear it in grown children's memories of treasured moments with parents, as Elizabeth recalled the fun, even the smells and taste, of walking to church with her father, or Jackie, when talking about golf with her dad.

Moments when we see a parent's passion, sense of values, and awe in the world can shape our own spirituality. A glimpse of a mother's or father's deeper values and meaning-making can be the bedrock of our own ways of finding value and purpose in the world. One older man now himself struggling with questions of meaning and finitude in the world understood his father in a new way as he wrote about an event that happened fifty years earlier:

"When I was about 9 or 10 years old, my father, one Christmas Eve, sat with me and read aloud the entire *Christmas Carol* by Charles Dickens. I knew that this was his way of giving me something of the spirit of Christmas. My mother would not allow Christmas to be celebrated in our home, as we were Jewish—agnostic, but Jewish!

"As I write this now, I realize that by reading the story to me, my father wanted me to know about the gift, the possibility of redemption."

There is a deep sensory root to spirituality that comes from our childhood and that can sustain us through our lives. That is perhaps the most important gift of all for us and our children. What matters to our children is to feel the tactile, sensory richness of belief—the wonderful smell of the church or temple itself, holding hands, playing a game on the way there, or simply the feel of leaning against a parent.

There's a simplicity to these stories. They resonate with sights and sounds and smells. The rituals mean so much to us precisely because of their sensory richness: the sights and sounds and smells of faith.

Family rituals can be a source of great renewal and satisfaction for parents as well as children—the Sabbath candles, a dream catcher, a special way of walking to church and laughing together. The trick is to use our creative imaginations to make playful, heartfelt rituals that capture and woo our children. In so doing, we may restore and enliven the part of our own hearts gasping to feel awe and gratitude once again.

Hidden Wisdom You Can Use

- Religion and spirituality are not always the same. Think about the places and experiences that provide you with a sense of wonder and awe in the world.
- We role model the development of religious faith and spiritual awe for our children. Don't be shy about expressing your sense of appreciation and wonder in the beauty of the world, of nature, of your relationships, your work, and wherever else you find it in your life.
- There are opportunities every day to nourish a child's sense of spirituality.
- You don't have to have all the answers as a parent—sharing some of your puzzlements about god, faith, and meaning can be helpful to your child.
- Children find comfort in the consistency of rituals and like to be involved—the Shabbot candle lighting, for example, or painting Easter eggs, lighting the advent wreath, or preparing latkes during Passover.
- Creating meaningful ritual is important for parents as well as children. If the rituals are not heartfelt for parents, they won't be for the children. Engage them. When in doubt, be playful. Humor helps.

- Keep the lines of religious communication open. TV, movies, and real-life situations can be times for asking questions and imparting values. Avoid the "right answer" format; good questions are better than rote answers.
- Our childhood experience of religion shapes how we respond to our children. On the other hand, we don't have to believe and worship exactly as our parents did, nor do our children need to become clones of us.

chapter   twelve

Growing Up with
Our Children

L ife always has lessons to teach us, if only we hear them. As parents, we grow along with our children. Often *they* teach *us*. Isn't that one of the ironies of parenting? By raising our children we bump into the unfinished parts of ourselves.

"Having kids and being a parent makes you realize how ordinary and human and broken you are," observed one mom. There's nothing like a dose of parenthood to temper our cockiness. One father remarked at a writing session, "There's a divide between those who are parents and those who are not. For me, BC refers to Before Children. Back then I thought I knew all the answers; then parenting happened, and I realized all I didn't know."

From such realizations come better parents, more mature adults, who are less likely to act out the past on their children. Some of the most delicious times in parenting consist of moments when we find *we* can change—we can let go of a familiar anger or sullenness or withdrawal or denial.

At first, though, we may feel stumped at something we said or did and wonder, "Where did" *that* "come from?"

Larry: "My Mother had a very effective punishment technique:"

Consider Larry's story. He is a professor of business administration, in his late 40s. At a parent group with his wife, Ellen, a nurse, he was one of the first to speak, eager to reflect on a lesson he learned from his teenage son John. Larry told his story with a friendly smile, reflecting his lively sense of humor. Larry and Ellen are very principled people, who hold their children accountable as they themselves feel bound by values of honesty, straightforwardness, and caring for others. So a lesson for Larry, of course, started with a lie told by his teenage son. Ellen nodded knowingly as her husband told the details.

When I was a kid, my mother had a very effective punishment technique: the silent treatment. It was a way I've learned since of withholding love. Right from the time I was 3 or 4 years old, she would send me to my room when I misbehaved, in the most stern fashion. She'd extend her arm and point upstairs and order me there in a very cold, icy voice. Then she wouldn't say anything more to me, even if I yelled and cried from my room.

The technique worked wonders with me, even into my teen years. I'd stop whatever I was doing. I couldn't stand her silence. I'd always come crawling back down the stairs, crying and pleading, asking her to please talk to me, please talk to me. I've come to see that my mother's withdrawal was very costly to me. It made me unsure of myself and afraid of losing people's love. However, when my son was younger, I hadn't realized all that. And the technique was so effective with me that I saved it up to use with my kid, figuring it had worked like a charm with me.

Then John entered his teenage years. I figured this was the right time. I had the height still and the power. So one day, when he was 13, we found out that John had cut an after-school drama club practice and gone to a friend's house, telling us he had been in school.

Well, I figured this was the moment! Time for the silent treatment! We were in our living room when this all came out and I said, "Okay, John, you're going to get the silent treatment!"

"What's that?" he asked, confused.

In my sternest voice I announced, "You are to go to your room and I will not be talking to you for quite a while."

I thought: *Wow, this has finally come full circle! How great! My mother gave me the silent treatment, and now I'm doing that to my son!* And I figured that he would soon be coming back to me, repentant for his lie and asking me to please talk to him.

Well, he went up to his room as I ordered, and he just stayed there. About two hours went by and nothing happened. I read some magazines, watched TV, talked with my wife. Finally I couldn't stand the suspense anymore. I went upstairs and walked into John's room. He was quietly doing his homework at his desk. I sat on his bed.

Silence.

Then I asked, "Aren't you going to ask me to talk to you?"

He turned and replied, "Dad, just because you decided to talk to me, doesn't mean that I've decided to talk to you.'

My first response was fury! I stormed out of the room! I was so confused and hurt. How could he be talking to me like that? I was the father here.

We all went to bed without another word. The next day he apologized for the lie, and we talked about lying and all. After thinking about that night's events for a while, I felt this wonderful gift in what my son had said. My son would not accept the unhealthy piece my mother had given to me: the fear that if I pissed people off they'd no longer love me. He stopped it in his tracks.

About a month went by. Finally I got up my nerve to talk with my son about "the silent treatment." We were alone in the kitchen eating breakfast, and I asked him how come it didn't rattle him when I told him that I would not be talking to him that night. He said to me: "Because I trust you. I know you love me. I feel safe with you and knew it would be okay even if you weren't talking to me, even if you were angry at me."

Well, I was really gratified, and also puzzled. I decided to confide in my son, who seemed quite mature and wise at that moment, "Well, your grandma always used it on me and it scared the hell out of me. How come I couldn't say to grandma what you just did?"

"Dad, I know grandma. She's not safe to say that to. That's why you didn't say it."

Can you imagine? He was right. My mother was a wonderful woman in some ways but very scary in others. He could see that, and he could see the difference between me and her. I realized that I didn't have to be just like my mother, that I could discipline my son and set limits without humiliating him. And best of all, I saw what a strong, thoughtful young man my son was becoming, how much he loved and trusted me.

Larry gets a gift from his son and gives one back to his boy, on the lip of manhood. The struggle began with John lying to his father. We can imagine what might be going on in this family that pays a lot of attention to responsibility and obligation. Lies from teens who are generally responsible are often a part of the adolescents beginning to separate themselves from their parents. It's a way of saying, "I know who I am and what I do, and you don't. I'm a separate person from the family." John very well may be making a statement about his growing autonomy. He's going to be in control of his afternoon and not be controlled by things like a drama club practice. And I don't even have to tell you the truth, either!

Father and son are dancing to the music of separation and connection, the child trying to assert difference from parental rules and obligations, even as he loves his family. Larry, as the parent, is of course concerned about the lie, perhaps more so because it's from a teenager and who knows what will happen if the boy starts lying now . . . where will it stop as he confronts drugs, sex, and rock 'n' roll?! Teens can seem so on the edge of growing out of bounds. Larry may want to keep John a little boy even as he's so proud of his growing up. So, of course, this was the "right time" to bring out the heavy guns—

the same old withdrawal of love that had shamed and frightened young Larry into staying overly connected to his mother, wanting to be a good boy. *Let's do it now*, Larry thinks, *before I lose my height advantage and power.*

There's also ancient family music here for Larry. John's separating brings back for Larry echoes of his own struggle to be different from his mother as a young boy. In Larry's experience, beginning at an early age, his mother had brought out the big guns when he tried to be different from her. When he "misbehaved" (which is another word for doing or saying things that parents don't like)—she blasted him with the silent treatment, disappearing into an icy coldness that left young Larry willing to do anything to please her, including not separating emotionally from her. So, of course, when his own son starts to separate, Larry imagines becoming like his icy, cold mother. We all are drawn back in parenting to our most ancient ways of making contact with our mothers or fathers.

Except it doesn't work. In this case, Larry's son thaws him out. The 13-year-old boy says that he will not be shamed and guilt tripped, and tells his father that, in fact, he is not an Ice Mother—he is a loving, trustworthy parent who the boy, thankfully, feels safe to defy. John gets a priceless gift—the message that he is not the angry, abandoning parent he fears he is and that the silent treatment really doesn't kill. The boy is showing the father that you can stand up to guilt tripping and shaming. Part of what Larry may savor in this experience is the lesson that you don't have to buckle inside when the silent treatment happens, from a mother, a wife, a friend, or a boss. This successful, competent father may even feel that *if my son can do it, so can I!*

By accepting this gift from his son, Larry gives something equally important back to John: the knowledge that his father can bear being rebelled against, that the son can stay in his room and ignore his father without the old man falling apart. This is a priceless gift for an adolescent to know about their parents—that his or her attempts to separate will not kill or damage their parents. Sons and daughters need to know that their fathers and mothers can bear their attempts at being different and separate, without striking back too much or crumpling inside. Only then can the child really get on with the work of becoming his or her own person.

From this one moment, Larry and John are, of course, not permanently changed. These are gifts and lessons that have to be re-given and re-learned over and over through our lives. Yet Larry's energy as he tells his story makes clear that even one moment can sometimes reverberate loudly in our lives.

What does parenting have to teach us, if we'll listen? The lessons usually have to do with unfinished parts of ourselves—pressure points from our own growing up. Parenthood brings us through our own childhoods all over again, this time as adults. Whatever your wound was when young, you will likely find it again when you have children, along with the opportunity for some healing. In the stories that follow, we find parents at many different ages and stages—from new parenthood to becoming grandparents—struggling with anger and envy, with loving a child who is so different from us, with partings and transitions, with how oblivious we can be to what we are doing, sometimes in the nick of time realizing we are doing the opposite of what we intended, perhaps with the inadvertent aid of our children, who help us see in the most miraculous ways that we can be different, that we can continue to grow even though we are supposed to be "all grown up."

Ginny: "Become a mother, and die of cancer."

Thirty years old, Ginny is a housewife and mother. Over the past year, she made a decision to be at home with her newborn rather than continue to work as a legal secretary.

I felt so proud of myself when I did not give up on breastfeeding my son. Breastfeeding and becoming a mother was not a small thing for me. I was 18 when my mother died of breast cancer. She didn't talk about her cancer with us, even though she was sick for several years. At age 15, while she was dying, I went to a counselor to talk about my terror of my mother dying. My mother couldn't talk to me. In the hospital, I told her I needed to talk about what was happening, about her dying. She said, "Everyone is going to die some day."

After my son's birth I had a breast lump. The surgeon talked to me about breast cancer. *Oh, great,* I thought, *become a mother, and die of cancer, just like my mother.* Well, I had the biopsy, and the tumor was removed; it was not cancerous. I kept thinking about what my mother went through, about how she handled all this. Did she cry over it? She left eight children. That was the scariest thing, thinking about leaving behind children. I had all these thoughts in my head, and I was angry that my mother didn't write anything down about what her struggle was. All the fears and worries I've had as a mother I've had to learn for myself, with my friends.

I came home with my newborn from the hospital and instantly felt inadequate as a mother and care provider. The second day home, Ricky was asleep for about five hours. All the books say not to let a new baby go longer than three to four hours without food. I was a mess! I tried to wake him, but it didn't work. He would not latch on. Frustration and a sense of failure set in. I was also panic-stricken because I thought dehydration, sickness, and perhaps brain damage might result from my utter lack of ability to nurture this baby.

I began to cry. My husband took our baby out of his sleeping outfit, and we tried to wipe him with a face cloth to get him to respond. He still did not awake. We put in a call to the doctor's office and had to wait because it was Saturday. The answering service told us someone would get back to us ASAP. I was so scared—as a first-time mom, I needed reassurance. Just then, as if sent by God, the doorbell rang. My girlfriend Janine showed up for a visit, a bit unexpected. Talking with her calmed me down. We sat in my living room with the baby in my lap and suddenly the most amazing thing happened: My son latched on!

I feel proud of myself that I have made a commitment to breastfeed him. I am often asked by people when I will stop and get my life back, get back to work. But I am proud to know I am doing the right thing.

The overwhelming neediness of the newborn can plunge us back into our most basic, primitive hungers as well. Ginny learned that being a mother didn't mean abandoning your child, as she had felt by her mother. In choosing motherhood, Ginny confronted her longing for her mother and her anger at her, wending her way through these scary feelings to a place of pride in, not fear of, being a mother. Perhaps, too Janine, with her unexpected visit, became—if only briefly—a calm, reassuring mother-figure for her friend Ginny.

Ramon: "At 2 a.m. in the morning, it's so dark, and things can fall apart in your mind."

A tall and well-dressed man, with his dark hair combed straight back, Ramon has not lost his Brooklyn accent even though he has lived in Texas for many years. He is the head of a large nonprofit organization and tries to find time to work out daily at a local gym, where he likes to box.

In the family I grew up in, my mother was pretty borderline. She would yell hysterically about dinner not being ready, about us being late for school, about whatever was happening. There was always a sense of chaos in our family, even though no one talked about it. My father was always saying, "Keep it quiet, make dinner, keep things calm because Mommy is sleeping." I spent a lot of time as a kid trying to protect Mommy, make sure she didn't get upset.

So the time I smashed our stove in anger, when I was up all night with our baby daughter, is a very painful story. Sandy is 4 now, and this happened when she was just an infant. I had Sandy in my arms, and I was trying to heat up her bottle. She was crying uncontrollably. She was so hungry, and we were trying to wean her. My wife Gina was exhausted, sound asleep in the other room. I really didn't want to wake her.

When Sandy cries and cries and I can't comfort her, I can't deal with it. Maybe that night I should have just put her down in her crib and walked away, but I so much wanted to prove myself as a nurturer that I could heat up this bottle and hold this baby. But no amount of walking was helping, and I wasn't sure of the bottle temperature. I knew if it was too cool, Sandy would push it away like she already had done several times. Well, the milk was all over me, and Sandy kept crying. I wanted to do it all right but, I was half-asleep. And I was afraid I was not going to get enough sleep and I would not be able to work out in the morning, that I would be exhausted before I even got to work. Then I realized I couldn't work out the day after either and, so, felt that my whole week was ruined.

At two in the morning, it's so dark, and things can fall apart in your mind pretty fast. I took the heating pot for the bottle, and I threw it across the room as hard as I could, in frustration. It smashed right into the stove. The front of the stove was made out of glass; it shattered into ten thousand little pieces. There I was, standing there holding this baby in my arms. Some of the glass shards could have hit her! I turned on the light. I couldn't even walk because there was glass all over the floor, and I had no shoes on. I realized that I had hit bottom.

My wife heard the noise. The glass stove smashed as if it had exploded. She came out. I cried and apologized, and she helped calm me down and listened to how frustrated I was. One of the things we came up with was that during the transition from breastfeeding to bottle, if Sandy wouldn't take the bottle from me, instead of giving her the bottle, we'd give her some love.

Soon after that I'd just hold her close to my chest and walk her around, loving her, not expecting that I could just make her stop crying magically. Sometimes, too, there are times when I have to walk away or give her to my wife. Sometimes I put her in her crib, but that night, with the stove incident, I said to myself, I will not go that way, with the explosions, like my mother.

So Ramon learned how to manage the "chaos" of family life. There are few moments so hard as not being able to soothe a crying baby. At these moments, we can fall into our internal chaos, as Ramon did when he exploded. He slowly learned, with his wife's help, how to manage frustration and disappointment of the most profound kind.

Mike: "I never knew what 'transition' meant myself."

A successful accountant in his mid 50s, Mike is also a little league baseball coach in his hometown in Indiana. His office is in his home; he converted a two-family house into a first-floor office for himself and his staff, with his family living right above, in a spacious apartment he and his wife have renovated through the years. Although some might find the closeness of home and office confining, Mike loves it. "It's such an easy transition," he said.

When Annie was 5 years old, I would carry her kicking and screaming out of the house. She had a terrible time with transitions. She wouldn't go out to school, to the park. I refused to be controlled by her, and I behaved badly. *I* was going to do what *I* wanted to do— if I wanted to take her to the park and she cried and didn't want to go, I'd pick her up, sling her over my shoulder, and take this hysterical child out of the house.

We had a wonderful baby-sitter back then, an older woman who was very skilled with kids, who wound up not taking Anne out of the house very much because it was too much trouble. But much of the trouble was with me. In those early years, I was too self-interested. I wanted to do what I wanted to do, and if that meant we were going to the park now, we were going now.

I never knew what "transition" meant myself. I got into personal therapy several years ago and found out that I had trouble with endings and leavings, with going to and starting new things.

I was among the first of the latchkey kids. Beginning in 1952, my mother went back to work to help support the family. I'd come home alone after school to an empty house. I was in the third grade in suburban New Jersey, which is not an unsafe place, but I was very lonely and scared. I decided to stay by myself rather than walk a few blocks to the baby-sitter's. I'd be in our little ranch house, frightened and not able to go out, trying to decide what I'd do if someone came in through the window, what knife to use.

Little things like going out of the house and coming back really gave me trouble as I grew up. Even in college, I often would study long periods in my dorm rather than go out on the campus. And I've been successful as an adult. But that's because I have a home office. For a while after we were married I couldn't go out of our house sometimes. I'd make up excuses—too much work to do—but really it was because I didn't want to go outside.

By the time our second child, Jessica, was born, seven years ago, I'd become a better parent. She too had trouble with transitions, but I had learned to talk with her about change. My wife and I both did. We could tell Jessie that change can be scary, but here's how we can deal with it. Annie still has a fit every year going to soccer, even though she is one of the best players on the field. She worries each year she goes and frets about whether anyone will like her, whether she'll play very much on the team. I've learned to just let the kids talk about their fears. I don't have to say very much. The best thing is for me *not* to be too reactive.

The topic of "transition problems" has become a big joke in our family. We'll be driving somewhere and can't decide on which restaurant or where to go and someone will say, "Uh-oh, the big T, not the big T!" It's really helped to realize that I had severe transition problems, as a kid and even as an adult. When I began to see that I struggled like they do, then I could let them have their struggles and not get so angry. So we make it into a humorous thing. When we laugh about it, it's not a big psychological issue, which turns my daughter off pretty fast.

Every transition is a kind of parting, an ending. They take place every day in many small ways. What may look like a simple transition with children can echo a deeper struggle for parents that touch on our own earliest childhood partings from our mothers. Mike's vulnerability to transitions ultimately helped him give his kids what they needed. Sometimes in helping a child master a scary moment, we heal some of our own pain about that very issue.

Jackie: "Sometimes I would bite my tongue."

A veteran chemical researcher, Jackie works in the laboratory of a distinguished scientist, helping run a research laboratory for a large pharmaceutical company. She has coauthored many scientific papers but has never written one on her own. She's a smart, cheerful lady, filled with insights. Telling her story to the group, she would occasionally pat her skirt with the palms of her hands.

I was so proud of myself when Monica, this tiny person in high heel shoes, skipped on to the stage in her senior class play in high school and made all our heads turn toward her. She could command a house full of spectators. She rehearsed for the play—it was *South Pacific*—by standing in front of the mirror and unabashedly and unself-consciously admiring herself while she sang lyrics about how she was the most beautiful of them all. And I applauded her when she rehearsed, told her—rightly so—that she was great, encouraged her, even though a part of me was twisted up inside like a knot. I wanted to turn away, yell at her, "No, no, stop it! Don't do that! Don't be so *out there!*"—for putting herself in the limelight like that. Sometimes I would bite my tongue!

In my family, any such drive to shine was seen as an unrightful aggrandizement. "Hide your light under a bushel," the bible says, and in my family we took that seriously. My parents would rebuke me, "Who are you to be angry?" "You're just a little nothing." "Don't show off, be better than others." In my family, you had to pretend not to be too out there. It's partly because I had a younger sister with Down syndrome, and there were these constant comparisons to her diminished ability. I was and am smart and talented and have made my way in the world, but my own brightness must have made the gap with my sister Lucy only seem bigger, and so it had to be diminished.

Now here is my 17-year-old daughter, glowing with self-worth and accomplishment, clearly aware of her power to draw others into her world and to delight them. When asked how she could sing in front of so many people, she said the limelight actually energized her—such a different outlook.

I cannot imagine such presence and courage in my own adolescence. I didn't even make the church choir, a long tradition in my extended family, because my voice faded during a crucial audition. And here she is, radiant and competent. How I wish and hope that some of that real spunk and self-joy will never leave her. Monica is in college now and still enjoys acting. She still seems to have no fear of the stage, of raising her voice in a large group, of directing her peers and commanding the kind of attention that I wonder whether

I will ever have. I am very proud I have not kept my daughter out of the light!

How wonderful that Jackie is able to give her daughters what she herself didn't get—encouragement to shine in public. And it didn't come easily. Like many of us, Jackie struggled to quiet the angry voices inside herself, ghosts from her own past, telling her not to stand by her daughter.

Albert: "I had the jarring realization that I was screwing up badly."

Albert and his wife are the parents of two children. He heads the public library system in a large city in the Pacific Northwest. She is a schoolteacher. In his book-lined office, there is a separate shelf devoted to first editions—Jack London, Melville, Twain—proudly displayed. A trace of his native Queens, New York, no-nonsense accent punctuates Albert's storytelling.

We have two children, and our daughter is much more verbal than our son, Danny, who is on the quiet, shy side. From the time our kids were 5 or 6, every time we went on our summer vacation, I would stop at the local college and take them to see it. I enjoy seeing colleges, but I was also giving them, I later found out, the not-so-subtle message that they were supposed to go to college.

I saw this simply as the way that Jewish parents behaved, and I never saw the question of how this little boy was going to deal with keeping up with the rest of his family. Things came to a head when our daughter went to college. It was a long day's drive to her new school, and the whole family went. What an emotionally wrenching day! My wife was in tears, my daughter was in tears, her roommate was in tears, her roommate's mother was in tears. I was the only one not in tears, because I was so happy to be rid of her after this awful summer between high school and college.

Danny observed the whole good-bye. He looked pretty sad too; I knew he'd miss his sister. On the way home, we stopped for dinner at a small country restaurant. I asked him if he had any sense now of where he was going to go to college. He replied, "I am never going to go to college! I can't deal with any of this—leave me alone."

At that moment, I had the jarring realization that I was screwing up very badly. I was doing the opposite of what my parents did with me, and that was what I thought was the right way to do it. My mother graduated from high school and my father went as far as the sixth grade. Their attitude was that whatever I wanted to do was fine. If I wanted to go to college, that was fine; if not that was also fine.

I decided to go to college three weeks before college started; I could just as easily have not have gone. I felt so indebted to my parents for making it possible for me to go to college. But I always had the desire not to leave it up to chance with my children. Going to college seemed so important, and I didn't want to leave my kids without guidance. And, of course, I gave them too much guidance!

On the ride home from the restaurant I felt really frightened. We didn't say much, we let it lie. What was so scary to me was that I thought I was being very appropriate all these years, and I was realized I was being just the opposite. I had to really look at the pressure—it had always been there, in little league, in school. I heard the message for the first time.

We decided to leave Danny alone about college. He went into his sophomore year in high school. His teachers had said that when his older sister went away, he'd begin to develop, which in fact did happen. But I backed off from what I thought was helpful, appropriate behavior. I even stopped taking him on trips to colleges.

When he ultimately decided to go, we told him in as friendly a way as possible, "You apply; you decide."

He applied to college as far from home as he could go. At first we couldn't figure out what kind of crazy pattern there was to his choices. but then it became clear that all were as far away as possible from home. And that's ultimately what he did. That was fine for him.

The kids are both in their late 20s now. I wish I had realized earlier that our kids are all works in progress and they work out if you don't screw up, or . . . you know—even if you do.

Albert's jarring realization helped him break an intergenerational legacy. Albert's father made college possible for his son; to be a loyal son, Albert had to continue the tradition; but he proceeded to do so in an overbearing fashion. By stepping back and saying to his son "You decide," Albert found a new, more satisfying paternal stance.

Sara : "I felt great pleasure in just being present for Mary."

Sara is a bus driver for an urban metro transit system. She arrived in blue uniform for the early evening focus group, having just gotten off from work. She said it was worth it to skip dinner to tell the story about the moment when her 28-year-old daughter made her own decision about religion and faith.

Religion has always been a war in my family; it must be my fate. I managed to avoid one battle, though, with my daughter. I left the Catholic Church at age 20 for some very painful reasons, among them the fact that the reality of women seemed completely ignored. My family is still very Catholic. When I told my parents I was leaving the Church, it was very painful. After my father died, my mother said, "You know, you almost killed your father when you left the Church." When my father was still alive he said, "You know, you almost killed your mother when you left the Church." I wasn't sure who was in more pain when I made that decision, me or them. I felt so guilty and alone and scared and sad, but I knew it was the right decision for me. When I had children, I joined an Episcopal Church and raised them in that tradition.

However, my eldest daughter Mary, at 28 has joined the Catholic Church. She was just confirmed in the Church two months ago. She loves the structure, the forms, the liturgy, and the ritual of the Mass. Can you imagine? After all I'd been through, here was my daughter telling me that she wanted to go *back* to the Catholic Church. That was really hard. But I also respected her—she was taking classes, talking to the priest. One day about a year ago, we were alone at home, and I was questioning her about the decision. She took my hand and said,

"Mom, I feel like this is home."

So I felt we really needed to support her. We went to her confirmation, we took her out to dinner, we had a celebration—a big party, it was a real event. I felt great pleasure in just being present for Mary, recognizing that her path wasn't my path, that this is where she is at this moment, and that it wasn't the end of the world, no matter what she chose.

For my parents it was very different. They couldn't do that for me. I felt very good about being able to respect Mary's choices and being present for her. At her confirmation I told her, "Wow, this is wonderful. I'm glad you feel at home here," so she didn't have to feel that loneliness.

A grown child's decision can open up differences between the generations that give us an opportunity to redo our past and sense of ourselves. Sara is able to be the kind of mother she wished she had herself had. Instead of punishing Mary for making different choices, Sara looked inside herself to realize what her daughter needed from her mother.

Nick: "I could get angry and make it better."

A physician, Nick is an intense, wiry man with curly black hair, who finds time to jog every day. He's the chief of medicine at a downtown hospital on the East Coast and always carries with him his beeper. He's a no-nonsense sort of person, which made his tears as he told this story all the more dramatic.

The other day I was cranky and tired. I was putting my 7-year-old daughter, Betsy, to bed. She was tired, and it was about 8:30, but I had another agenda for putting her to bed. I wanted to get to my reading of several medical journals that were piling up on my desk. So I was really impatient. Betsy was fidgeting in her bed—arranging her Beanie Babies, not being able to find one, getting upset and looking all over for it. Just as I had all the covers neatly arranged, she had to get up to look for "Moosey." That did it! I was really angry—all that work in getting her settled, and I felt like I was going to have to start all over! I started to criticize her for not keeping track of her animals. I said she had too many. Then she got scared that I meant she had to get rid of some, which I really didn't. But she was near tears and protested, "Daddy, I won't throw out any of my Beanie Babies, or give any away!" So I told her I didn't mean that. But I was still pretty angry that bedtime had to be such a major production. I hurried her to get settled once again. By the time she was at last all tucked in with everything arranged just so, Betsy turned her back toward the wall and wouldn't give me a kiss goodnight. I was so cranky and upset I said, "Okay, fine, just go to sleep then," in an angry tone. Then I just walked out of the room without a kiss.

I felt pretty wretched, though, because I remembered how often my mother would just explode at me when I was a kid and walk out at bedtime and never come back to make it right or fix things at all between us. There was a constant feeling of anger in my house growing up, and I hate feeling that way now as a father.

The next morning I went in to wake Betsy up for school. She sleeps so soundly it's often a struggle getting her up in time for the bus. So I left a few extra minutes, and I went in and woke her very gently, telling her it was morning time. I rubbed her back, which I know she likes, and she started to stir. When she gave a big stretch, I said to her: "Gosh, I was so cranky last night, and I missed getting a kiss from you." She opened her eyes, smiled, sat up and gave me a real hug and big kiss. I said I was sorry and so did she.

This was very important because I realized that same thing had happened with my mom. But she'd never come back to me and make it right or share what was going on with her. That morning Betsy let me do that and helped me see that I could get angry and make it better—something that never happened between my mom and me.

There may be little else more important to learn as a parent than "repair"—that hurtful words or deeds can happen between us and our children, but that we (and they) can take active steps to make up for, to heal, the hurt that results. If there's a break in the relationship, you can fix it. From his daughter, Nick learned that he can get angry and make things better, an important lesson for us all and especially for a man scared of becoming like the angry version of his mother, whose explosive anger did not lead to reconnection or repair but resulted rather in just "wretched" feelings. As a child, Nick didn't learn how to make things better when anger took over his house.

Marianne: "There is surprise and startling feelings in becoming a grandmother."

Thoughtful and reflective, Marianne still runs the bookstore she started with her husband over 30 years ago. She's recently become a grandmother.

There is surprise and startling feelings in my becoming a grandmother that are still going on even though it was over two years ago. I've felt jealousy and anger that I really did not anticipate.

My son Stan's baby made a big impact. No, my son *and* daughter-in-law's baby actually—did you catch that slip? I'm still trying to make the grandchild a possession of our family and not hers.

Prior to the birth, I felt so connected to my daughter-in-law, Rachel. She's the one who would call me, not my son. We saw a lot of each other for many years. The arrival of a grandchild felt like such a blessing. One of my other children had great difficulties after college—drugs, hospitalizations. One of the most painful experiences in life is not being able to take away the problems of those we love so dearly. So, anticipating the baby's arrival I wanted to connect with this new fresh baby who had nothing to do with the pain of the past. It was another chance to help somebody who really needed it—my daughter-in-law and my grandchild.

I figured that the openness between Rachel and me would continue. But things changed once the baby was born. I felt closed out. I'd offer to take care of the newborn: "Don't feel like you're imposing. I'm here to baby-sit whenever you need me. When you hire another baby-sitter, I feel some regret." I was trying to make myself available without being too pushy.

My daughter-in-law's parents live in Boston too. We all do. But it's easier for her to drop her baby off at her mother's house.

We all want a piece of her, to make sure that she knows us and is connected to us. My son and Rachel went away for a weekend recently. I told them that I would be glad to take her, that I had no work and it would be my pleasure. My daughter-in-law kept hemming and hawing. Stan wasn't saying much. Finally she just said, "I think I'll leave her with my mother."

I blurted out, "Oh, I'm so disappointed!"

My son finally said, "Look. It's her baby, and she's just more comfortable with her mother."

I realized that indeed my daughter-in-law was more comfortable leaving her with her mother. Rachel made every effort to bring Chris over in the following weeks. She knew I felt bad.

I feel a lot of sadness as I'm telling this story. There's a connection to my own mother here. My mother was a tough, outspoken woman, and I have tremendous respect for her. I could never have made the bookstore the success it is without her toughness inside me. I was very close to her. We'd sit when I was a kid and play with her jewelry and talk. We'd sort through all the earrings, bracelets, and necklaces—red and green and gold and silver colors flashing in the light. It's not that the jewelry was worth so much; it's rather that it reflects all the warmth and liveliness of the women in our family. It had been my grandmother's, handed down to my mother and then to me. She left me her jewelry after her death. I miss her.

Now with the grandparent thing. I've never really been sure as a mother-in-law what my role with Rachel is. And I feel so close to her. I've raised several sons and never had a daughter. When we found out she was pregnant, I wanted to give Rachel all my grandmother's jewelry. I'm realizing she's the daughter I never had. I imagined showing it to Rachel, looking at it together, her trying on all the pretty pieces. That's how close I felt to her. I thank God I finally have a daughter whom I can give my special things to! My grandmother's jewelry may not be worth more than ten cents, but to me it was special stuff. I think to really be at peace with grandparenting, I'm also going to have to let my daughter-in-law be different from me—and share the jewelry with her anyway!

With the transition to grandparenthood, we dance once more with separation and connection, having a chance to learn new steps yet again. In the course of her story, Marianne found that becoming a grandmother meant learning about differences from those she loves, as well as her connection to them. Through her granddaughter and daughter-in-law, Marianne has a chance to come to terms with her sad-

ness about the daughter she never had and her continued sadness at the death of her own mother. Marianne learned to become a "good enough" mother for her daughter-in-law, even if the relationship is not perfect.

DIFFERENCES, SEPARATIONS, AND GROWING UP

There's so much to learn as a parent, but a lot of what we struggle with may boil down to two matters: differences and separation. How do we respond to the ways our children are different from us, and how in turn we are different from our parents? Difference, finally, means separation, separation from our own deeply held wishes and needs for those we love to be like us. The recognition of differences and similarities between our parents, our children, and ourselves is also a harbinger of growth and change.

We are each like our parents in some ways, and as we deepen and age, we find new and different ways our parents are alive within us. The timeless cycles of raising children honors and links the generations. There are, though, often troublesome ways in which we feel like our parents and want to be different—wishing not to put our parents' needs, disappointments, anger, passivity, or pain on the shoulders of our children or trying not to be bound to the elder generation in ways that feel burdensome to us. Yet we may be drawn to being like them in just the ways that caused us pain, because we don't know how to be different or for fear of betraying them if we are different.

We may not be aware of what we are replaying and repeating until our children, by their refusal to go along, bring it to our attention. A son, for example, won't accept the treasured (and painful) silent treatment a father trots out just like his mother did for him; a daughter chooses her own church, leaving the mother facing the possibility of turning into an overbearing version of her own mother.

As parents, we struggle too in accepting the way that our kids are different from us, different from the way we want them to be or even *need* them to be. For Mike, the "first" latchkey kid, home life was very chaotic. And as a parent, he may need his young children to conform to his schedule, his way of making transitions. But they are not going to. Ramon, so frightened of the angry mother within himself, may need his daughter to be quiet and nurse just so at 2 a.m. so that he can feel like a Good Mother. But in the midst of her own rhythms, she isn't going to.

In delicious, special moments of grace and opportunity, we may find we can ourselves change, be different from how we were. Mike learns that he can grow beyond the chaotic feelings provoked by simple transitions during his day. He learns to manage his need for stability and order amidst what is the inherently messy experience of raising children. His first attempts to force his daughter through transitions gives way to his ability to look at himself and calm himself when his daughter is different than he wishes she would be. As always in difficult moments in parenting, a sense of humor helps. "Uh-oh, the big T, not the big T!" becomes a playful way of managing a common separation struggle in families, endings and beginnings.

From these struggles we may find new parts of ourselves. Nick learns about restitution, for instance, amidst the "Beanie Baby Battle" with his daughter Betsy. Nick's mother would disappear into her angry outbursts when he was a child. Nick as a parent finds that he can go back to his daughter and make things okay in a way that his mother was unable to. His daughter Betsy accepts his apology for his anger and so "helped me see that I could get angry and make it better." How to make things better was something he had never learned from his mother, who struggled to simply contain her anger, much less repair the damage it caused.

From our kids' struggles to be different from us we may learn that attempts to separate really don't kill or maim those we love. Our shame or guilt over what *we* did as children can be lessened. Watching our children can give us new insights into our parents. All the responsibility for our childhood family difficulties need not be on our shoulders; our parents had *choices* how to respond. One father, Gus, wrote movingly in a focus group about the pleasure he takes in his son's adolescent cockiness.

"He sits and strums his guitar, plays Grateful Dead songs, and tells me to forget college, he's going to buy a VW bus after high school and just drive around the country. He informs me he's going to marry Claire Danes."

Gus tells the group that he feels delight in being able to joust verbally with his son, encourage his imagination, in the process freeing up a playful part of himself that was frozen in an unfinished stalemate with his own father, who was unable to play with the young Gus in that way.

It can help to see that often we are struggling with the same issues our children are. So much of parenting is a reworking for ourselves as well as our kids. We redo our childhood in doing things differently with our kids. For Mike the beginning of learning to be a better parent, for example, was to realize that he felt as shaky about "simple" transitions as his young children did. Recognizing that he had trouble getting out of the house, about feeling safe in the world, helped him respond more helpfully and lovingly to the needs of his children.

We learn, as parents, all through our lives how we are similar to and different from our parents and our children. And so we face the reality of endings and partings, that our children grow up and lead separate lives from us, that we are no longer ourselves little children living in the bosom of our own parents.

Hidden Wisdom You Can Use

- Be mindful of the fact that you are still growing up even as your children are too.
- We all are working something out from our past when we become parents.
- Where is your "growing edge" now as a parent—dealing with being an authority for your children? Is it in managing separations and transitions, or in the sorrow and loss of what you didn't get from your own parents, or in calming your frantic, angry feelings?
- As our children grow into different stages, they demand different things from us. We may be better with kids at one stage of life than another. Dealing with a teenager is easier for some parents than dealing with a toddler, and vice versa. Parenting is a constant stream of transitions and changes.

- Never underestimate the value of apology and restitution. If you feel you've blown it at some time with your child, apologize. If you mean it, your kid will know and accept it.
- Think about the intergenerational legacies in your family. How much of your parenting style is connected to being like or unlike your own parents? Try to be conscious about what you'd like to take from your parents and what you feel okay about leaving behind.

p a r t   f o u r

Enjoying the Rewards
of Parenting

chapter   thirteen

Our Everyday Gifts

W e work hard to take care of our families. Sometimes we feel we don't get much back. Yet children give us gifts of love every day, often in a hidden, secret way. Young children do, teens do, grown children do. Being able to see and hear and receive these gifts is a bonus for parents and is good for the kids. They're important for our well-being. Moments when our children, perhaps unexpectedly, show their love, or push us in new ways to see and acknowledge them, can be a source of nourishment for the whole family. We may wait for a Big Show of Love and miss what's right in front of our eyes.

Molly, my neighbor down the road, told me her experience recently of feeling a typical morning frustration with her 5-year-old daughter, Natalie—rushing to get to preschool, hurrying to make her lunch, get her dressed for the cold day, and into the car. All the while her daughter dawdled at the breakfast table. Molly wondered, *Why is she so slow, unfocused, can't get it together in the morning?* She had a busy work day ahead and she was feeling her "typical going-to-work-blues, leaving my daughter and the warm house to get to the office." Her daughter was playing with some paper at the table while her mother hurried around the kitchen. Finally, my friend rushed over, prepared to scoop up the detritus of breakfast and get her daughter going. Molly's daughter looked up at her with a folded piece of paper in her hand, "See, Mommy, a bird I made for you. To take to work with you."

The girl had been folding an origami bird as she had learned to make in preschool. "I realized that here was this gift my daughter had made for me, such love, and I almost hurried right by it. I did take the little colored bird to work with me, and it made my day, really—to think I almost missed it!"

These are the kinds of gifts that can pass between parents and children of all ages. Small moments, almost missed, sometimes overlooked, that are invaluable. There are key times and marker events with our children that undo and heal the past or point to a new and better future. Then there are times, equally important, that simply bring us out of our gloom at the day's chores, remind us of the hope threaded into every decision to have children, point to ways that we already succeed, too easily overlooked as we try to live up to impossible standards of "real life success." Their happy laughter, bright eyes, warm touch absolve us of our flaws, remind us of a brighter future.

As parents, we live so much within a cocoon of adult preoccupations—get the kids fed, dressed, and out the door to school (we hope in that order), get ourselves to work on time, get the kids *back home* before 1 a.m. when they get older, attend to grades, college applications, keeping our own relationships and work commitments viable. The habits and routines of our life can blind us to the wonder around us, the miracle of children, their love for us and ours for them. Sometimes children woo us out of our cocoon or break through our mindlessness and restore us.

Stuart: "It added a real joy to the morning."

Stuart, a pharmacist in a large urban hospital in California, talked about the long commute he faced every day for a job that doesn't feel as successful as he had hoped, at age 33. His story began in response to the writing prompt "A time with your child that you hold close to your heart."

It was 7 a.m. last Monday morning, and I was in the kitchen, still waking up, making my lunch and preparing myself for the day. I knew I had a long drive ahead of me and a long drive back, plus a whole day of work before I was going to be home again. I was sitting at the table eating a bowl of oat bran flakes with raisins and reading a magazine by myself. My son Danny came downstairs and began to prepare his breakfast, also a bowl of cereal.

I was still reading, filled with my typical morning gloom. It was like I was oblivious that he was there. Danny reminded me that no reading is allowed at the table when there is more than one person there— family rule. We both ate our cereal, making sure that each of us was not secretly reading one of the cereal boxes, periodically accusing each other of just that.

"Hey! You were reading the comics on the back of the box."

"No, I wasn't. But you were looking at that picture of Michael Jordan on the front of the box."

"No way!"

Then Danny started his regular game of asking me percentages and micrograms of fat, sodium, vitamins, and so on, in the cereals were eating. I found myself laughing, my spirits lightening.

We laughed continuously throughout—he roared when we found out his cereal had three times as much sugar in it as mine. Usually I'll get on him about eating too much sugar—my word, the next health concern as the younger generation gets older will be insulin insufficiency!—but Monday I just forgot about that and played with him. I made a joke out of my shock, giving him a look of mock horror, really giving it all it was worth: "Three times!!" He roared with laughter, milk dripping out of the corners of his mouth as he tried to eat and laugh at the same time.

It added a real joy to the morning and cut through my gloom at starting the day.

Stuart feels his son's love through the boy's questions and prodding and playing around. For these moments, he's not just an employee about to go off for the day to his office but also a father who can chuckle with his son, who can hear the love twinkling in his son's laughter. He gets more nourishment, perhaps, from the humor than from the breakfast cereal.

What's so special and unpredictable about these moments is that both parent and child are fed by "the gift" they are giving each other. Danny gets the knowledge of being valued and loved and appreciated by his father. After all, they're on parallel tracks—the boy is leaving the house, going to his "work" just as his father is.

They may not be able to put it into words as clearly as we can, but our children get ready for their day just as we do, around the breakfast table. They think about how to deal with assignments, teachers, the playground, and friends. Danny going off to school can now carry with him an energized version of his own father to hold on to through the day. Instead of leaving for the school bus with a sorry sense of Dad, the unpleasant thought perhaps that "my dad faces the day with defeat and I'm his son so I do too," Danny can carry with him a touch of his father's potency and power and good humor as a part of himself as well.

My hunch is that we are surrounded daily by opportunities for such moments, which we sometimes see by luck or happenstance and sometimes by being mindful, as we see in the following stories.

Erika: "I found myself laughing out loud."

Red haired and lively, Erika is a social worker married to the chief of police in a metropolitan city. Her children are grown now, but she wrote about a moment when her then-young son Eddie punctured her familiar bubble of worry. The story she crafted began in response to the invitation to write whatever comes to mind about "My son made me laugh out loud when . . . "

My son made me laugh out loud when he was coming home from school and was late. I called the school to ask where the bus was, and they said it took a different route—but he was only 5½ years old! So I started down our street to see if I could find him. All of a sudden, there he was walking toward me. He looked very serious as I approached and threw my arms around him.

"What happened?" I asked. "You're a half hour late."

"Oh," he said. "The bus got here awhile ago, but I found a little dead bird by the road and went to bury it and say a prayer. You know, like that other time with the crushed rabbit."

I hugged him tight, thinking only that we better get home to wash his hands, just in case the bird was decaying. Mostly I found myself laughing out loud with relief that he was safe. I was delighted—no, awestruck—that a small lesson in compassion had been learned, taken in by this little boy's being so completely there that he would delay coming home to honor a small animal. Eddie remains—at age 25—affectionate, creative, and given to moving to the beat of a different drummer.

Here was a moment of grace found amidst a time of worry and concern. Often these gifts from our children bring us a new way of seeing them, or the world. It may simply have to do with the comic, the way our children have a direct line to our funny bone. Erika finished her story by telling us about "the time one December when Ed ran outside with his magic carpet, stuck his tongue out toward the sky and then ran down the driveway, and sat on the magic carpet. When asked what he was doing, he said, "I'm waiting for snow." I laughed out loud.

Parents who travel on business know what a bittersweet pleasure such trips are. It's nice to be away, but you miss the family at the same time. Bruce is a 43-year-old father and husband whose work for a large bank takes him away from home a lot.

I am very blessed as a father. There are many memories I treasure. Most all of them involve my son telling me, often in his own way, that he loves me. I told Justin Thursday night that I would be away this past weekend. I said I would miss him, and be home for dinner Sunday.

He responded by telling me that I could take his stuffed dog, which he often cuddles at night. He told me I could "pet him and everything," but that I must be "careful when you carry him, not to squeeze him too tight."

Needless to say, I brought the stuffed dog, and I am grateful for my son's love.

Sometimes when we are leaving, we need to hear we are loved and will be missed. Our kids need to hear that from us. And what a gift when they can communicate the same thing back to us.

The father of several teenage boys, Ernie gives voice to a father's need to feel competent in his son's eyes.

Ernie: Recently I was driving my teenage son and a friend of his to school. We were talking about the Wimbledon tennis matches going on. As I often do, I tried to teach him something—I started to explain about "byes" and why you have them in sports competition. It got complicated, and my son started to rag on me, "Yeah, yeah, okay Dad. Stop trying to impart information, will you!" Then a few days later I heard him explaining to another friend about how in sports competition there are often an uneven number of matches and so "you have to have byes on the first round." I felt effective and listened to.

The gift to Ernie was the opportunity to see how much his son was taking in from him even as he seemed disinterested in what his old man has to offer.

A grandmother now, her gray hair in a bun, Annette remembers back to a moment over thirty years earlier, treasuring still a gift from her son.

I'm 76 years old, and my son David is now grown up, in his 50s. One of the most moving moments in the parenting of David happened almost thirty years ago, during his freshman year at college. His father and I drove him north to Vermont on a sunny autumn day, and I knew all three of us had mixed, unexpressed feelings about loss, gain, and separation.

We toured the campus briefly, had a fast lunch together, and then deposited David and his luggage at his dorm. My husband, always avoiding overt sentimentality, clapped our son on the shoulder, wished him well, and talked gruffly about leaving immediately to avoid traffic. I remember giving David a quick kiss on the cheek and smiling brightly through the window as we drove off. I was pleased with myself for not crying. We were proud of him, wanted the best for him, but I knew it was the end of his growing up years and the beginning of a different time for all of us.

David was always good about writing; his letters, addressed to either both of us or individually, were fairly frequent. (We did not use the telephone quite as much in those days.) A few weeks after he left, a letter came addressed to me. As I started reading it, I realized with a shock that it was a love letter—a warm and loving tribute from a perceptive, grateful son, telling me how much my caring support and understanding had meant to him throughout his childhood. It left me flooded with emotion and in tears.

I read that letter over several times, and when I had stopped crying, I tucked it back in its envelope and put it away in a safe place. It was such a safe place that I could never find it again, although I looked for it many times. David says that he *did* write it, although he doesn't remember exactly what he said—so at least it wasn't a figment of my imagination. But it would have been nice to read again.

Timothy, David's son and our eldest grandson, is starting to talk about college, and when the time is right, I will take him aside and explain that a bouquet of flowers on Mother's Day is fine but a letter of love and gratitude to his caring and supportive mother during his freshman year would be very, very meaningful. Perhaps it should be a national act.

How often do grown sons have an opportunity to say "thank you—I love you!" to their mothers, in a heartfelt manner? How often do mothers hear it? Yet such words can be a gift that a mother will treasure for decades. How interesting too that Annette would lose the letter even while trying to keep it safe! Is there a way that such direct expression of love between mother and son (or father and daughter) makes us uncomfortable even as we love it?

WHAT KEEPS THE REWARDS OF PARENTING HIDDEN?
What else do we miss? What are the things that keep us from receiving love from our children? Across the room at the parent focus group, Abby, a mother of a young daughter, listened to Stuart's story and said, "I get caught up in the feeling that I have to be the parent. My son colored me a picture on a napkin in the restaurant where we were having dinner last night. I was so busy paying the bill, keeping the kids organized, and wiping chins that I almost threw the picture in the trash with everything else."

Being the parent does not mean that you can't stop to smell the roses, or notice the pictures your child draws for you. Yet it *can* feel that way. Sometimes it takes more courage to slow down with our children than it does to hurry through life trying to live up to all our responsibilities.

Our busyness is one block to receiving the gifts our children offer us—the real-world responsibilities that we have to provide, to take care of our kids, *to be vigilant when they can't be*. Another block comes from the conceit that *parents don't need things from their kids*. We're supposed to give to them, not them to us, and sometimes we may feel we don't really deserve it. Yet when we accept these gifts, we are nourishing our children's self-esteem, helping them realize that they are capable of lighting the light of love in our eyes.

How special when we can relax from the parent role—having to protect and provide and get things done—and lean into those moments of wonder with our children, the small moments throughout our lives, often overlooked, when we express our love and caring to each other.

Mattie: "I retrieved my true self as vulnerable as anyone else."

Mattie is unlikely to attract attention in a crowd; she's short without dramatic features, except for her steel blue eyes, which stand out when you watch her. "People always say I'm very observant—that my eyes seem to get bigger and bigger as I pay attention to things." She's clearly a confident lady, an English teacher at a private girl's school, with a reputation as a tough but fair grader. She's the kind of teacher you go back years later to visit.

I have always played the role of caretaker in my relationships with others. I am the one who holds my friends' hands when they cry, who brings meals when they're sick. I do a lot of listening and nodding and consoling, and I touch—someone's arm when she tells me something sad, a child's head as he runs past. I believe in listening and touching, in letting people know that they are real to me. But I have also set it up so that *I* am never the one confiding, never the one calling for help, never the one being held. I remember even when I was in labor, in absolute agony, I would not let anyone touch me.

And then, when I was 45, I had to have a hysterectomy. I was terrified. I had several very large, possibly malignant tumors, and, as I had legal custody of my teenage daughter, the doctor suggested that I make out a will. He suggested it in the same tone of voice in which he told me not to eat ahead of time, a tone he might have used to set a tennis date. And I signed the release form detailing all the things that might happen to me while I was under anesthesia: I might wake up paralyzed, brain-damaged, I might never wake up at all. As a single mother, you *can't* die, you're not allowed to!

But I did wake up, and when I did I was not alone. A friend of mine, Anna—an older woman—had arranged to be in the recovery room, and she had brought my daughter, too. I was in a lot of pain, and the two of them stayed with me the whole night, on opposite sides of the bed, behind me. They supported me—literally—all through the night. I had just lost my uterus and ovaries, and I was in a birthing position—in the same posture, with the same location of pain in my body as when I gave birth to my daughter—and now my daughter's hand was on my back, massaging me, and I could hear her gentle voice, and my friend's—the two of them holding me, touching me—and it felt wonderful.

Somehow I could let Anna be the mother, the grandmother, the woman-in-charge. I could let her be responsible for me and for my daughter for that time so that I did not worry about whether or not it was okay for my teenage daughter to be in there, caring for me. I have always felt *solely* responsible for Beth, as if she did not even have a father, and it's been hard for me to receive from her because I am obsessed with what I needed to be doing for her. I felt guilty about being ill and needing the surgery!

When she was little, making presents for me, I thanked her and praised her, but I wasn't really *getting* her gifts, because what I was truly thinking about was whether or not I had boosted her self-esteem enough and what she had for lunch and what she needed for supper, had she gotten enough fresh air today? I saw other mothers handing their kids off to their own mothers for the afternoon and truly letting go, having a breather, getting refreshed. But my mother wasn't the kind you could do that with, and I certainly never trusted anyone else.

And yet that evening, coming out of surgery, I did let go. I let myself be held and consoled; I let Anna take charge; for the first time I understood my daughter's strength and generosity. I didn't have to do anything about it. *I wasn't in charge.* And I realized that in not-being-responsible I actually gave my daughter something I'd never given her before: I *got* who she was. Later she told me how much the experience had meant to her. And for a moment I let go again and it was as if all the drawings, the collages, the special rocks, and the specially folded up pieces of paper were spread before me, a feast of gifts, an absolute celebration of motherhood and childhood.

So it was good for Beth, and it was great for me—those four hands on my back, all that love, that journey first into hell and then into my daughter's arms, a reverse-labor from which I retrieved my true self, as vulnerable as anyone else.

In taking a gift from our children, we are also giving back to them. Sometimes children need to take care of us in order to feel that they have something to give to the world. One of the "silver linings" in Mattie's surgery and recovery was that it became a coming of age marker for her daughter Beth. Mattie explained, "She was just on the edge of leaving home. What better way for a child to establish her independence than to have her parent depend on her? I remember praising her for her ability to take care of things, to make meals, clean the house. She loved it! I think every child loves to have a parent in trouble so they can rescue them!" If a parent rejects the nurturing and loving impulses of the child, how is the child to know that what they have to give is of value to the world?

I remember the pain as a 12-year-old of buying my father a long cigar at the souvenir store of the Baseball Hall of Fame in Cooperstown in 1957 and then having him yell at me when I presented it to him in the car on the way home. Why? Because it cost over a dollar, and money was tight in our family then. He worried it was a waste of money. Years later when I first saw Red Auerbach, coach of the Boston Celtics, light up his traditional victory cigar as yet another winning basketball game drew to a close, I realized what he missed, and couldn't say at that age. He missed my desire to show him how much I loved him and wanted him to feel successful and proud of himself. Light up your own victory cigar! In my eyes you are a winner! Remembering the inchoate pain I felt at age 12 in having that gift rejected helps me try to be mindful of moments when my children are trying to *give me something*. It's as important for our kids' self-esteem as for ourselves that we be able to take these gifts they offer.

GIFTS FREELY GIVEN—AND NOT

How else do things go awry? Some presents may not be freely given and thus have a hidden message addressed to the recipient. Then either the act of giving or act of receiving is not really a free one. My "victory cigar" gift to my father, for example, may have had a hidden message: *You have to live up to my expectations for you!* People are very good at intuiting hidden messages. My father may have, somewhere in his being, picked up my 12-year-old wish that he be different in some way and rebelled against that invalidation of who he was, simply a father struggling to support his family and not (in his eyes at least) a hero.

There is too a difference between freely given presents from children to their parents and the parents who *demand* gifts from their children. Sometimes parents demand that their children be or act a certain way. While all parents, of course, want their children to reflect parts of them, and to live up to important values, the situation is different when a parent's narcissistic needs are so great that they override the child's sense of self. Verbal insults or physical threats or subtle psychological consequences such as profound sulking or emotional withdrawal may follow for the child who does not conform to his mother and/or father's needs. In such cases, children will fashion their lives into a sorrowful gift to their parents out of fear of losing the parents' love. As a therapist, I've learned from many grown children who have fashioned their work lives, career choices, and marital choices into gifts to parents who seemed to demand that they be a certain way, even at the cost of sacrificing a part of themselves. We need to be attentive to the gifts we are getting. Are they joyfully, happily given, or is there a dutiful, sorrowful air that indicates it reflects a defeat for our child, not a triumph?

It's a delicate balance. We need to shape our children and get something back, but we don't want to misshape our children and stunt their individuality, forcing them to be like us. Yet you *can* tell the difference between freely given gifts and ones extracted at a price. Be aware of the feeling tone surrounding the gift. There is a sense of joy and pleasure for both parties in the freely given gift exchange.

Sometimes slowing down to let our kids show their love may do more for us (and them) than thousands of dollars in increased salary at work or better "parenting strategies." Ironically, as parents there may be so much attention to our role in raising our children and the responsibilities of parenthood that we may miss our need to feel loved and beloved of our children. That doesn't mean that we're supposed to demand that from our kids or coerce it from them, but it does mean that it can be important to open yourself to the love and gratitude that children of all ages want to display to their parents. Gift giving spans the ages and all ranges of difficult circumstances. The stories in this chapter affirm once again that it is never over as a parent. The opportunity to be given to and to give to our children is present no matter what our age or theirs. The past is not written in concrete, and a moment of connection can help thaw out years of disconnection or alienation.

Hidden Wisdom You Can Use

- Every day with our children has moments of specialness just for us—something they say, a trinket made, an experience shared—that can deepen our sense of wonder in the world, as well as our self-esteem and feeling of competence.
- We may be so rushed or harried or preoccupied that we overlook a treasured moment right in front of our eyes. Try taking a deep breath when you are feeling harassed when with (or by) your kids and just look at them. You may see them or what they are doing in a new way.
- Children get a gift when they give to us. The opportunity for a child to display love in concrete form to parents is important for their self-esteem. When we respond with a smile or gratitude it acknowledges that they have something important to give to the world. When we take a gift of love from our child, we are giving a gift back to them.
- Think back to your own childhood, to a moment when you wanted to give something to your parents—something you made, words you wanted to say, an action you wanted to do for them—and they missed it.
- What was the feeling you had back then? What had you wished they had done differently?

c h a p t e r   f o u r t e e n

Hard Times Have a Silver Lining

W hat do these stories teach us about the "silver linings" of parenting? *Webster's* defines a silver lining as a "hopeful prospect." The moments of parenting that really stick with us have some hopefulness to them. And hope comes from struggle. Many of the stories have "grit" to them—a difficulty overcome, some sadness mixed in with the happiness, a recognition of the deeper rhythms and currents to the relationship. They are not of the Pollyanna, "don't worry, be happy" variety. That's the first lesson from these stories— that what really counts to us as parents are moments of active engagement, not passive involvement, with our children. The second lesson is that parenting is inherently stressful and that there are no "magic bullets" or magical charms that will take away the demanding-ness of this most intense of activities, of raising a younger generation, the young who carry *us* forward, with whom we are so inextricably enmeshed. We fail, we say things we can't believe, we injure those we love, and they injure us.

Yet through all that are many blessings in parenthood, rooted in the very difficulty or adversity that pains us. The stories in this book offer several kinds of silver linings. First, adversity can serve the process of differentiation in families. Parents and children may come to see each other as real people, not as fantasized ideal (and therefore unreal) versions of people. All parents and children start out in a hazy, merged soup of projection and yearning. Children see their parents in larger than life, cartoon images as great heroes or as demons. Parents similarly distort their children. We imagine they will become "better" versions of us, maybe carry out our dreams or unfulfilled parts of ourselves. When our children disappoint, frustrate, or injure us, or when we do the same to them, there is also a process of "growing up" at work for both generations. One mother, looking back many years on the suicide attempt of her daughter, a teen at the time, reflected that "she had to break my heart in order to get me out of my adoration of her. I absolutely adored her and, in so doing, put a lot of expectations and pressures on her. We've both changed a lot since she almost killed herself, and in fact I wonder if that event was a way for us to go on with our life together, with her no longer being my adored little child but really a person very different from me."

Difficult moments and hard times can also be a way for parents and children to give messages to each other, to say things that—for whatever reason—cannot be said directly. Often they have to do with a parent and/or child saying that "you need to see me more clearly, let go of your illusions and overbearing expectations, see and value who I really am, different from you."

Getting through difficulty may also be a part of the process of finding out more who *we* are as parents. We become more authentic. A father pushing at his teenage son to be a better version of himself, to achieve in ways he never could, suddenly sees, via his child's protest, how in the face of his teen he is, and—more—how he has to deal with his own sadness at what he has not achieved in his life, instead of putting it on his kid. Moments of adversity stretch us. Parenting, like so much of life, has many lessons to teach us, if we can only hear them.

Each stage of our children's growing contains lessons for us as parents. The normal adolescent struggles of our children means that we have a chance to work out our own unfinished adolescent struggles, for example. Being aware of what resonates within us from our own past can be helpful to intuiting what our kids need and can help us be better parents, less likely to mix ourselves up with them. Each stage of parenting—newborns, toddlers, latency age children—offers a chance to "rework" whatever in the past that left us stuck. We go through it with them.

Often, too, difficulties with and for our children provide opportunities for parents to reconnect with each other. In the process of raising young children, we can lose ourselves in them, become so enchanted with our children that we hardly invest in our parenting partner. One of the big tasks of parenting is how to safeguard your marriage so that as your kids age, you have a partner to turn back toward. When our kids back us into a corner, they often back *both* parents into it. We may find a new togetherness with the very partner we've felt most split off from. That can be fortunate. As we get older, we can't always rely on our children to meet the intimacy needs that are more appropriately met in marriage or with our life partner.

Many of the most important moments with our children involve few words between parent and child. A lot of talk is not crucial to an important, transforming moment. In our verbal, psychologically oriented culture, we may feel we have to say just the right thing. That's not true. In fact, it's part of the pressure that actually blocks us. Clumsy attempts to make things right or awkward words on our part can show our kids or our parents that we care. Being awkward may in itself be good, a silver lining to our own discomfort. It shows the effort we're making, and makes the value of what actually happens most apparent. *And* when parents model the courage to do what makes them feel awkward, it helps their children learn that going the extra mile emotionally is a part of what adults do. Parents communicate to their children how important they are precisely by the effort they put in to make a difficult situation work out okay.

It can help to talk. Often our secrets or difficulties are more known than we think. Finding age-appropriate ways to say what needs to be said can be one of the most rewarding parts of parenting as *we* learn as parents how to deal with family matters that might at first leave us feeling stumped.

As parents, we may feel that we have to be in control and have the answers. We may feel we're being weak by showing our feelings and needs, and we strive not to show "weakness" to our children. The "All-Knowing, All-Powerful" model of parenting is still alive and well—and it is often one that we try to live up to, even as we know it doesn't really make sense.

It is true that parents have a primary importance as protectors and providers for their young. And, of course, overwhelming children with *our* needs is not helpful. However, we need to model interdependency in our families. it is clear that children need to feel that they can contribute to their parents' lives, can give something back to them. In taking care of us, children are learning mastery and competence and a sense of having something valuable to offer those they love. Aloof, unneeding parents can deprive children of their opportunity to learn generosity. The silver lining in allowing our children to comfort us, to take care of us at times, is that they become more independent and confident.

Actually, we're learning a new kind of strength—the courage to acknowledge limits and ask for help. Isn't it ironic that many of our most treasured moments as parents are also ones that were difficult in some way? Much of parenting is not black or white, all good or all bad. We may yearn, like our children, to know that either we're a "good person" or a "bad person." We fear that we're a "bad parent" and hope we're a "good one." We yearn for family moments where everything is "perfect."

In fact, reality is messier, and parenting is one of the messiest parts of reality. The good moments, the ones that really stick with us, are also wrapped up in difficulty. There's tremendous hope and possibility in this insight. All parents are good in some ways and bad in others. Parents have strengths and weakness at different times. We might be very good with one age child or one gender or our firstborn or our second born and then find stress at different ages or with different children. We might be a better parent in our 30s than our 40s, or vice versa. There is not a one-size-fits-all kind of parenthood.

When we think things are bleak or at their darkest, there is present too the potential to turn things around, to find some light and opportunity to make things better. Often such turnarounds have to do with the ability to come at things from a new direction, to change our own way of seeing rather than waiting for the other person to change, to nurture within ourselves the changes we demand from those around us. Playfulness helps a lot, as does taking manageable risks and a sense of humor. That's why the unpredictability of raising children also offers us hope and freedom: Outcomes are not written in concrete, as evidenced by so many of these stories. A parent may think matters are hopeless, or will never turn around and then be happily surprised by what lies around the corner in his or her family.

And, don't hold out for Enormous Changes and miss the important ones right in front of your eyes. Sometimes small changes in family patterns can bring big consequences. We may think we have to completely rewrite the family script, but, in fact, most often we take small steps as parents; we are different from our parents by degrees.

Difficulties in parenting can teach us about our own resourcefulness. One heritage of our own childhood is that many of us wait around as adults for someone to come and fix things, for Big Daddy or Mommy to come and make things right. The moments of distress helped many of the mothers and fathers in these stories see that *they* had to do something, take action, that no one was going to come and sort it out, that there may not even be a perfect answer. By taking action, they learned about a new, more empowered part of themselves. And sometimes they learned to tolerate uncertainty and messiness in a new way.

Perhaps most often we learn forgiveness from parenting, giving up our need to look and be perfect. We transform narcissism into love— the need to be perfect and adored and looking good becomes the wish to help and nurture and contribute to the lives of others. It's in facing what seems beyond us that we learn to be different.

Maybe too, at bottom, parenting is as much about getting as giving. Let's not forget the everyday gifts that children bring to us. Parenting is truly a treasure trove, one that we may overlook or that may lie hidden away in our mental attics for a while. But, as I hope the stories in this book make clear, if we can open ourselves to the possibilities, even simply once a day or a few times a week, there are wonderful gifts available for the taking.

Create Your Own Parenting Stories

Now that you've seen just how important parents' stories can be—offering invaluable insight and perspective into parenting issues, priorities, and values—you may want to learn how to develop your own stories. For many of us, writing raises performance anxieties. Will I have anything to say? Will it be good enough? Fortunately, you don't need to climb Mt. Everest, stage a dramatic heart-to-heart talk, or sail across the Atlantic together in a small boat in order to have something to write about. Some of the best stories can be about very ordinary moments. Put your worries aside, and let yourself explore your family stories without worrying about how your stories will measure up. You'll do fine! Here's how to do it.

STEP 1: GET STARTED

Find a quiet place, free from interruption. Take your phone off the hook if you need to! You may work best at your kitchen table with a cup of coffee or sitting in the living room. Or you may prefer to go to a local coffee shop or the town library.

You can use these exercises alone. However, some people find they work best with a partner or in a small group. If you are in a small group make sure that you've all introduced yourselves and talked a little bit about your parenting experiences and what you hope for from the group. In each case, we'll begin in the same way—by warming up.

STEP 2: WARM UP WITH FREE WRITING

Let's begin with an invitation to free up our imaginations about parenting. Free writing is a common technique used in writing classes; it goes back to Dorothea Brande's classic work, *On Becoming a Writer,* first published in the 1930s.[7]

In free writing, you take a preset amount of time to write about whatever comes to mind on a given topic. I'd suggest fifteen minutes for the free write. Set your alarm to go off at the end of fifteen minutes and stop writing at that point! I'm going to offer you a phrase to begin writing about, but first I want to make clear what you do when you free write.

When you begin the fifteen-minute free write, *do not* think about what to write. Just start writing, putting down whatever comes to mind. Don't worry about grammar or punctuation or making sense. Just write whatever words come to mind. Here's the hard part: Try to keep your pen moving the entire time! If nothing comes to mind about the phrase, that's okay. Just write the phrase or your name over and over until something comes.

Remember that this is just a warm-up exercise. If it feels irrelevant or meaningless as you write, that's okay. At times, free writing is a great memory loosener, at other times it just tires out the hands! There is no right or wrong end product from a free write. I try to give myself fifteen

---

[7] D. Brande, *On Becoming a Writer,* Los Angeles, CA: Tarcher, 1934.

minutes to free write most days, and sometimes I just write my name over and over or feel very irritated by the exercise. Other times it is a source of great joy and insight.

Okay, ready? Below are a list of some prompts that I invite you to free write about for fifteen minutes. Choose one (put them in a hat on individual pieces of paper, and pick one out if you'd like) and remember that once you've started, keep your pen moving!

Free-Writing Prompts
My son's/daughter's hands . . .
When she says NO! I feel . . .
My son's/daughter's skin . . .
I could hear myself screaming at . . .
My son's/daughter's posture . . .
I laughed out loud when . . .
Everyone was clapping . . .
My son's/daughter's breath . . .

If the free write produces an image or story that you want to pursue, that's fine. If not, you can try different free-write prompts to explore other images.

More Free-Writing Prompts
When I see my son/daughter naked . . .
A time when my child broke a taboo . . .
A gift I got from my child happened when . . .
I felt so proud of myself as a parent when . . .
A time when I was called on something by my kid . . .
I felt so proud of my child when . . .

After the fifteen minutes is up, I'd encourage you to read the free-writes aloud, whether you're by yourself, with a partner, or in a group. Remember there is no right or wrong answer. The purpose is simply to warm up and to stimulate images about parenting that can be explored to create a story. The purpose is not to see who's the best writer!

Here are a few more tips on getting started on your story.

A Treasured Memory

Another way to focus in on a story image is to explore your most treasured memories, as a parent or as a child. Think of a time together with your children that gives you special pleasure. This may have happened a long time ago or as recently as today. It may involve something you both did or said. It may be something that you've never told anyone else. It may take place in the home, or at work with your child, or in a special place you all share outdoors, or at an unexpected time. Take fifteen minutes to free write about that memory, including as much detail as you can.

A Childhood Treasure

If you wish, you may choose to write instead about your childhood, about yourself and your parents. Think of a memory with your mother or father or both of them from any point in your life that you particularly treasure and hold dear to your heart. It may involve something they did or said. It may have to do with a tool, a picture, a song, a trip together, an object, or something else. It may be a memory that you've never told anyone else. Free write for fifteen minutes, including as much detail as you can.

What If Nothing Comes to Mind?

Suppose you want to write down a story or free write, but nothing comes to mind. Where should you start? Many parents have found that a "clustering" technique—based on the methods described by Gabrielle Rico in her excellent book *Writing the Natural Way: Using Right Brain Techniques to Release Your Expressive Powers*,[8] a great way to get started. Here's what's involved.

Find a quiet place free from distractions. Take a blank piece of paper. Let a beginning stimulus word come to mind. In the middle of the page write the word and then draw a circle around it. The word might be a child's or parent's name, or any person, place, or image from your life. Now write down without thinking very hard as many

---

[8] G. Rico, *Writing the Natural Way: Using Right Brain Techniques to Release Your Expressive Powers*, Los Angeles, CA: Tarcher, 1983.

new thoughts as you can about that word. For each thought, you may place a summary word or two on the page and then draw a circle around it, with a line radiating out from the original stimulus word in the middle. Some thoughts will produce their own set of associations, and you can follow them, with circles radiating out from them. Don't worry about whether the associations "make sense" or not. You want to feel almost as if you're doodling. You don't really know where you're going at this point, so just play around.

For example, Audrey is a recently remarried wife in a blended family situation. She began—without knowing why—by writing her 14-year-old stepdaughter's name, "Stephanie," in the center of the page. Then she radiated outward in a circle with "remarriage," "difficulty," "Lily" (her daughter's biological mother), "Lily's house, "our new house," "Jim" (her husband). From "our new house," she had a line that went off on its own and included "all together—some of time," "painful," "fighting," "outside house," "Great Meadows Bird Preserve."

You're not trying to make sense. Instead you're doodling on the sheet, paying attention to your bodily sensations, perhaps feeling a slight sense of tension as we do when trying to complete a puzzle or searching out a direction we're not entirely sure of.

As you doodle, see if an "ah-ha" experience happens—a theme suddenly clicks in and emerges. You'll know this happens because you may feel a shift in bodily tension, a sense of relief as you get to where you wanted to go. What you're looking for is called a "felt focus" by psychologist Eugene Gendlin.[9] The "felt focus" is a visceral shift in the body—satisfaction, relief from tension—as you focus on an experience that is important to you.

So, Audrey clustered from "Great Meadows," a large Audubon bird sanctuary about a quarter mile from their home. "Great Meadows" led to "nearby," "birds," "sanctuary," "invitation," "walking together," "Big Bird," "laughing," "how I felt."

After she doodled some about walking at the bird preserve, Audrey stopped and realized what she wanted to write about: the Saturday a

---

[9] E. Gendlin, *Focusing*, NY: Everest House, 1978.

week earlier when Stephanie had invited her to go for a walk at Great Meadows, just the two of them, after many days of her stepdaughter having ignored her. This was the first real acknowledgment by Stephanie that Audrey had felt after the remarriage. It was a pivotal moment she needed to get in focus—that in her own cautious, tentative way her stepdaughter was making a place for her stepmother. And she was doing it in the neutral site of the beautiful bird sanctuary. The bird sanctuary became a sanctuary for the two women, free from the turmoil of blending families in several homes. They hadn't talked a lot on the walk, just enjoying the beautiful outdoors, the trees, swamps, and meadows, and the dirt trail running through them. At one point, one of them had made a joke about seeing Big Bird from Sesame Street in the preserve, and their shared laughter was the first real connection Audrey had felt with her stepdaughter. As her story unfolded, Audrey then wondered if her initial difficulty in finding a story reflected her own reluctance to make room herself for a new stepdaughter! And in telling the story that came from this clustering exercise, Audrey began making that place.

So, take a blank piece of paper and doodle around. See if you have a similar "ah-ha" experience! If you are working with a partner or friend or in a small group, work on the clustering exercise for about ten to fifteen minutes and then stop. Take the page with your doodles on it to the other person and describe what you have done. Often in talking over our associations, a story will begin to emerge.

STEP 3: CRAFT THE STORY

Now that you have a memory or image to work on, you can explore and refine it. Create now a beginning, a middle, and an end to the story. Written stories are different from told ones. What can be very helpful in writing is *detail*—stories come alive when we include details that often get left out of spoken stories or when we simply talk to each other about our day—the weather that day, the color of the car or the wallpaper, what our kids were wearing, the look on someone's face. Don't shortchange yourself—think of as many of the details as you can while also now trying to be direct and to the point.

Here are some suggestions to think about:

How did the experience start?
You may want to note the weather or temperature that day. Was it overcast or sunny, hot, warm, chilly, or very cold, raining or snowing?
What were the smells that come to mind from that day?
List all the sounds that you can remember from the experience. Then list all the tastes you can associate with the experience.
How did your children (or your parents) look and act? What other visual images come to mind from the time?
What were you wearing? What were they wearing?
What did you say to each other?
What did your children (or parents) do that felt most special?
Was a parenting partner involved in any way?
Were friends involved?
What do you most remember about the experience?
What in particular makes this story important to you?
How did the time together end?
Looking back, what feelings come to mind about it?

STEP 4: USE YOUR STORY
Now that you've worked on a story, what do you do with it?

If you've been working alone, think about what new parts of yourself you can discover in the story. Can you see ways in which you succeed as a parent that you particularly treasure? Can you see some things you did or your children did that make you feel good about yourself and them? Did you find a way to spend time with your children that simply felt satisfying to you and them? Has a new perspective emerged—a way around or through some old conflicts or dilemmas with them?

If you're working with a partner or friend, you may each want to read your story to the other. I strongly suggest writing the story down rather than simply telling it as you go along. Writing allows us to rehearse and think through a story and, generally, to finish with a much deeper version than if we simply tell a story that comes to mind.

After you've finished the writing, decide who'll go first. Then agree that each person will read their story *without interruption* by the other. Agree also to try not to hurry, so that whomever is reading can feel the story they're telling and its importance. After one story has been completed, the partner or friend can respond and give his or her reactions if the reader feels that would be helpful. Then the other person has the chance to read his or her story, again without interruption or undue haste. As you discuss each story, think about new parts of yourself and each other that you can discover in the story. Can you see ways in which you each succeed as a parent that you particularly treasure? Have new perspectives emerged—ways around or through some old conflicts or dilemmas with your children? If you are partners in parenting, have you gotten new insight into your partner as a parent? Are you pleased in having shared some element of yourself? Is there some insight you wish your partner will help you remember from your story?

If you're working in a small group, it can be very valuable to share your stories. Here's how I'd suggest doing that. Make sure all are comfortable with having stories read aloud. It is fine for those who don't want to share their own stories to simply listen to the others. You can pass on this one! You may want to agree beforehand about the order of who'll read. You can simply go clockwise if you want or leave it to each person to read when he or she is ready. Agree that each person who reads does so without being interrupted and that they can take their time. Some groups prefer to go around the group reading all the stories first and then discussing them; other groups prefer to discuss each story after it's been read before going on to the next. Decide on that before beginning.

In discussing the stories, try not to make judgments about what you hear. The point is not to decide whether a story or event or experience is "good" or "bad" but rather for you and the other person to understand the meaning and importance of the story. What new parts of himself or herself did the person discover in the story? What did they particularly feel good about in the story? After sharing stories with the group, do you and the others feel less alone in parenting? In the discussion you may want to share what you learn from the other person's story and experiences that are similar to what you've just heard.

STEP 5: CONNECT THEMES

Regardless of whether you're working by yourself or with others, look for the repetition of themes across stories you write. There may be values, moments, ways of being together that keep reappearing in the stories you write. You may discover that a theme from a story about being outdoors in nature with your children is similar to one from a different story, a different time.

As you identify recurrent positive, satisfying themes, you will be nourishing and enlivening yourself as a parent. And as you identify stories that cause you pain, you will be clarifying the stuck places in parenting that you can work on, by yourself or with others.

Index

SAMUEL OSHERSON, PH.D., is a psychologist and writer, and received his Ph.D. in clinical psychology from Harvard University. He directed the Adult Development Project at Harvard, has taught at the University of Massachusetts, MIT, Harvard University, and the Harvard Medical School, and is chairperson of the psychology faculty of the Fielding Institute. He has written for *Newsday, Boston* magazine, *The Boston Globe*, *The Chicago Tribune*, and *Cosmopolitan*, and offers regular Stories for Parents seminars in Boston, Philadelphia, Washington, D.C., Houston, and other major cities. He lives in Cambridge, Massachusetts.